Instructional Strategies for Improving Students' Learning

Focus on Early Reading and Mathematics

A volume in
Psychological Perspectives on Contemporary Educational Issues
Jerry S. Carlson and Joel R. Levin, *Series Editors*

Instructional Strategies for Improving Students' Learning

Focus on Early Reading and Mathematics

edited by

Jerry S. Carlson
University of California–Riverside

Joel R. Levin
University of Arizona

INFORMATION AGE PUBLISHING, INC.
Charlotte, NC • www.infoagepub.com

Library of Congress Cataloging-in-Publication Data

Instructional strategies for improving students' learning : focus on early
reading and mathematics / edited by Jerry S. Carlson, Joel R. Levin.
    p. cm. – (Psychological perspectives on contemporary educational
issues)
  Includes bibliographical references.
  ISBN 978-1-61735-629-2 (pbk.) – ISBN 978-1-61735-630-8 (hardcover) –
ISBN 978-1-61735-631-5 (ebook)
  1. Reading (Elementary) 2. Mathematics–Study and teaching (Elementary)
I. Carlson, Jerry S. II. Levin, Joel R.
  LB1573.I6335 2011
  372–dc23
                                                              2011038814

Printed in the United States of America

CONTENTS

SECTION 2

MATHEMATICS INSTRUCTIONAL STRATEGIES

EDITORS' INTRODUCTION

The twin objectives of the series *Psychological Perspectives on Contemporary Educational Issues* are (a) to identify issues in education that are relevant to professional educators and researchers; and (b) to address those issues from research and theory in educational psychology, psychology, and related disciplines. The format for the series involves a focal chapter followed by commentaries and a "final words" response by the author(s) of the focal chapter.

The first two volumes in the series, *The No Child Left Behind Legislation: Educational Research and Federal Funding*, published in 2005, and *Educating the Evolved Mind*, published in 2007, dealt with broad educational issues. The present volume is more focused, targeting specifically instructional strategies for improving students' learning in two of the traditional "three R" areas, reading and 'rithmetic (mathematics), in the elementary school grades. Few would dispute the essentiality of these two curricular domains in laying the foundation for the development of students' competencies in a vast array of academic disciplines in both the in- and out-of-school years that lie ahead. Because of its dual curricular emphasis, the present volume contains two focal chapters, two sets of commentaries, and two "final words" responses.

In the reading section of the book, Cathy Collins Block's focal chapter offers a comprehensive review of the literature on effective strategies for enhancing the reading skills of primary- and upper-elementary school-aged children. Citing research studies (including her own programmatic work on designing and evaluating reading strategies), Block provides evidence for both "proven" and "promising" reading instructional strategies, with

Instructional Strategies for Improving Students' Learning, pages vii–ix
Copyright © 2012 by Information Age Publishing
All rights of reproduction in any form reserved.

the former referring to practices "based on many years of research... and [that] have full, chapter-length discussions of their value in handbooks or articles that review reading research and instruction"; and the latter referring to practices "that have also been shown to contribute to students' literacy-skill improvement... but have had a briefer and more recent history of research testing." These practices follow from informed decisions about the content, instructional strategies, lesson characteristics, and teacher actions related to the development of students' reading skills.

Although all commentators are complimentary about the general substance of Block's recommended practices, they each extend the discussion by adding to or taking issue with her specific recommendations. Rollanda O'Connor, for example, argues that even following a careful review of the reading-instruction literature, one person's "proven" is an other's "promising," and vice versa, and so she proceeds to give examples of her own preferred switched-category choices. Similarly, in Margaret McKeown's focus on reading comprehension strategies and teacher actions, she questions whether the research-evidence picture that underlies Block's recommended practices is as strong or as clear-cut as she paints it. James Baumann focuses on the various definitions, components, and teaching of reading fluency, including the influential role that reading fluency plays in the process of becoming a skilled reader. Finally, Virginia Berninger, concerned that both neurological and sociological factors involved in the reading process are given short shrift in Block's considerations, provides some thought-provoking anecdotes about the sociological aspects by drawing from her early indoctrination to teaching in suburban and rural schools.

In the mathematics section of the book, Douglas Clements and Julie Sarama's focal chapter provides an extensive and detailed analysis of, and their perspectives on, learning and teaching mathematics. They provide extensive reviews of the literature on general as well as domain-specific pedagogical strategies, notably "learning trajectories" that integrate skills learning with conceptual development. They also provide a detailed review of, and recommendations for, effective approaches to professional development.

Commentators on the Clements and Sarama chapter offer critiques as well as extensions of the theses developed in the focal chapter. For example, Arthur Baroody, David Purpura, and Erin Reid support the main aspects of the Clements and Sarama chapter but argue for including in their descriptions of learning trajectories discussion of how information is assimilated and how knowledge is constructed. Karen Fuson expands Clements and Sarama's learning trajectory model to the Common Core Standards and National Council for Teaching Mathematics process standards. James Stigler and Belinda Thompson agree with Clements and Sarama that false dichotomies, such as skills versus conceptual development in mathematics education, are not useful. They suggest that mathematics education, practice, and research should (a) focus on integrating skills with conceptual development, (b) construct clear learning goals and subgoals, and (c) be domain-specific. Anita Wager and Thomas Carpenter also acknowledge the value of learning trajectories as described in the focal article. They suggest, however, that aspects related to the learner need to be taken into consideration, including recognition that assumptions of developmental level and readiness to learn are age related but not age determined. In addition, they suggest that cultural factors and how children experience mathematics outside of school should be taken into consideration when designing and implementing instructional sequences.

Both the reading and mathematics sections of the book conclude with a response to the commentators by the section's focal authors.

—**Jerry S. Carlson and Joel R. Levin**

SECTION 1

READING INSTRUCTIONAL STRATEGIES

CHAPTER 1

PROVEN AND PROMISING READING INSTRUCTION

What We Know and What Works

Cathy Collins Block
Texas Christian University

We believe that literature helps young people experience the great stories that lead to a deeper understanding of what it means to be truly human. They need to learn [how] to read nonfiction to know the world and [how to read] literature to know themselves.
—Scholastic, 2010, p. 1

The goal of this chapter is to provide research summaries of proven and promising reading instructional practices in early and upper elementary grades. Realizing that numerous books have been written about this topic, this single chapter cannot propose to report every advancement that has been or is being made in reading instruction. Rather, its intent is to provide compact syntheses of highly important facets of today's instructional programs. Proven practices differ from promising ones in several ways. Principally, the former have been studied for several years and have provided evidence on many dependent measures that they reliably and validly play a part in improving students' literacy skills. The number of empirical stud-

Instructional Strategies for Improving Students' Learning, pages 3–41
Copyright © 2012 by Information Age Publishing
All rights of reproduction in any form reserved.

ies that document their effects, as well as the variety of students with which they have proven their worth, is larger than those that exist for promising practices. Proven practices are based on many years of research; they have full, chapter-length discussions of their value in handbooks or articles that review reading research and instruction.

Although promising practices have also been shown to contribute to students' literacy-skill improvement, they have had a briefer and more recent history of research testing. These approaches are based on theoretical foundations that are as solid as those underlying proven practices. Yet, they are viewed by a large segment of the reading research community as more newly evolving, hybrid methods that hold the potential to further advance the effects of past, proven methodologies for today's students.

The syntheses in this chapter were designed (a) to begin a discussion upon which chapter commentators could both amend and expand; and (b) to assist educators, policymakers, parents, and laypersons to make more reliable educational decisions. Throughout my career, interested persons representing the latter group have asked, "Where can we find research to support highly effective instructional practices?" Educators want to share these resources with their colleagues. Policymakers seek original sources of research to establish new directions for American education. The summaries and tables in this chapter were created to address these needs. Lastly, the information and tables in this chapter are presented in such a way that laypersons with limited knowledge of technical terminology can benefit from its contents.

The discussion of proven and promising instructional practices is divided into four sections: the content of instruction, strategies to be taught, lesson characteristics, and exemplary teacher actions. Instructional content is defined as what students are taught to do to become better readers; instructional strategies are defined as how students are taught to read; lesson characteristics are defined as the features within single lessons, as well as the order in which events in instruction occur; and exemplary teacher actions are defined as educator behaviors that have been demonstrated to assist students in achieving statistically higher levels of literacy success than that of control groups. The chapter ends with suggestions for future research.

PROVEN AND PROMISING PRACTICES
IN EARLY READING INSTRUCTION

In this section of the chapter, the content of instruction will focus on research that informs what should be taught in early reading classrooms, how it is best learned, and why increased attention is being given to nonfictional texts. Instructional strategies will be described that enable young readers to apply more than one skill to a reading challenge and to use the superstructures in authorial writing patterns during the earliest stages of their reading development. Lesson characteristics will be reported that enable students to use their multicultural and linguistic resources (with oral and kinesthetic supports) to comprehend at deeper levels. Finally, the specific actions that exemplary teachers take at all and at specific grade levels to increase student achievement will be highlighted. A summary of these discussions appears in Table 1.1.

TABLE 1.1 Proven and Promising Early Reading Instruction and Instructional Strategies at Work

Name	Research-Based Examples in Classrooms	Research Supporting Their Effectiveness
Proven Content: *Teaching the five domains of phonemic awareness, phonics, comprehension, vocabulary, and fluency in early grades and showing students how to apply them interactively*	Interactive instruction in phonemic segmentation and phonics through the manipulations of letters (Ball & Blachman, 1991; Bradley & Bryant, 1985; Ehri, 1991; Ehri & Wilce, 1987, Griffith, 1991; Tangel & Blachman, 1992)	Dole, Sloan, & Trathen, 1996; Droop & Verhoeven, 1998; Duke & Pearson, 2002; Games et al., 2008; Moss et al., 2008; NRP, 2000
Promising Content: *Using more nonfiction and student selection of two books on the same subject back-to-back*	"Two Books Back-to-Back on the Same Subject" (Block, Parris, Reed, Whitely, & Cleveland, 2009); Creating conceptually rich instruction (Guthrie et al., 2000)	Bodrova & Leong, 1996; Chall & Jacobs, 2003; Chall et al., 1990; Duke, 2000; Gersten et al., 2001; NEGP, 1999; NETA, 2004; Williams et al., 2005
Proven Instructional Strategies: *Teaching multiple comprehension strategies in single lessons*	"Experience-text-relationship method" (Au, 1979; Tharp, 1982); "K-W-L" (Ogle, 1986); QAR (Question-Answer Relationships, Raphael & Au, 2005); Reciprocal Teaching (Palincsar, 1986; 2006; Palincsar & Brown, 1984; Rosenshine & Meister, 1994)	Block, 1999a; Block & Pressley, 2002; Brown et al., 1996; Cummins, Stewart, & Block, 2005; NRP, 2000; Pressley et al., 1991; RAND, 2001; Snow, Burns, & Griffin, 1998;
Promising Instructional Strategies: *Teaching authorial writing patterns and text structures*	Teaching authorial writing patterns for individual paragraphs, full texts' super structures and text features (Meyer et al., 2010; Williams, 2008)	Collins, 1991; Dalton & Rose, 2008; Flavell et al., 1981; Meyer et. al., 2010; Pressley, 2006; Snow et al., 1998; Taylor, 1980; Williams, 2008
Proven Lesson Characteristics: *Using multicultural content and students' own multicultural and linguistic resources as lesson features*	Culturally relevant pedagogy, instructional strategies for ELLs, family literacy projects (Edwards & Turner, 2009), and mentor texts (Au & Carroll, 1997; Lacina & Block, in press)	Au, 2002; August & Shanahan, 2006; Banks, 2002; Damon, 2008; Ehmann & Gayer, 2009; Fairbanks et al., 2009; Florida, 2008; Hart & Risley, 1995; Jacoby, 2008; Prater, 2009

(continued)

TABLE 1.1 (continued) Proven and Promising Early Reading Instruction and Instructional Strategies at Work

Name	Research-Based Examples in Classrooms	Research Supporting Their Effectiveness
Promising Lesson Characteristics: *Scaffolding to increase students' active learning during whole class instruction*	Comprehension Process Motions (Block, Parris, & Whiteley, 2008), peer discussions, collaborative learning groups (Slavin et al., 2009), cross-age/same-age tutoring, paired interactions (Block & Dellamura, 2001/2002) and Invitational Groups (Keene & Zimmerman, 2007).	Bond & Dykstra, 1967; Block et al., 2009; Cazden, 1991; Gardner, 1999; Guthrie et al., 1999; Morrow et al., 1999; Paivio, 1986, 1991, 2008; Porter & Brophy, 1988; Rosenblatt, 1978; Vygotsky, 1978; Wigfield, Metsala, & Cox, 1999; Yuill & Oakhill, 1991
Proven Teacher Actions: *Using exemplary literacy teacher research to significantly increase early reading achievement*	Characteristics of highly effective teachers, their schedules, grouping systems, and types of literacy methods they use (examples in Table 1.2).	Pressley et al., 2001; Block et al., 2002); Taylor et al., 1999; Wharton-McDonald et al., 1998
Promising Teacher Actions: *Implementing six domains of exemplary literacy competencies that are important at individual grade levels*	*Using a different teaching style* at specific developmental levels; *motivating students* differently at distinct age levels; *relating to students* in different ways; *re-teaching* effectively; *creating successful lessons,* and *building effective classroom milieus.*	Anderson, 1992; Block & Mangieri, 2009; Block et al., 2002; Guthrie et al., 2000; Morrow et al., 1999; Parris & Block, 2007; Ruddell, 1997; Snow et al., 1998; Wharton-McDonald et al., 1998

Content for Young Readers

Proven Content: *Teaching the five critical reading components in early grades and showing students how to apply them interactively.* These components are (a) *phonemic awareness,* the ability to focus on, isolate, and manipulate single sounds in words; (b) *phonics,* the ability to match sounds to letters; (c) *comprehension,* the ability to derive meaning from print; (d) *vocabulary,* the ability to deduce the meaning of individual words; and (e) *fluency,* the ability to read with appropriate speed, accuracy, and phrasing so that the flow of English syntax can aid in determining meaning. Prior to 1960, it was believed impossible (or at least unwise) to teach comprehension to children who were still learning to decode individual words. This belief stemmed from the assumption that phonics and word identification should be the sole instructional focus during the primary grades (Smith, 1978).

In 2000, the National Reading Panel (NRP) conducted a comprehensive review of 481 studies published from 1980 to 1998 in peer-reviewed, scientific journals (NRP, 2000). This analysis found that phonemic awareness, phonics, comprehension, vocabulary, and fluency are the proven critical components to be taught in early reading instruction. Since 2000, we have discovered that students must also be taught how to apply these components interactively (Duke & Pearson, 2002). Interactive instruction enables students to understand the full concept of what reading is and to realize that it is not just phonics, word calling, and oral recitation. When such full conception emerges, young readers are more likely to confirm when they understand a sentence and reread and reflect when they do not (metacognition). Such lessons do not detract from children's decoding development; they strengthen it. Such interactive presentations demonstrate that comprehension and decoding have a reciprocal, synergistic relationship (Droop & Verhoeven, 1998).

True interactive instruction occurs when students are taught how to use these five components in conjunction with one another (e.g., how to use phonics and summary abilities to infer the meaning of an unknown term at the end of a paragraph; see Dole et al., 1996). To cite one example of the effect of such conjunctive instruction, when kindergarten students were taught phonemic segmentation (phonemic awareness) as they learned both to match graphemes to phonemes (phonics) and to write/draw the meanings of words learned, they scored statistically higher in their abilities to store words in memory, spell more words correctly, and use phonemic segmentation to learn and write more words in comparison to students who received extensive instruction in phonics in which subjects wrote words that were to be learned (e.g., Ehri, 1991; Griffith, 1991). The effects of instruction in phonemic awareness, phonics, and meaning making, interactively, also resulted in statistically significant differences in overall beginning reading abilities as measured by standardized tests (Ball & Blachman, 1991; Bradley & Bryant, 1985; Ehri & Wilce, 1987; Tangel & Blachman, 1992). Interestingly, statistically significant effects did not occur in studies in which students were exposed to phonemic awareness and phonics as separate instructional components. To further this example, when the 52 empirical tests of phonemic awareness reported in the National Reading Panel report (2000) were meta-analyzed, it was found that the manipulation and vocalizing of letter names and sounds (phonics) in conjunction with phonemic awareness resulted in an effect size of .67 (a mean difference between experimental and control conditions amounting to two thirds of a standard deviation), compared to an effect size of .38 for studies that taught these components separately.

More support for interactive instruction occurred in the recent findings from studies of the national Reading First Program (Gamse et al., 2008;

Moss et al., 2008). These studies found that students in Reading First Programs were not taught how to use comprehension and decoding strategies interactively from the earliest stages in their literacy development. Most often, they were taught reading components separately, with an emphasis being placed on phonics instruction above the other components. Such instruction had small effects on first-grade decoding measures and no impact on comprehension assessments in grades 1–3.

Promising Content: *Using more nonfiction and student selection of two books (or electronic versions of them) on the same subject back-to-back.* The promise here is that teachers are moving early-reading instruction beyond traditional thematic units and the integration of reading instruction into content areas. They are teaching and modeling *how to read nonfiction.* This content focus has only recently evolved. In 1959, the National Council of Teachers of English and the International Reading Association published *Critical Reading: An Introduction* (NCTE & IRA, 1959). In this summary of research to date, the Council concluded that "Primary level children do not appear to be ready to deal with much more than is in their immediate environments, even with instruction and use of all their thinking processes" (p. 5). As a result, for many years after 1960, nonfictional texts that described concepts beyond young children's neighborhoods were omitted from K–3 curricula. In 2000, Duke examined the types of materials used in K–3 instruction and found that expository texts and how to read nonfiction were still almost nonexistent.

Today, several needs to increase early readers' abilities to read nonfiction have been documented. After the primary grades, students must (a) learn from expository texts predominantly (e.g., Gersten et al., 2001); (b) comprehend expository text to be successful in life and academics (NEGP, 1999); and (c) take standardized tests that contain mostly nonfiction selections (NETA, 2004). The difficult transition some students experience in shifting from reading narrative to comprehending expository texts is described as "the fourth-grade slump" (Chall, 1983) and it often occurs as early as grade 2 (Chall & Jacobs, 2003). As Chall, Jacobs, & Baldwin (1990) have noted, "By third grade, children who do not comprehend nonfiction tend to fall further behind their peers [in overall reading abilities] even if they are very successful decoders" (p. 98). Moreover, after repeated failures, many struggling readers, as early as the kindergarten level, have been shown to retreat to only "good enough reading," even when reading fictional text (Mackey, 1997). As a result, such students acquiesce to a lifetime of reading haltingly, making so many compromises in comprehension that only minimal meaning is ever attained. The promising practice reported here holds the potential to not perpetuate this detrimental habit. Today, young readers are asked to read more nonfictional text, whose structure have been shown to create even greater comprehension challenges for most younger students than do fictional texts (Gersten et al., 2001; Williams et al., 2005).

Reading two books back-to-back on the same subject and creating conceptually rich instruction (Guthrie et al., 2000) are promising methods being used in early elementary classrooms to produce impressive literacy gains (Block et al., 2009). Such learning environments provide opportunities for students to read two self-selected expository texts back-to-back about a topic of their choice and to initiate metacognitive problem-solving and clarifying processes to resolve inconsistencies between conflicting information that may appear in their contents (Block et al., 2009). The use of this new research-tested-content method occurs when teachers introduce a subject with two or more selections of expository texts. With the first, teachers ask students which sections of the book they want to read and discuss together, as the teacher (and students who are tracking the same text) turn page by page, pausing to read and converse about the content that is of greatest interest to students. Then, teachers allow children to select another book on the same topic to be read and discussed either with a partner or in a small group. Research results have indicated that the Two Books Back-to-Back method makes it easier for less-able readers to accomplish this goal (Bodrova & Leong, 1996). Specifically, students who experienced this instructional approach achieved statistically higher scores on the Stanford Achievement Vocabulary and Comprehension Subtests than treated control groups who received interventions that included either extended time with basal reading instruction (one exposure to a content subject before moving to a new topic) or silent reading of short passages on one subject after another (Block et al., 2009). The effect sizes of this intervention were large, ranging from .79 to .91 for students in grades 3 and 4.

Instructional Strategies for Young Readers

Proven Instructional Strategies: *Teaching multiple comprehension strategies in single lessons.* K–3 comprehension instruction has a long and rich research history dating back to the early 1970s. These studies have concluded that multiple comprehension strategy instruction should begin in early elementary grades. Such instruction should be delivered through "transactional" strategy lessons, a method of teaching in which multiple abilities are learned and applied to one's own cultural and experiential base through self-regulated processes, "developing students who, on their own, use the comprehension strategies that excellent readers use [as identified by Pressley & Afflerbach, 1995] (NRP, 2000; Pressley et al., 1991, p. 5; RAND, 2001; Snow et al., 1998). Such multiple comprehension strategy lessons have proven to be learned best when teachers (a) model (show students how to think when they are trying to comprehend); (b) think aloud (stop to tell students what they are thinking to comprehend a sentence, paragraph, or passage); (c) scaffold (help students develop independence in comprehension by giving as much support as needed and gradually removing teacher supports as student independence is achieved); (d) provide guided practice (allow students to practice a strategy in a teacher-led group before they are asked to apply it independently); (e) deliver direct instruction (teach students explicitly what they are to learn rather than asking them to deduce key comprehension strategies without instruction); and (f) allow for independent silent reading time for pupils to use strategies independently and metacognitively (i.e., helping students become aware that they are using a comprehension strategy; for a review of research, see Block & Pressley, 2002). By teaching readers how to use more than one comprehension process in a single lesson, K–3 students have been able to view their comprehension and meta-comprehension as a unified, self-controlled ability, and their comprehension increased considerably (Block, 1999b). Even kindergarteners can use multiple strategies, and through them, they were able to achieve higher levels of achievement than occurred for treated control groups (Brown et al., 1996; Cummins et al., 2005).

Four approaches demonstrate how this research is being used in classrooms. Among the first to teach multiple comprehension strategies in a single lesson was the "experience-text-relationship method," in which strategies of building experiential background and text cues are taught together to construct meaning (Au, 1979; Tharp, 1982). The second, "K-W-L," teaches readers to use the thought processes of what do you Know already, what do you Want to know, and what did you Learn from your reading? to comprehend (Ogle, 1986). Third, QAR (Question-Answer Relationships) teaches readers to assess whether authors are providing information explicitly or whether the reader has to go beyond what the author provides (i.e., to infer) in order to fully comprehend (Raphael & Au, 2005). Last, reciprocal teaching teaches students to query each other on their use of predicting, questioning, clarifying, and summarizing (Palincsar & Brown, 1984). Palincsar and Brown's work has been extensively expanded to include nonfictional instructional settings (Palincsar, 2006), as well as more extensive teacher modeling and scaffolding, so that even kindergarteners can lead a reading group, use strategies without teacher prompting, and independently apply the strategies that were taught (Palincsar, 1986). To demonstrate the effects of these approaches, Rosenshine and Meister (1994) conducted a review of 16 studies of reciprocal teaching and found statistically significant growth of experimental over control subjects on standardized tests of reading comprehension, as well as on experimenter-developed assessments, with an effect size of .72.

Promising Instructional Strategies: *Teaching early readers to use authorial writing patterns to learn new terms and to predict upcoming events and facts.* The goal of K–3 reading instruction is to "produce students who not only understand what they read but also know when they are not understanding; that is, they monitor their comprehension" (Pressley, 2006, p. 322). Recently, researchers discovered that students who had taught themselves to follow the structure that an author used in a text recalled more textual information than those who had not acquired this ability (e.g., Taylor, 1980). In other studies, students have been taught authorial writing patterns and how to use these superstructures to build vocabulary, comprehension, and fluency. In these lessons, teachers modeled and expected students to "get on author's train of thought (the placement of main idea and detail statements in paragraphs and in full texts) during the first few pages of a text" (Block, 2004, p. 89). Once this ability was practiced repeatedly, teachers helped develop students' independent use of other superstructures, such as how to recognize when authors repeat the same pattern in their paragraphs and how authors create an overarching structure for their full texts. For example, teachers would model how the book *Volcano* (Lauber, 1983) follows a paragraph structure in which every first sentence includes a main idea, and how a new vocabulary word is boldfaced and defined through a parenthetical expression that appears after it. The second sentence and all remaining sentences in this author's paragraphs provide "what" details about each paragraph's main idea. Next, teachers would point out how a different book about this same topic, *Why do Volcanoes Blow their Tops?* (Berger & Berger, 2001), follows a different paragraph structure. Its first sentence contains a main idea, but vocabulary words are not bolded nor do they have parenthetical expressions to define them. All subsequent sentences in this book's paragraphs report "how" details. Such lessons enable pupils to predict what kind of detail will appear in an upcoming sentence.

When pupils learned how to follow authors' trains of thought throughout to gain meaning, statistically significant gains on standardized tests of reading ability (effect sizes were above . 67) resulted (Collins, 1991; Dalton & Rose, 2008; Flavell et al., 1981). This line of research has continuously expanded to include the development of new computer-based methods of teaching students text structures. A recent study even demonstrated that Internet avatar tutors can teach these structures to adolescents as well as human tutors, with results on standardized tests of content knowledge and authorial writing superstructures tests to be statistically significant (effect sizes were above .50; Meyer et al., 2010). These effects with older readers have stimulated research into computer-based instruction in text structure for young readers at the Cognition and Technology Group at Vanderbilt University.

Lesson Characteristics for Young Readers

Proven Lesson Characteristics: *Using multicultural content and students' own multicultural and linguistic resources as features in literacy lessons.* A vivid array of principles influence reading instruction today: (a) metacognitive (teaching students to think about what they are thinking as they read); (b) multicultural (including familiar cultural content in reading lessons); (c) social (including student interactions and discussion in lessons); (d) linguistic (teaching language features); and (e) constructivist (strengthening students abilities to create their own meanings from text) (August & Shanahan, 2006). Moreover, today's lessons must be cognitively, socially, and pedagogically richer for a more widely diverse student body than ever before (Au, 2002; Banks, 2002). For instance, in 2008, for the first time in history, the majority of U.S. students attended low socioeconomic, urban schools (Florida, 2008). Many of these children were at risk for reading failure and were being raised by parents who did not speak English (Damon, 2008; Jacoby, 2008). The majority of today's students also have learned substantially fewer words, had fewer books read to them, had less independent reading time, and have spent considerably more time with nonprint activities than in reading continuous text, in comparison to peers who were raised in more affluent neighborhoods (Damon, 2008; Hart & Risley, 1995).

Numerous research-tested methods have been created to increase the opportunities for students to bring their own multicultural and linguistic resources to bear in learning to read. These methods are labeled "culturally relevant pedagogy" (for a review, see Fairbanks et al., 2009), instructional strategies for English Language Learners (ELLs; for a review, see Prater, 2009), and family literacy projects (for a review, see Edwards & Turner, 2009). One culturally relevant method is to use mentor texts (books in which an immigrant main character is learning to speak English). Lessons with these texts have been built so that both ELLs' and monolinguals' literacy abilities and human empathy increase (Au & Carroll, 1997; Ehmann & Gayer, 2009; Lacina & Block, in press). When native English speakers read about the challenges faced by their ELL classmates, empathy and appreciation of classmates' language-learning trials have increased. When ELL students read about main characters that have difficulty learning English, they have demonstrated an ability to comprehend better and connect with the text because they were living its contents. By teaching Mentor Texts Lessons (and increasing students' abilities to replicate the specific features of English syntax and semantics through them), teachers reported not only an increase in both ELLs' and monolinguals' reading abilities but a building of stronger bridges between these students' lives and the schooled literacy in U.S. academic culture (Lacina & Block, in press). Similarly, below-grade-level readers who were taught through multicultural content and their multicultural and linguistic resources achieved greater improvements (relative to control subjects) in reading comprehension on grade-level benchmark tests and portfolio assessments (Au & Carroll, 1997).

Promising Lesson Characteristics: *Scaffolding to increase students' active learning during whole class instruction*. Listening, speaking, reading, and writing are interrelated domains in a child's literacy development (Cazden, 1991). Young children who develop proficiencies in listening comprehension will possess advanced speaking vocabularies and have a greater likelihood of success in reading comprehension and writing (Cazden, 1991; Yuill & Oakhill, 1991). Information received through a variety of pathways (e.g., auditory, visual, kinesthetic) enhances short-term memory and retention (Paivio, 1986; 1991; 2008). Moreover, both action and activity are important in children's learning processes, as "merely passive experiences tend to attenuate and have little lasting effect [on independent comprehension of text]" (Gardner, 1999, p. 82).

Comprehension Process Motions (CPMs; Block et al., 2008), more advanced peer discussions, and collaborative learning groups (for a review, see Slavin et al., 2009) are ways to scaffold whole-class instruction so that students become more active learners and use more than one learning input system. CPMs are hand motions that students make to depict the unseen mental processes that they use to comprehend. These motions are designed to stimulate active learning during transactional strategy lessons by engaging both linguistic and nonlinguistic input systems. They provide young readers with concrete images to learn the unseen cognitive processes that make meaning. Students initiate a CPM while they read silently or when their teachers read orally to large or small groups to show that they have used a comprehension process that improved their understanding. To ensure that all students initiate all comprehension processes metacognitively and without teacher prompting, checklists are kept to mark which students signal their use of each comprehension process.

After 18 weeks of instruction, CPMs led to statistically significant increases in experimental students' scores on the Stanford Achievement Test (SAT-9) standardized comprehension and vocabulary tests, with moderate effect sizes of treatment on students scores on SAT-9 Vocabulary Subtest ($r^2 = .52$), abilities to recall main ideas on SAT-9 Comprehension Subtest ($r^2 = .66$), retaining details ($r^2 = .49$) and applying information in texts to life experiences ($r^2 = .53$). CPM-instructed students also increased their verbal activity in large-group settings (relative to control students who received typical reading lessons from their regular reading curriculum) by tripling both the number of comments made and the number of questions posed during guided practice session (Block et al., 2008). Teachers reported that CPMs enabled them to call upon students based on the type of thinking they wanted to discuss. Equally effective scaffolds are cooperative learning groups, cross-age and same-age tutoring (two students of different ages or the same age working together, with one acting as a tutor and the second as the tutee); structured peer-to-peer interactions (different lessons in which pairs of students work together to complete lesson objectives; for review, see Block & Dellamura, 2001/2002); and Invitational Groups (small groups in which student elect to become members to discuss and learn together; see Keene & Zimmerman, 2007). Slavin et al. (2009, p. 1332) found that "if students work in small groups to help one another master reading skills and if the success of the team depends on the learning of each team member, highly statistically significant gains in reading abilities, as measured by standardized test comparisons to control subjects, occur."

Teacher Actions for Young Readers

Proven Teacher Actions: *Using the behaviors identified in exemplary literacy teacher research to increase early reading achievement.* A large body of exemplary literacy-teacher research exists. Over the past dozen years, substantial data have been obtained to conclude that there are specific actions that teachers can take to enable their students to achieve at higher levels on standardized and criterion-referenced assessments than schoolmates who are taught by good teachers who do not include these actions in their reading instruction (Morrow et al., 1999; Pressley et al., 2001; Taylor et al., 1999; Wharton-Mc-Donald et al., 1998). Some of these teacher behaviors are valuable for all literacy educators to exhibit regardless of the grade level at which they teach.

Exemplary literacy-teacher research supports the theory that the power of the teacher (as opposed to the dominance of a particular set of instructional materials or organizational plans) is a major contributor to students' literacy growth (e.g., Bond & Dykstra, 1967; Porter & Brophy, 1988). This focus has not discounted the active role that students play in the construction of their own literacy (Rosenblatt, 1978). What students do, however, depends greatly on the instruction they receive, the instructional actions driven by their teachers, and the pupil-to-teacher interactions used to support their literacy (Vygotsky, 1978).

Exemplary literacy research has revealed 88 characteristics of highly effective teachers, their schedules, grouping systems, and the types of literacy methods that they use (Block & Mangieri, 2009; Block, et al., 2002; Taylor et al., 1999). Table 1.2 summarizes this research, presenting exemplary teacher actions that contribute to young students' literacy success at all grade levels. Data indicate that these actions have contributed to students' higher scores on standardized literacy tests, more positive reading attitudes, reading of a greater number of books, and more time on task than has occurred for schoolmates who are in classes where teachers do not include these actions in their reading instruction.

TABLE 1.2 Examples of Exemplary Literacy Teachers' Actions that Have Increased Students' Literacy Achievement at All Grade Levels

Exemplary literacy teachers...

1. ... *plan thoroughly and effectively so that they present a wide variety of enriched instruction.* For example, they teach reading as parts and wholes every day; they teach word decoding in three different ways (as letter-to-sound correspondences, word patterns, and context-sensitive semantic links in sentences).

2. ... *teach more content each day in comparison to their less exemplary peers.* By maintaining a continuously challenging, rapid pace in daily lessons, the content is (a) constantly varied; (b) of great interest to students; and (c) tied to students' interests. By such teaching actions, students stay engaged with learning constantly, and learning time increases significantly in these classrooms. Students do not engage in "busy work." Students are learning every day for 90%–100% of the time.

3. ... *teach numerous literacy strategies in single lessons and teach them interactively,* with as many as 22 strategies being discussed and answered immediately when students query (e.g., they use students' names, students' words, and complete sentences to label classroom objects, to teach phonics, and to capitalize on semantic clues interactively in decoding).

4. ... *re-teach with new examples and methods,* using as many as six or more enriched and unique re-teaching lessons a week (if needed) to ensure student mastery of a concept. On a daily basis, they post words and charts that students generate so that students can see words that they know.

5. ... *set aside time to read and write real texts,* which are constantly monitored. As many as two 30- to 45-minute periods are scheduled in many of these teachers' rooms, in which students can sustain independent writing of continuous text every day.

6. ... *monitor the writing process and reading instructional process daily so that new concepts are learned in three days* (as opposed to automatically scheduling a full week to teach each new concept). They (a) use generative fast mapping and generative learning as features in every literacy lesson; (b) use students' ideas for prewriting; (c) give more choices and modified methods of writing; (d) show three examples before students start to write; (e) require all students to master strategies, and they do not stop their individualized instruction until all meet this requirement; (f) check each writing and reading experience for students' integration of two or more taught literacy skills; and (g) use clipboards that they carry with them constantly to check that every child has received positive reinforcement each week.

7. ... *stimulate students' initiation of literacy learning* by using 12 statements from Table 1, such as "What question do you think I would ask about this story and why?" and "Do you want to pass, think about it for one minute, or ask a friend for a clue?"

8. ... *use the PAR (Praise, Assist and Return feedback cycle—see pages 161–163, 165–166, 168, 175— to meet individual students' needs.* They meet with students individually each week, and they personalize their modeling and think aloud to use their students' multicultural and linguistic resources. They make every member of the class an expert in one of the student's talent areas so that every student knows that their teacher "knows them by heart" and cares for them deeply.

9. ... *maintain superb classroom management, and they employ inventive methods by which students manage their own learning.* They prepare for anticipated interruptions or distractions in advance so all students know that everyone's learning is important to their teacher at all times. They attend completely to one student at a time. Outside their classroom doors are daily-prepared checklists of the exact items that students will need to carry into the room so that classes may often begin before the bell rings. Teachers tie discipline statements to learning so that when students stop misbehaving, they instantly realize that self-discipline leads to increased learning.

Source: Block & Mangieri, 2009

Promising Teacher Actions: *Implementing six domains of exemplary teacher competencies at distinct grade levels.* Besides the exemplary actions that literacy teachers at all grade levels exhibit, other competencies contribute to students increases in literacy test scores when used at specific grade levels (e.g., Block, Oaker, & Hurt, 2002). These competencies fall into six domains (Block et al., 2002; Block & Mangieri, 2009; Parris & Block, 2007; Wharton-McDonald et al., 1998). These domains are (a) executing a *dominant teaching style* that creates greatest growth at students' specific developmental level by communicating high expectations effectively (Ruddell, 1997); (b) *motivating students* with methods that are most valued by pupils at distinct age levels (Guthrie et al., 1999; Guthrie et al., 2000); (c) *relating to students* in different ways by understanding each learner's potential (Snow et al., 1998); (d) *re-teaching* by effectively supporting pupils' attempts to learn new concepts (Snow at al., 1998); (e) *creating successful lessons* by providing clear purposes (Anderson, 1992); and (f) *building highly effective classroom milieus* (Morrow et al., 1999). Table 1.3 presents the domains of competence (from these six) that have produced the largest growth in student achievement at specific grade levels. When these actions are included in reading instruction, students have exhibited literacy growth on end-of-year standardized tests that amounts to an average of 2.3 years more than that of schoolmates at the same reading ability levels who did not receive instruction that incorporated these actions (e.g., Block et al., 2002).

PROVEN AND PROMISING PRACTICES IN UPPER ELEMENTARY READING INSTRUCTION

In this section, research investigating proven and promising practices for upper elementary grades (focusing on comprehension instruction) is discussed. This research is presented in the following domains: (a) content advances in vocabulary and higher-level comprehension instruction; (b) the scope and sequence of comprehension strategy instruction, as well as methods by which such instruction is individualized; (c) lesson characteristics that meet the learning needs of today's upper elementary students and build their student "agency" (i.e., students' abilities "to imagine and create new ways of being in social settings" [Holland et al., 2001, p. 5]); and (d) teachers' actions that enable them to provide expanded explanations (providing students with more than a simple definition of an objective to be learned), elaborated feedback (providing students with information about which parts of their reading behaviors are valuable and which can be improved, as well as showing how to do so), and instruction at points of need (providing the intervention at the exact point in a reading episode when students' confusions or misunderstandings occur). These proven and promising practices are summarized in Table 1.4.

TABLE 1.3 Most Important Contributor to Exemplary Reading Instruction at Specific Grade Levels

Grade Level	Dominant Instructional Competence	Example of Exemplary Reading Instruction in Action
Kindergarten (Learning environment)	Instruction is filled with transcriptions of words into notes, messages and signs for students' use in class and at home.	Students write, draw, and record in their own "words" what they learned about reading this day, writing twice a day, and taking their best work home each day.
First Grade (Lesson characteristics)	Instruction shows how to use five domains of reading interactively; texts read are intrinsically valuable to children.	Individual lessons are rapidly paced and filled with playful analogies to teach difficult skills, with teachers answering students' questions as soon as they are asked.
Second Grade (Instructional strategies)	Instruction stimulates students' queries about literacy: "What did you learn best yesterday and what do you need to learn more about today?" which strengthens students' confidence to grow (regardless of their ability level).	Lessons are inventive and differentiated from earlier grade levels, because new methods that students have never seen before are created to teach the five skill domains interactively. That way, the "old" seems "new" and not failure-fraught (e.g., CPMs, Mentor Texts).
Third Grade (Teachers re-teach and individualize instruction)	Instruction motivates students to become active learners and to work with teachers so together they can be lifted over their unique literacy obstacles.	Teachers are masters at flexible grouping and re-teaching immediately until mastery occurs (attending to generative fast mapping), working with many varied groups simultaneously.
Fourth Grade (Students teach with teachers as peer experts)	Teachers begin lessons by stating differentiated goals and provide varied assignments masterfully so at-risk readers do not feel demeaned and students' choices are honored.	Teachers are coaches, using pupils as experts for peers' reference; collaborative learning teams work together to reach deep understanding of the material.
Fifth Grade (Student learning needs met)	Reading instruction requires students to organize their thoughts, to explore and learn on their own, and to think on their feet and on their own about abstractions.	Instill a desire to produce reading that is excellent by always holding students accountable and teaching vast amounts of material while stimulating students' deep understanding of how all literacy strategies work interactively.

TABLE 1.4   Proven and Promising Upper Elementary Reading Instruction and Comprehension Instructional Strategies at Work

Name	Research-Based Examples in Classrooms	Research Supporting Their Effectiveness
Proven Content: *Teaching vocabulary strategies that unravel the complex relationship between students' abilities to discern word meanings and comprehend*	Teaching vocabulary strategies for frequently occurring words, affixed words, content area terms, and unusual-appearing or unusual-sounding words (Baumann et al., 2002; Beck, McKeown, & Kucan, 2007; Beck, Perfeti, & McKeown, 1982; Block, Hasni, & Mangieri, 2005; Block & Mangieri, 2004, 2006; Block et al., 2010)	Baumann, 2009; Baumann et al., 2003; Baumann et al., 1998; Bertram, Baayen, & Schreuder, 2000; Biemiller & Boote, 2006; Biemiller & Slonim, 2001; McKeown, Beck, Omanson, & Pople, 1985; NRP, 2000; Willingham, 2006/2007
Promising Content: *Teaching higher-level thinking strategies of inference and metacognition*	Accountable talk and peer tutors (Collins, 1991; Dalton & Rose, 2008; Gee, 2008; Kintsch, 2003; VanDijk & Kintsch, 1983; Verhoeven, 1990); and "Buddy Beside Me" (Block, 2004; Block & Dellamura, 2001/2002; Cain, Oakhill & Lemmon, 2004; Zinar, 2000)	Baker, 2008; Cartwright, 2008; Leu et al., 2008; Mangieri & Block, 1994; Paivio, 2008; Reznitskaya et al., 2008; Rosenblatt, 1978; Schraw, 1998; Smolkin, McTigue, & Donovan, 2008; Swaab, Baynes, & Knight, 2002; Vygotsky, 1978; Williams, 2008
Proven Instructional Strategies: *Teaching nine research-based comprehension strategies*	Teach students to predict/infer; monitor metacognitively; questioning, imagery, look-back, rereading, and fix-it strategies; apply content to life; find main ideas, summarize, and draw conclusions; evaluate; synthesize (Dewitz, Jones, & Leahy, 2009; Willingham, 2006/2007)	Block & Duffy, 2009; Bond & Dykstra, 1967; Hoffman et al., 1994; Holmes & Singer, 1964; Jitendra et al., 2001; Miller & Blumenthal, 1993; NRP, 2000; Schmitt & Hopkins, 1993; Slavin et al., 2009; Yuill & Oakhill, 1991
Promising Instructional Strategies: *Individualizing comprehension instruction (generative fast mapping, generative learning, and helping students set their own purposes for reading)*	Mid-Year Surveys, "Read 2 Pages and Set Your Purpose," and Discovery Discussions (Block, 1999b; Block et al., 2008, 2009; Block, Mangieri, Knudson, Rose, & Kirby, 2010; Morrison et al., 2004; Rose & Block, 2010; Wittrock, 1974)	Anderson & Roit, 1993; Betts & Welch, 1963; Block, 1993, 2004; Block & Mangieri, 2004, 2006; Duffy, Roehler, & Hermann, 1988; Gee, 2008; Schmitt, 2005; Wilkinson, 2006; Woodward & Talbert-Johnson, 2009

Name	Research-Based Examples in Classrooms	Research Supporting Their Effectiveness
Proven Lesson Features: *Creating methods that match Generation Y's special learning needs*	Generative fast mapping, generative learning, helping students set their own purposes for reading	Damon, 2008; Doctorow, Wittrock, & Marks, 1978; Glowacki, Lanucha, & Pietrus, 2001; Hahne, Eckstein, & Friederici, 2004; Jacoby, 2008; Kandel, 2006; Manset-Williamson & Nelson, 2005; Neuborne & Kerwin, 1999
Promising Lesson Features: *Teaching comprehension and decoding strategies at exact points of need*	Individualized schema-based learning (Kelley & Clausen-Grace, 2007; Moss & Young, 2010) and PAR (Praise-Assist-Return) (Block et al., 2009; Block, Schaller, Joy, & Gaine, 2002)	Block et al., 2009; Hacker & Tenet, 2002; Paris & Hamilton, 2009; Raphael & Au, 2005
Proven Teacher Actions: *Delivering expanded explanations and elaborated feedback more effectively*	Detailed examples of expanded explanations and elaborated feedback can be found in Block & Israel (2004); Duffy (2009); Meyer et al. (2010); Keene & Zimmerman (2007); and Paris & Jacobs (1984)	Anderson, 1992; Anderson & Roit, 1993; Block, 1993, 1999 [1999 a]; Brown et al., 1996; Cain et al., 2004; Collins, 1991; Duffy et al., 1988; Meyer et al., 2010;
Promising Teachers' Actions: *Increasing student agency through the use of more student-led groups and scaffolds during whole class instruction*	Teacher Reader Groups (Block, 2004; Block & Pressley, 2007; Tyner, 2009), and literacy practices identified in survey of Blue Ribbon schools (Block, 2009)	Block & Pressley, 2007; Block, Rodgers, & Johnson, 2004; Clark, Blackburn, & Newell, 2010; Holland et al., 2001; Woodward & Talbert-Johnson, 2010

Content for Upper Elementary Grades

Proven Content: *Teaching vocabulary strategies that unravel the complex relationship between students' ability to discern word meanings and their ability to comprehend.* NRP (2000) found that vocabulary instruction contributed to increases in students' reading abilities. These studies (e.g., Beck, Perfetti, & McKeown, 1982) indicated that

acquiring a broad vocabulary and a rich base of background knowledge will yield substantial and longer-term benefits, but doing so is more difficult and time consuming [than once supposed]. This knowledge must be the product of years of systematic instruction as well as constant exposure to high quality books that provide incidental exposure to a great deal of new vocabulary and knowledge. (Willingham, 2006/2007, pp. 45, 50)

For example, McKeown et al. (1985) found that even as many as 12 high-quality encounters with words was not enough to create mastery of a word's meaning. Such mastery required robust instruction using the research-based vocabulary-acquisition approaches discussed in this section (Beck et al., 1983; Stahl & Fairbanks, 1986).

The method by which this research is applied in exemplary classrooms is to teach vocabulary-building strategies and allow students to select which would be the most valuable to try first (Block & Mangieri, 2004, 2006). To infer the meaning of an unfamiliar "target" word, students are instructed in the following strategies. First, *Vocabulary Strategies to Learn Frequently Occurring Words* teaches students to use (a) syntax clues (the role that the target word performs in a sentence); (b) semantic clues (the meanings of other words that surround the target word); and (c) the sounds of the target word's onset (first consonant[s] and vowel[s]) to deduce meaning (Bertram et al., 2000; Block et al., 2010). Next, *Vocabulary Strategies to Learn Affixed Words* teaches students to reflect on the meanings of the affix and root of a word, and to infer how these meanings combine to make sense in the sentence in which they appear (Biemiller & Boote, 2006; Biemiller & Slonim, 2001); *Vocabulary Strategies to Learn Content-Specific Words* teaches students that these words are likely to be nouns that describe very specific aspects of the subject being read, and before selecting a meaning they should read to the bottom of the page (Baumann et al., 2003; Beck et al., 2007); and *Vocabulary Strategies to Learn Words with Unusual Letter Orders or Sounds* teach students to recognize that when a word has an unusual letter pattern or blended sound that does not sound like any English word that they have ever heard before, these words may have an unusual word history, may be derived from a foreign language, or are idiomatic. Students will be best served to ask someone the meaning of these unknown words, as expert readers do, to derive meanings from strange-sounding or strange-appearing words. Then students are taught to create their own personalized mnemonic devices (memory aids) to remember that word's meaning (Block & Mangieri, 2004, 2006). When students were taught at least one of these strategies (e.g., Baumann et al., 2003) or all of these strategies (Block et al., 2005, 2010) experimental subjects substantially outperformed uninstructed peers on their ability to derive meaning of unfamiliar words (r^2 ranged from .79 to .46), with slight but statistically significant effects on comprehension scores on standardized tests (r^2 ranged from .16 to .40).

Promising Content: *Teaching higher-level thinking strategies of inference and metacognition increases reading abilities.* Within the last 2 decades, researchers have examined methods by which students' higher-level thinking abilities can be initiated during reading (see Mangieri & Block, 1994, for summaries of 13 bodies of research in this field). These data have proven that students' more complex, higher-level thinking comprehension abilities can be developed when students are taught how to place the making of meaning under their own control (Rosenblatt, 1978) and are supported in their application of these during reading (Vygotsky, 1978). More specifically, the following reviews of research demonstrate the variety of ways in which these higher-level thinking abilities are being used to increase students' literacy competencies: Dalton & Rose's (2008) research on methods of scaffolding digital comprehension; Gee's (2008) research relative to the use of specialist language in comprehension; Leu et al.'s (2008) research in developing students' comprehension of new literacies for online reading; Paivio's (1986, 1991, 2008) use of metacognitive and inference instruction based on neuroscience; Reznitskaya et al.'s (2008) development of inference and metacognition through argument schema theory (developing higher-level comprehension by debating opposing viewpoints); and Smolkin et al.'s (2008) and Williams' (2008) application of higher-level thinking strategies to expository texts.

Examples of how this research is being applied in today's classrooms is through the use of accountable talk (students' initiation of discussions of topics, controversies, and concepts of their interest) and peer tutors (Kintsch, 2003; Van Dijk & Kintsch, 1983; Verhoeven, 1990) such as the "Buddy Beside Me" approach (Block, 2004; Block & Dellamura, 2001/2002), a hybrid of assisted/repeated reading (i.e., methods of instruction in which teachers read a page and students read the next page or the same page over again) and a modification of reciprocal teaching. In this instruction, teachers create many opportunities for pairs of students to practice complex advanced higher-level thinking strategies. If the lesson is designed so that the teacher selects the books that students are to read, pupils are allowed to select the partner with whom they will read the book. In these lessons, students sit side-by-side and read from the same book. The first student reads three pages orally as the partner follows along, reading silently. The partner then summarizes, in two sentences, what was read. Next, the reader of the pair asks the listener a question from the three pages' content. As soon as the next page is turned, the listener predicts what is likely to appear and tells what strategies were used to make that prediction. Then students' roles switch. As Rusty, a fifth-grader in Atlanta stated, "We like 'Buddy Beside Me' because we want someone beside us to say 'Wow' to when we read something that is really neat!" Many pupils also need their partners' help on words and concepts that are difficult for them to understand alone.

Several fields of research have suggested that teaching problem-solving abilities (Collins, 1991), inference (for a research review, see Kintsch, 2003) and metacognition (e.g., for a review of these studies, see Baker, 2008 and Cartwright, 2008) lead to increases in students' literacy as measured on standardized achievement tests (see reviews of these data in Schraw, 1998 and Swaab et al., 2002). For instance, in a longitudinal analysis, elementary students were assessed on a battery of tests measuring vocabulary, decoding, verbal ability, working memory, inference-making skill, metacognition, and knowledge of story grammar (Cain, Oakhill, & Lemmon, 2004). Inference-making and metacognitive abilities were the only two independent variables to contribute unique variance to comprehension after removing the effects of working memory, decoding, and verbal abilities (Cain et al., 2004, with an effect size of .89). Moreover, Zinar (2000) examined the extent to which instruction in metacognitive skills influenced inference abilities. Fourth-grade students read passages containing embedded inconsistencies, which called upon the students' metacognition and problem-solving skills. Data indicated that students who slowed down their reading when encountering an inconsistency and employed a taught problem-solving process (e.g., looking back at the sentence that preceded the inconsistent statement) scored statistically higher on a standardized comprehension test than control subjects (Zinar, 2000).

Instructional Strategies for Upper Elementary Grades

Proven Instructional Strategies: *Teaching nine research-based comprehension strategies.* Bond & Dykstra's (1967) and Holmes & Singer's (1964) landmark works on the effects of various reading programs on students achievement found that a curriculum panacea is not the answer to improve all students' comprehension. More recently, Slavin et al. (2009) conducted a meta-analysis of 79 upper elementary reading instructional studies. Data revealed that "programs designed to change daily teaching practices have substantially greater research support than programs that focus on curriculum or technology alone. The salience here is that the 'fixes' that rely on either texts or technology alone will not be as likely to help students learn as much as those that involve thoughtful instructional interventions involving the manner in which teachers and their students work together" (p. 1331).

Other researchers found that core reading programs actually teach too many strategies and can interfere with students' abilities to comprehend. They promote the instruction of more strategies than can be substantiated by empirical evidence or effectively taught in a single year (Dewitz et al., 2009; Miller & Blumenthal, 1993; Schmitt & Hopkins, 1993). In particular, if present basal manuals are followed explicitly, 18–45 comprehension skills would have to be taught each year (Dewitz, et al., 2009). Further, certain strategies are easier to learn than others. For example, inferring is a more difficult skill to learn than visual imagery or predicting (Yuill & Oakhill, 1991), meaning that many scopes and sequences should be altered to incorporate recent research findings (Jitendra et al., 2001; Hoffman et al., 1994).

The method by which this research is applied in exemplary classrooms is to include the nine empirically validated comprehension strategies described in the bottom section of Box 1.1. The top of Box 1.1 contains labels of the 18–45 strategies that are contained in many core reading programs, but they have not been shown to increase students' comprehension reliably and consistently on standardized literacy tests. One of the reasons that these strategies have not proven to produce substantial student growth is because many of these strategies represent the same ability. By teaching any strategy through the use of several different labels, students have become confused as to which process they are to use to comprehend and how a newly taught strategy differs from another that they were taught previously (Dewitz et al., 2009; Jitendra et al., 2001).

BOX 1.1   COMPREHENSION STRATEGIES

Sample of the Recommended Strategies Taught in the Past (From 120 in the *Wisconsin Design for Reading Skill Development* (1976) to the 45 contained in today's Core Reading Programs)

Setting a purpose, interpreting the structures in texts that authors use to divide content and communicate emphasis (e.g., subheadings, boldfacing, labeling, table of contents), being alert to main ideas, knowing the most important ideas attached to author's goal, relating what one reads to prior knowledge, asking questions, drawing conclusions, changing the hypothesis, adding to themes as the meaning of a text unfolds, predicting, mental imagery, making images to relate text by using one's own and the prior knowledge presented in that text, identifying the gist, learning to choose which strategy would be helpful, interpreting author's intentions, paraphrasing, pausing to reflect, interpreting and generating insights using fix-up strategies, monitoring while reading, re-reading when something isn't clear, evaluating the text as to how well it is or is not written, noting whether you should recommend a text to others, consciously constructing a summary, self-regulating one's own comprehension, internalizing text, corroborating text, contextualizing text, being retrospective about text, actively listening, using mnemonics, organizing text, independently engaging one's own metacognition, using study skills while reading, reorganizing text, completing content analyses through main idea pattern/conceptual pattern/problem-solution/cause-effect/story plot/compare-contrast, using and being aware of the seven parts of story grammar as aids to comprehending, constructing self-explanations, elaborating on one's understanding, and clarifying meanings.

Strategies That Have Been Researched and Validated To Be Highly Successful Since 2000

1. Predict and infer: Using titles, text features, sections, pictures, and captions, continuously updating and re-predicting what will occur next in a text.
2. Monitor metacognitively: Activate many comprehension strategies to decode and derive meaning from words, phrases, sentences, and texts; and by personally, independently building background knowledge.
3. Question: Stop to reread and initiate comprehension processes when the meaning is unclear and to integrate large units of meaning.
4. Image: Construct meanings from text by wondering, noticing, and generating mental pictures.
5. Look-backs, rereads, and fix-it strategies: Continue to reflect on the text before, during, and after reading, continuously deciding how to shape the knowledge base for personal use.
6. Apply to life: Connect ideas in text based on personal experiences, knowledge of other texts, and general world knowledge; making certain that inferences are made quickly so as to not divert attention from the actual text but rather help the reader better understand it; activate one's own background knowledge and connections.
7. Find main ideas, summarize, and draw conclusions: Make sure to include information gained from story grammar or textual features; if students can't make a valid summary of information read to date, this is the signal to go back to reread; story structure, authorial writing patterns.
8. Evaluate: Come to a fictional text expecting (and ascertaining) that students note the setting, characters, and story grammar early on and recognize problems, solutions, and resolutions as they reveal themselves throughout the text.
9. Synthesize: Come to an informational text watching for textual features, access features, unique types of information, sequence of details, and conclusions, combining all of these authorial clues and superstructures to make meaning; create one's own graphic organizers.

The nine strategies at the bottom of Box 1.1 have sufficient scientific basis to be considered valid and essential. Of these, the first five were verified through extensive empirical tests for inclusion in comprehension instruction (NRP, 2000); the last four have been found to improve comprehension since the NRP report (for a review, see Block & Duffy, 2009). For example, question generating (students generate questions so they can infer and apply content while they read) and multiple strategy instruction produced the highest effects on standardized comprehension tests (averaging effect sizes of .90 and .88, respectively, which may be interpreted as "large" effects of these two strategies on overall comprehension ability) and "comparable to students moving from the 50th to the 82nd percentile [on the standardized test]" (Willingham, 2006/2007, p. 42). These effect sizes were computed from a meta-analysis of research studies relative to these strategies, as reported in Willingham.

Promising Instructional Strategies: *Individualizing comprehension instruction.* Many teachers have difficulty re-teaching comprehension strategies to grades 3–6 struggling readers (Anderson & Roit, 1993; Woodward & Talbert-Johnson, 2009). When such instruction is too teacher-dominated, students do not learn how to apply strategies without prompting. Alternatively, when individualized instruction is too sparse, pupils do not develop the tools necessary to comprehend independently (Duffy et al., 1988). Comprehension instruction can be individualized by teaching (a) pupils to *want* to correct their confusions, tie new information to prior knowledge, and apply relevant information to their lives; (b) specific strategies and how to select the ones needed to fully understand increasingly complex texts; and (c) how to think about one's own thinking (Block, 1993).

Mid-Year Surveys and *Discovery Discussions* (Block, 2004, 2008) have proven to help teachers individualize instruction for struggling readers. The surveys are a formal means by which students can report how they feel about their reading abilities and which methods they find to be of greatest value. Mid-year surveys ask students what they need, individually, to become better readers. They are conducted each year before students leave for winter vacations. They contain questions to which upper grade students respond in writing and early-grade students reply orally. The questions are (a) Which of the activities that we have completed thus far this year have enabled you to learn the most and why? (b) What activities have *not* helped you learn as much and why? (c) What new methods would you like to add when we return from winter vacation that would help you learn? and (d) How should we change our class to have time for these new activities, and why would these changes assist you to learn more? Use of this instrument is particularly important when it is determined that teachers do not know which methods students judge to have most improved their reading abilities (Block, 1999b, 2004; Rose & Block, 2010).

Discovery Discussions is a new type of one-to-one conferencing. Through these discussions, students have a voice in the next direction their instruction will take. Discovery Discussions can be scheduled by a teacher or a student. At any time during the conference, either the teacher or student can explain things that (s)he has learned (or ask specific questions to gain more information) about the pupil's reading abilities. After the student has asked any questions that he or she has about reading, teachers ask, (a) "What do you need *me* to do to help you comprehend better?" (b) "What have you learned about your reading abilities since we last met, and how did you learn it?" and (c) "What do you want to learn next to become a better reader, and what do you judge to be the best action we could take to help you learn it?" Then, the teacher and student develop a plan to individualize this student's instruction, which is revisited at month's end. Discovery Discussions enable students to work at their best pace and to become more actively engaged in methods that they judge to be best. Mid-Year Surveys and Discovery Discussions attain high levels of success because today's students know and can express the level of their drive and how internally motivated they are to become better readers. Research has shown that only 4% of teachers who did not use these methods could determine the instructional strategies that their students judged to be most effective in increasing their reading abilities. In contrast, when these methods were incorporated into lessons at least twice a year, 89% of teachers correctly identified the instructional strategies that their pupils judged to advance their reading skills most effectively (Block, 1999b; Rose & Block, 2010).

Lesson Features for Upper Elementary Grades

Proven Lesson Features: *Creating methods that match today's students' special learning needs (generative fast mapping, generative learning, and helping students set their own purposes for reading).* Since 1948, lessons have included features designed to meet individual student needs (Betts & Welch, 1963). The first feature was to vary lessons based on students' overall ability levels through the creation of three different reading groups. The features of lessons taught to these groups varied by depth and pace of instruction. During the 62 years of research since then (for a review, see Schmitt, 2005), other lesson features have been added to meet the special learning needs of Baby Boomers, and Generation Xers.

Today's Generation Y students, born from 1982 to 2001 (Jacoby, 2008), have profited from more specific changes in their lesson features than was true of previous generations (Damon, 2008). Today's students appear to require these more specialized lesson modifications because the students (a) are greater in number and are more racially and ethnically diverse; (b) have had access to technology as a learning tool from the time they were born; (c) more often view peers as reliable sources of new information; (d) value immediate answers; (e) do not want or need to memorize information as much as previous generations did; (f) learn more visually/

kinesthetically/independently; (g) favor customized learning experiences in which they create their own purposes and are allowed to choose what they read, as well as the format of their projects; and (h) desire education to be entertaining (Neuborne & Kerwin, 1999). They enjoy peer learning because they tend to look to classmates to determine "what is worth paying attention to, what is fun, and what is work" (Damon, 2008, p. 208). Research also suggests that today's students' brains have developmental differences, which contribute to these more specialized learning needs (Hahne et al., 2004; Kandel, 2006).

Without the instructional modifications of historical practices, today's students' multilevel, hypertexted thinking leads many pupils to seek only snippets of information rather than to dig for deeper understanding (Damon, 2008). For example, they do not like to be asked a question for which their teacher already knows the answer. Thus, when teachers use pictures on book covers to ask, "What do you think this book will be about?" most Gen Yers pick a detail in the picture about which they want to learn. When their specific topic is not discussed by the end of the text, these pupils, more often than previous generations, come to judge that the time spent reading a full text has been wasted, making the reading of full-length texts less valued by the end of the lesson than before it began. Also, when asked a question based only on a picture and title, Gen Yers tend to answer with a one-word response so as either not be wrong and embarrassed before their peers or not to appear as "know-it-alls." Unfortunately, classmates who hear such one-word answers assume that they are being asked to learn single terms or facts during this lesson. Therefore, many do not use their higher-level thinking strategies, such as inferring, comparing, or evaluating the book's information. Thus, using practices that were effective for previous generations of readers often creates more negative than positive effects on reading attitudes and achievement for today's generation (Block et al., 2008).

Instead, using new lesson features, such as helping these students to set their own purposes for reading, generative fast mapping, and generative learning, have proven to produce statistically significant increases in gen Yers' reading achievement (Block et al., 2008, 2009). For instance, to incorporate students' desires to set their own purposes, one lesson adaptation is to ask Gen Yers to read three pages and then to stop and set their own purposes for continuing to read. This is because the students will have gotten on that author's train of thought so that they can more reliably predict what content will appear in the book. Then, to meet students' needs to interact with peers, books read by a large or small group are halted before the last chapter is reached. When the book is stopped, peers discuss their thinking to this point and their proposed endings (as well as the comprehension strategies used to reach these decisions). Such lesson features have proven not only to increase generation Yers' literacy abilities but to make learning more enjoyable because their learning needs are being addressed (Block & Mangieri, 2009; Block et al., 2008).

Equally effective is adding generative fast mapping as a lesson feature. Generative fast mapping is a lesson characteristic that accelerates students' metacognition and self-management (Doctorow et al., 1978; Manset-Williamson & Nelson, 2005; Wilkinson, 2006). It provides students with several consecutive opportunities to demonstrate their success in independently applying a single, directly taught strategy before they are taught a second major strategy (Morrison et al., 2004). It focuses lessons on a single target—one major strategy—until students can independently apply it without teacher prompting. Only when such independent use is demonstrated in novel, untaught texts will a new strategy be taught. Generative fast-mapped instruction has successfully increased at-risk, urban, and ELLs' comprehension and vocabulary at statistically significant levels on the Stanford 9 Reading Achievement Test, the Northwest Evaluation Association Assessment, and ability to write longer sentences (writing 4.4 more words per sentence), use multisyllabic words in their composition ($r^2 = .40$), and exhibit positive literacy attitudes as measured by the Title 1 Reading Attitude Assessment (Block et al., 2008, 2010; Block & Mangieri).

Following Wittrock's (1974) research, generative learning is applied as a lesson feature in which students (a) describe how they comprehended or (b) give examples of independently applying a strategy in texts. Students read novel texts and tell their teachers how they applied a strategy (that was just taught) to a selection of text that was not used in instruction. Such generative learning has been demonstrated to create a higher level of student cognitive and affective involvement in reading, as measured through standardized instruments. These changes in lesson characteristics also resulted in statistically greater retention than lessons that engage lower levels of student ownership when tests over material taught were administered several months later (Glowacki et al., 2001).

Promising Lesson Features: *Teaching comprehension and decoding strategies at exact points of need.* Many educators are "unsure of how to teach different comprehension strategies at specific points in a text when it is needed to obtain a full understanding of the text" (Raphael & Au, 2005, p. 208). Even after 5 months of transactional comprehension instruction, many students could not transfer comprehension strategies independently without teachers prompting them to do so (Hacker & Tenent, 2002).

The method by which this research is applied in the classroom is *individualized schema-based learning or PAR* (Praise-Assist-Return; Block et al., 2009; Kelley & Clausen-Grace, 2007; Moss & Young, 2010). When students come to an unknown word or a confusing concept while reading silently, they are being asked to raise their hands. Teachers praise students individually for

(a) wanting to become a better reader, (b) knowing what comprehension strategies they have already tried, and/or (c) the correct aspects of students' efforts. This first step in teaching at point of need, *Praise*, is designed to build students' self-regulation and affect. The second step, *Assist*, provides support through a personalized re-teaching experience. Immediately following the *Praise* statement, teachers describe (through a brief think-aloud) the most effective strategy to use at that particular point in the text. They begin this mini-lesson with the phrase, "When I have this problem while I'm reading, I think..."

The last step, *Return*, is designed to build students' self-efficacy and meta-cognitive use of the re-taught strategy. This *Return* step occurs during the last few minutes of that day's 20-minute silent reading or at the beginning of the next day's period. During this step, teachers return to each student who had been assisted during the silent reading period and points to a new but similar word or sentence in a text. The teacher requires students to demonstrate and describe the re-taught strategy and how they will use it to overcome such reading challenges independently in the future. When personalized instruction such as this is provided at point of need, students have performed at statistically higher levels on standardized reading tests, with an effect size of .91 (Block et al., 2002, 2009). As Paris & Hamilton (2009) concluded, "During the past 20 years, researchers have shown that comprehension can be increased significantly when it is taught explicitly, when it is intertwined with engaging activities, when it is focused on learning new content, and when it is assessed and re-taught to a deep level of new understanding. In this view, enhancing children's reading comprehension is synonymous with teaching children to be thoughtful, strategic and independent learners" (p. 49).

Upper Elementary Grades Teacher Actions

Proven Teacher Actions: *Delivering expanded explanations and elaborated feedback more effectively.* Prior to 1990, many teachers taught reading by merely (a) giving directions, (b) telling students to "read carefully," (c) assigning workbook pages, or (d) asking literal questions after a text was read (Duffy et al., 1988). Only a few educators were highly skilled in explaining comprehension processes, or what Paris & Jacobs (1984, p. 2085) labeled, "making thinking public." These teachers presented descriptions of what they were thinking and expanded explanations or think-alouds to describe what, how, and when to apply the strategies that they taught (Block & Israel, 2004; Keene & Zimmerman, 2007).

Teachers must be "relentless. When an explanation does not work the first time, it must be adjusted, and teachers have to try again. They must give students multiple opportunities to use what they've learned while in the pursuit of real reading" (Duffy, 2009, p. 13). Similarly, feedback must be elaborated and not simply stated as "your main idea and details were incorrect. Try again." Teachers should describe what is good or how to correct errors: "Your main idea was not quite right. You're missing some details. Check the pattern for the main idea [shown in the graphic of this comprehension strategy] to make sure you understand what is being asked for and rewrite your details including all that you can remember from the text" (Meyer et al., 2010, p. 87). When such expanded explanations and elaborated feedback are given, avatar Internet tutors have proven to be as effective in getting students to use a text-structure strategy as trained human tutors (Meyer et al., 2010). Detailed examples of expanded explanations and elaborated feedback can be found in Block & Israel (2004), Duffy (2009), and Keene & Zimmerman (2007).

Such teacher actions have proven to be highly effective at all grade levels (Anderson, 1992; Anderson & Roit, 1993; Block, 1993, 1999; Brown et al., 1996; Collins, 1991;). For instance, in the Brown et al. study, the performance of even at-risk, low- performing students who experienced expanded teacher explanation and elaborated feedback for a full school year statistically outperformed control subjects who received regular reading instruction that adhered to regular reading curricula on standardized tests of word-level knowledge and comprehension abilities, with effect sizes that ranged from .69 to .94.

Promising Teachers' Actions: *Increasing student agency through the use of more student-led groups and scaffolds during whole class instruction.* Literacy stakeholders are asking educators to include students as active agents in planning, implementing, and assessing their learning (Block, 2009). More frequently, the most agency that students exercise in literacy instruction is whether or not they will "do school well, play by the rules, take up the curriculum as it is designed, and work hard to master the skills required to perform well on standardized tests. Agency in today's classrooms lies primarily with teachers; they have the power to choose texts and activities and to decide what the acceptable ways to engage are" (Clark et al., 2010, p. 124).

A survey of Blue Ribbon schools, which are schools that are recognized by the U.S. Department of Education for high student achievement, found several methods by which student agency has moved these schools from "good" to "great" (Block, 2009). Students usually work in groups for a portion of every class, discussing and generating new ideas. Students, and not their teachers, create the mental-model graphics for strategies learned, which are displayed on class and hallway walls (Clark et al., 2010; Woodward & Talbert-Johnson, 2010). School milieu includes what Gen Yers want to learn in the ways that they learn it best. The same strategies are presented throughout the day in all classes to enable rapid, generative fast mapping and generative learning. Students create needs-based reading groups. They also select important expository reading experiences in which they want to engage. For example, in October of 2009, students in one Blue Ribbon school in New Jersey elected to join reading groups to develop (a) a new school policy to overcome bullying, (b) community impact projects, and (c) their artistic abilities. Perhaps as a result of these agency actions, the stifling feel of student suppression did not permeate the reading rooms in these buildings. Student energy was boundless. Students would rather have been in their reading classes than in hallways; they smiled, genuinely greeting visitors because they wanted to share the important reading projects that they initiated.

Teacher Reader Groups is another method by which student agency is being built in exemplary classrooms (Block, 2004; Block & Pressley, 2007; Tyner, 2009). These are student-led groups that enable Teacher Reader leaders to re-teach the reading strategy that their teachers just presented so new voices enter the instructional process. Teacher Reader Group leaders verbalize the processes they used to apply reading strategies, and they put the steps in their thinking in their own words (Block, 2004; Block et al., 2004). To begin, teachers prepare prompts for each group leader to follow. These prompts are instructions about how far to read in the text, when to stop, and what questions to ask peers so they can describe how they applied the strategy taught. Teachers select books that require students to use the strategy repeatedly. This lesson frees teachers to walk around and hear what children say about the comprehension strategy. Based on quantitative data, Teacher Reader Group members of high, medium, and low ability experienced statistically greater growth, relative to control subjects who received regular reading instruction in word knowledge, comprehension, and vocabulary, as measured by standardized tests (Block, 2004; Block & Pressley, 2007). Based on qualitative data, these students' attentiveness also increased, presumably because (among other things): (a) Teacher Reader leaders took seriously the job of generating new examples to clarify, (b) students felt as if their voices were heard more frequently, and (c) the number of pupil-generated questions rose substantially (Block & Pressley, 2007).

Several directions for new research remain. The most prevalent are (a) How long does it take to develop automaticity (LaBerge & Samuels, 1974), the automatic ability to employ comprehension strategies for various levels of reading ability? (b) How can we best vary the density/depth of instruction throughout a student's career? (c) How can we teach students to think metacognitively more often? (d) How can we develop more targeted and effective interventions, especially for older and ELL students? (e) How can we better meet the reading needs of English Language Learners? and (f) How can we best teach the new reading skills that will be needed by ever-evolving technology?

SUMMARY OF PROVEN AND PROMISING READING INSTRUCTIONAL PRACTICES

In this chapter, research supporting promising and proven instructional practices in today's schools was described. The message is clear: We know a lot about reading instruction and a lot about how to prevent reading failure. We are much closer to helping all students attain literacy success. At the K–3 level, we know how to teach basic reading skills interactively and how to use nonfictional content more effectively. We know how to teach authorial writing patterns, to use more kinesthetic and oral supports in learning, and to employ exemplary teachers' actions.

In the upper grades, we know how to (a) improve vocabulary and higher-level thinking instruction, (b) teach the most effective comprehension strategies, (c) implement re-teaching strategies individually at exact points of need, (d) use expanded explanations and elaborated feedback, and (e) create methods through which Gen Yers' special needs are addressed and their agency increased.

In the future, changes in text features and density, the rapidity with which vocabulary is created, new ways in which individuals are positioned and sanctioned in our multicultural worlds, natural- versus second-language learning needs, and hybrid forms of virtual reading (many of which have yet to be created) will test the proven and promising methods presented in this chapter. Such new data and methods will advance our field and are welcomed. Bringing unity to our field was not the intent of this chapter. Providing syntheses of research that can be used to overcome ineffective practice was. This and the companion mathematics instruction chapter in the present volume were designed to broaden and deepen the effectiveness of present practices by providing an expanded research base that supports their use. Through this synthesis, may we better remember where we've been so as not to repeat past errors. May we welcome more student voices in the creation of future research-based methods designed to increase their literacy success. By 2024, before today's kindergarteners graduate from high school, may we have implemented more effective reading instruction at each grade level so that all students can use literature to help them experience "the great stories that lead to a deeper understanding of what it means to be truly human" (Scholastic Bill of Reading Rights, 2010, p. 1).

REFERENCES

Anderson, V. (1992). A teacher development project in transactional strategy instruction for teachers of severely reading-disabled adolescents. *Teaching and Teacher Education, 8,* 391–403.

Anderson, V., & Roit, M. (1993). Planning and implementing collaborative strategy instruction for delayed readers in grades 6–10. *Elementary School Journal, 94,* 121–137.

Au, K. (1979). Using the experience-text-relationship method with minority children. *Reading Teacher, 32*(5), 403–412.

Au, K. H. (2002). Multicultural factors and the effective instruction of students of diverse backgrounds. In A. E. Farstrup & S. J. Samuels (Eds.), *What research has to say about reading instruction* (3rd ed., pp. 392–415). Newark, DE: International Reading Association.

Au, K. H., & Carroll, J. H. (1997). Improving literacy achievement through a constructivist approach: The KEEP Demonstration Classroom Project. *Elementary School Journal, 97,* 203–221.

August, D., & Shanahan, T. (Eds.). (2006). *Developing literacy in second-language learners: Report of the national literacy panel on language minority children and youth.* Mahwah, NJ: Lawrence Erlbaum.

Baker, L. (2008). Metacognition in comprehension instruction: What we've learned since NRP. In C. C. Block & S. R. Parris (Eds.), *Comprehension instruction: Research-based best practices* (2nd ed., pp. 65–79). New York: Guilford Press.

Ball, E., & Blachman, B. (1991). Does phoneme awareness training in kindergarten make a difference in early word recognition and developmental spelling? *Reading Research Quarterly, 26,* 49–66.

Banks, J. (2002). *An introduction to multicultural education.* Boston: Allyn and Bacon.

Baumann, J. F. (2009). Vocabulary and reading comprehension. In S. E. Israel & G. Duffy (Eds.), *Handbook of research on reading comprehension* (pp. 312–340). Mahwah, NJ: Lawrence Erlbaum.

Baumann, J. F., Edwards, E. C., Boland, E., Olejnik, S., & Kame'enui, E. W. (2003). Vocabulary tricks: Effects of instruction in morphology and context on fifth-grade students' abilities to derive and infer word meanings. *American Educational Research Journal, 40,* 447–494.

Baumann, J. F., Edwards, E. C., Font, G., Tereshinski, C. A., Kame'enui, E. J., & Olejnik, S. (2002). Teaching morphemic and contextual analysis to fifth-grade students. *Reading Research Quarterly, 37,* 150–176.

Baumann, J. F., Hoffman, J. V, Moon, J., & Duffy-Hester, A. (1998). Where are teachers' voices in the phonics/whole language debate? Results from a survey of U. S. elementary teachers. *The Reading Teacher, 50*(8), 636–651.

Beck, I. L. McKeown, M. G., & Kucan, L. (2007). Different ways for different goals, but keep your eye on the higher verbal goals. In R. K. Wagner, A. E. Muse, & K. R. Tannenbaum (Eds.), *Vocabulary acquisition: Implications for reading comprehension* (pp. 182–204). New York: Guilford Press.

Beck, I. L., Perfetti, C. A., & McKeown, M. G. (1982). Effects of long-term vocabulary instruction on lexical access and reading comprehension. *Journal of Educational Psychology, 89,* 269–297.

Berger, M. & Berger, G. (2001). *Why do volcanoes blow their tops?* New York: Scholastic.

Bertram, R., Baayen, R. H., & Schreuder, R. (2000). Effects of family size for complex words. *Journal of Memory and Language, 42*(3), 390–405.

Betts, E. A., & Welch, C. M. (1963). *Betts basic readers* (Rev. ed.). New York: American Book.

Biemiller, A., & Boote, C. (2006). An effective method for building meaning vocabulary in primary grades. *Journal of Educational Psychology, 98,* 44–62.

Biemiller, A., & Slonim, M. (2001). Estimating root word vocabulary growth in normative and advantaged populations: Evidence for a common sequence of vocabulary acquisition. *Journal of Educational Psychology, 93,* 498–520.

Block, C. C. (1993). Strategy instruction in a student-centered classroom. *The Elementary School Journal, 94*(2), 137–153.

Block, C. C. (1999a). The case for exemplary teaching, especially for students who begin first grade without the precursors for literacy success. In T. Shanahan (Ed.), *49th yearbook of the National Reading Conference* (pp. 71–85). Chicago: National Reading Conference.

Block, C. C. (1999b). Comprehension: Crafting understanding. In L. B. Gambrell, L. M. Morrow, S. B. Neuman, & M. Pressley, (Eds.), *Best practices in literacy instruction* (pp. 98–118). New York: Guilford Press.

Block, C. C. (2004). *Teaching comprehension: The comprehension process approach.* Boston: Allyn & Bacon.

Block, C. C. (2009). *Site evaluations of National Blue Ribbon Schools of Excellence.* Newark, NY: State Department of Education.

Block, C. C., & Dellamura, R. Y. (2001/2002) Better book buddies. *The Reading Teacher, 54*(4), 364–370.

Block, C. C., & Duffy, G. G. (2009). Research on teaching comprehension: Where we've been and where we're going. In C. C. Block & S. R. Parris (Eds.), *Comprehension instruction: Research-based best practices* (2nd ed., pp. 19–37). New York: Guilford Press.

Block, C. C., Hasni, J., & Mangieri, J. N. (2005, December). *Effects of direct vocabulary instruction on students' vocabulary, comprehension and affective development.* Paper presented at the annual meeting of the National Reading Conference, Miami, FL.

Block, C. C., & Israel, S. E. (2004). The ABCs of performing highly effective think alouds. *The Reading Teacher, 58*(2), 154–167.

Block, C. C., & Mangieri, J. N. (2004). *Powerful vocabulary for reading success and Word forward.* New York: Scholastic, Inc.

Block, C. C., & Mangieri, J. N. (2006). *Vocabulary enriched classroom.* New York: Scholastic, Inc.

Block, C. C., & Mangieri, J. N. (2009). *Exemplary literacy teachers: What schools can do to promote success for all children* (2nd ed.). New York: Guilford Press.

Block, C. C., Mangieri, J. N., Knudson, K., Rose, M. L., & Kirby, K. (2010). Vocabulary instruction that significantly increases vocabulary, comprehension, writing abilities and reading attitudes for ELLs and urban youth. *Journal of Literacy Behavior, 49*(4), 203–219.

Block, C. C., Oaker, M., & Hurt, N. (2002). Exemplary literacy teachers: A continuum from preschool through grade 5. *Reading Research Quarterly, 33,* 115–134.

Block, C. C., Parris, S. R., Reed, K. L, Whiteley, C. S., & Cleveland, M. D. (2009). Instructional approaches that significantly increase reading achievement. *Journal of Educational Psychology, 101,* 262–281.

Block, C. C., Parris, S. R., & Whiteley, C. S. (2008). CPMs: A Kinesthetic Comprehension Strategy. *The Reading Teacher, 61*(6), 460–472.

Block, C. C., & Pressley, M. (Eds.). (2002). *Comprehension instruction: Research-based best practices.* New York: Guilford Press.

Block, C. C., & Pressley, M. (2007). Best practices in teaching comprehension. In L. B. Gambrell, L. M. Morrow, & M. Pressley, (Eds.), *Best practices in literacy instruction* (pp.220–242). New York: Guilford Press.

Block, C. C., Rodgers, L., & Johnson, R. (2004). *Comprehension process instruction: Creating reading success in grades K–3.* New York: Guilford Press.

Block, C. C., Schaller, J. L., Joy, J. A., & Gaine, P. (2002). Process-based comprehension instruction: Perspectives of four reading educators. In C. C. Block & M. Pressley (Eds.), *Comprehension instruction: Research-based best practices* (pp. 42–61). New York: Guilford Press.

Bond, G. L., & Dykstra, R. (1967). The cooperative research program in first-grade reading instruction. *Reading Research Quarterly, 2,* 10–141.

Bodrova, E., & Leong, D. J. (1996). *Tools of the mind: The Vygotskian approach to early childhood education.* Upper Saddle River, NJ: Prentice Hall.

Bradley, L, & Bryant, P. (1985). *Rhyme and reason in reading and spelling.* Ann Arbor: University of Michigan Press.

Brown, R., Pressley, M., Van Meter, P., & Schuder, T. (1996). A quasi-experimental validation of transactional strategies instruction with low-achieving second grade readers. *Journal of Educational Psychology, 88,* 18–37.

Cain, K., Oakhill, J. V., & Lemmon, K. (2004). Individual differences in the inference of work meanings from context: The influence of reading comprehension, vocabulary knowledge and memory capacity. *Journal of Educational Psychology, 96*(4), 671–681.

Cartwright, K. B. (2008). Cognitive flexibility and reading comprehension: Relevance to the future. In C. C. Block, & S. R. Parris (Eds.), *Comprehension instruction: Research-based best practices* (2nd ed., pp. 50–64). New York: Guilford Press.

Cazden, C. (1991). *Balancing whole language.* Portsmouth, NH: Heinemann.

Chall, J. S. (1983). *Stages of reading development.* New York: McGraw-Hill.

Chall, J., & Jacobs, V. A. (2003). The classic study on poor children's fourth-grade slump. *American Educator, 27*(1), 14–15, 44.

Chall, J. S., Jacobs, V. A., & Baldwin, L. E. (1990). *The reading crisis: Why poor children fall behind.* Cambridge, MA: Harvard University Press.

Clark, C. T., Blackburn, M. V., & Newell, G. E. (2010). From chasm to conversation: Bridging divides in research on adolescent literacies. *Reading Research Quarterly, 45*(1), 116–127.

Collins, C. (1991). Reading instruction that increases thinking abilities. *Journal of Reading, 34,* 510–516.

Cummins, C., Stewart, M. T., & Block, C. C. (2005). Teaching several metacognitive strategies together increases students' independent metacognition. In S. E. Israel, C. C. Block, K. L. Bauserman, & K. Kinnucan-Welsh (Eds.), *Metacognition in literacy learning: Theory, assessment, instruction, and professional development* (pp. 277–295). Mahwah, NJ: Lawrence Erlbaum.

Dalton, B., & Rose, D. (2008). Scaffolding digital comprehension. In C. C. Block & S. R. Parris (Eds.), *Comprehension instruction: Research-based best practices* (2nd ed., pp. 347–361). New York: Guilford Press.

Damon, W. (2008). *The path to purpose: Helping youth find their calling in life.* New York: Basic Books.

Dewitz, P., Jones, J., & Leahy, S. (2009). Comprehension instruction in core reading programs. *Reading Research Quarterly, 44*(2), 226–251.

Doctorow, M., Wittrock, M. C., & Marks, C. (1978). Generative processes in reading comprehension. *Journal of Educational Psychology, 70,* 109–118.

Dole, J. A., Sloan, C., & Trathen, W. (1996). Teaching vocabulary within the context of literature. *Journal of Reading, 38,* 452–460.

Droop, M., & Verhoeven, L. T. (1998). Background knowledge, linguistic complexity, and second-language reading comprehension. *Journal of Literacy Research, 30*(2), 253–271.

Duffy, G., Roehler, L., & Hermann, G. (1988). Modeling mental processes helps poor readers become strategic readers. *The Reading Teacher, 41,* 762–767.

Duffy, G. G. (2009). *Explaining reading: A resource for teaching concepts, skills, and strategies* (2nd ed.). New York: Guilford Press.

Duke, N. K. (2000). 3.6 minutes per day: The scarcity of informational texts in first grade. *Reading Research Quarterly, 35,* 202–224.

Duke, N. K., & Pearson, D. (2002). Effective practices for developing reading comprehension. In A. E. Farstrup & S. J. Samuels (Eds.), *What research has to say about reading instruction* (3rd ed., pp. 205–242). Newark, DE: International Reading Association.

Edwards, R. A., & Turner, J. D. (2009). Family literacy and reading comprehension. In S. E. Israel & G. Duffy (Eds.), *Handbook of research on reading comprehension* (pp. 622–642). Mahwah, NJ: Erlbaum.

Ehmann, S., & Gayer, K. (2009). *I can write like that!* Newark, DE: International Reading Association.

Ehri, L. C. (1991). Development of the ability to read words. In R. Barr, M. L. Kamil, P. Mosenthal, & P. D. Pearson (Eds.), *Handbook of reading research* (Vol. 2, pp. 383–417). New York: Longman.

Ehri, L. C., & Wilce, L. (1987). Does learning to spell help beginners learn to read words? *Reading Research Quarterly, 22,* 47–65.

Fairbanks, C. M., Cooper, J. E., Masterson, L., & Webb, S. (2009). Culturally relevant pedagogy and reading comprehension. In S. E. Israel & G. Duffy (Eds.), *Handbook of research on reading comprehension* (pp. 587–606). Mahwah, NJ: Erlbaum.

Flavell, J. H., Speer, J. R., Green, F. L., August, D. L., & Whitehurst, G. J. (1981). The development of comprehension monitoring and knowledge about communication. *Monographs of the Society for Research in Child Development, 46,* 1–65.

Florida, R. (2008). *Who's your city.* New York: Basic Books.

Gamse, B. C., Tepper-Jacob, R., Horst, M., Boulay, B., & Unlu, F. (2008). *Reading First impact study: Final report.* Washington, DC: U.S. Department of Education, Institute for Educational Sciences.

Gardner, H. (1999). *The disciplined mind.* New York: Simon & Schuster.

Gee, J. P. (2008). Games and comprehension: The importance of specialist language. In C. C. Block & S. R. Parris (Eds.), *Comprehension instruction: Research-based best practices* (2nd ed., pp. 309–320). New York: Guilford Press.

Gersten, R., Fuchs, L. S., Williams, J. P., & Baker, S. (2001). Teaching reading comprehension strategies to students with learning disabilities: Review of research. *Review of Educational Research, 71*(2), 279–320.

Glowacki, D., Lanucha, C., & Pietrus, D. (2001, May). *Improving vocabulary acquisition through direct and indirect teaching.* (ERIC Document Reproduction Service No. ED453542).

Griffith, P. (1991). Phonemic awareness helps first graders invent spellings and third graders remember correct spellings. *Journal of Educational Psychology, 76,* 1059–1064.

Guthrie, J. T., Cox, K. E., Knowles, K. T., Buehl, M., Mazzoni, S. A., & Fasulo, L. (2000). Building toward coherent instruction. In L. Baker, M. J. Dreher, & J. T. Guthrie (Eds.), *Engaging young readers: Promoting achievement and motivation* (pp. 209–236). New York: Guilford Press.

Guthrie, J. T., Wigfield, A., Metsala, J. L., & Cox, K. E. (1999). Motivational and cognitive predictors of text comprehension and reading amount. *Scientific Studies of Reading, 2,* 231–256.

Hacker, D. J., & Tenent, A. (2002). Implementing reciprocal teaching in the classroom: Overcoming obstacles and making modifications. *Journal of Educational Psychology, 94*(4), 367–389.

Hahne, A., Eckstein, K., & Friederici, A. D. (2004). Brain signatures of syntactic and semantic processes during children's language development. *Journal of Cognitive Development, 16*(7), 1302–1318.

Hart, B., & Risley, T. R. (1995). *Meaningful differences in the everyday experiences of young American children.* Baltimore: Paul H. Brookes.

Hoffman, J. V., McCarthey, S. J., Elliott, B., Bayles, D. L., Price, D. P., & Ferree, A. (1994). The literature-based basals in first grade classrooms: Savior, Satan, or same-old, same-old? *Reading Research Quarterly, 35,* 28–44.

Holland, D., Lachicotte, W., Jr., Skinner, D., & Cain, C. (2001). *Identity and agency in cultural worlds.* Cambridge, MA: Harvard University Press.

Holmes, J. A., & Singer, H. (1964). Theoretical models and trends toward more basic research in reading. *Review of Educational Research, 34,* 127–155.

Jacoby, S. (2008). *The age of unreason.* New York: Basic Books.

Jitendra, A. K., Chard, D., Hoppes, M. K., Renouf, K., & Gardill, M. C. (2001). An evaluation of main idea strategy instruction in four commercial reading programs: Implications for students with learning disabilities. *Reading and Writing Quarterly, 17,* 53–73.

Kandel, E. R. (2006). *In search of memory: The emergence of a new science of mind.* New York: W. W. Norton & Company.

Keene, E. O., & Zimmermann, S. (2007). *Mosaic of thought: The power of comprehension strategy instruction* (2nd ed.). Portsmouth, NH: Heinemann.

Kelley, M. & Clausen-Grace, S. (2007). Using think-alouds to examine reader-text interactions. *Reading Research Quarterly, 34,* 194–216.

Kintsch, W. (2003). *Comprehension: A paradigm for cognition.* New York: Cambridge University Press.

Lacina, J., & Block, C. C. (in press). Building ELLs and monolinguals English competencies: Using mentor texts in new ways to craft their language and writing abilities. *The Reading Teacher.*

LaBerge, D., & Samuels, S. J. (1974). Toward a theory of automatic information processing in reading. *Cognitive Psychology, 6,* 293–323.

Lauber, P. (1983). *Volcano.* New York: Aladdin.

Leu, D. J., Coiro, J., Castek, J., Hartman, D. K., Henry, L. A., & Reinking, D. (2008). Research on instruction and assessment in the new literacies of online reading comprehension. In C. Block & S. Parris (Eds.), *Comprehension instruction: Research-based best practices* (2nd ed., pp. 321–346). New York: Guilford Press.

Mackey, M. (1997). Good-enough reading: Momentum and accuracy in the reading of complex fiction. *Research in the Teaching of English, 31*(4), 428–458.

Mangieri, J. N., & Block, C. C. (1994). *Creating powerful thinking in teachers and students: Diverse perspectives.* New York: Harcourt Brace College Publishers.

Manset-Williamson, G., & Nelson, J. M. (2005). Balanced, strategic reading instruction for upper-elementary and middle school students with reading disabilities: A comparative study of two approaches. *Learning Disability Quarterly, 28,* 124–139.

McKeown, M. G., Beck, I. L., Omanson, R. C., & Pople, M. T. (1985). Some effects of the nature and frequency of vocabulary instruction on the knowledge and use of words. *Reading Research Quarterly, 20,* 522–535.

Meyer, B. J. F., Wijekumar, K., Middlemiss, W., Higley, K., Lei, P., Meier, C., & Spielvogel, J. (2010). Web-based tutoring of the structure strategy with or without elaborated feedback or choice for fifth- and seventh-grade readers. *Reading Research Quarterly, 45*(1), 62–92.

Miller, S. D., & Blumenthal, P. C. (1993). Characteristics of tasks used for skill instruction in two basal reader series. *Elementary School Journal, 94,* 33–47.

Morrison, R. G., Krawczyk, D. C., Holyoak, K. J., Hummel, J. E., Chow, T. W., Miller, B. L., & Knowlton, B. J. (2004). A neurocomputational model of analogical reasoning and its breakdown in Frontotemporal Lobar Degeneration. *Journal of Cognitive Neuroscience, 16*(2), 260–271.

Morrow, L. M., Tracey, D. H., Woo, D. G., & Pressley, M. (1999). Characteristics of exemplary first-grade literacy instruction. *The Reading Teacher, 52*(5), 462–476.

Moss, B., & Young, M. (2010). Teaching comprehension to young readers. *The Reading Teacher, 63*(6), 441–450.

Moss, M., Fountain, A. R., Boulay, B., Horst, M., Rodger, C., & Brown-Lyons, M. (2008). *Reading First implementation evaluation: Final report.* Cambridge, MA: Abt Associates.

National Council of Teachers of English and International Reading Association. (1959). *Critical reading: An introduction.* Urbana, IL: NCTE and Newark, DE: IRA.

National Educational Goals Panel. (1999). *Reading achievement state by state, 1999.* Washington, DC: U.S. Department of Education.

National Endowment for the Arts. (2004). *Reading at risk: A survey of literacy practices in America.* Washington, DC: NETA.

National Reading Panel. (2000). *Teaching children to read. An evidence-based assessment of the scientific literature on reading and its implications for reading instruction: Reports of the subgroups.* Bethesda, MD: NICHD.

Neuborne, E., & Kerwin, K. (1999, February 15). Generation Y. *Bloomberg Businessweek.* Retrieved from http://www.businessweek.com/1999/99_07/b3616001.htm

Ogle, D. (1986). K-W-L: A teaching model that develops active reading of expository text. *Reading Teacher, 39,* 564–570.

Paivio, A. (1986). *Mental representations: A dual coding approach.* New York: Oxford University Press.

Paivio, A. (1991). Dual coding theory: Retrospect and current status. *Canadian Journal of Psychology, 45,* 255–287.

Paivio, A. (2008). Looking at reading comprehension through the lens of neuroscience. In C. Block & S. Parris (Eds.), *Comprehension instruction: Research-based best practices* (2nd ed., pp. 101–113). New York: Guilford Press.

Palincsar, A. S. (1986). The role of dialogue in providing scaffolded instruction. *Educational Psychologist, 21,* 73–98.

Palincsar, A. S. (2006, December). *Multiple strategy instruction at work in science classrooms.* Paper presented at the annual meeting of the National Reading Conference, Los Angeles, CA.

Palincsar, A. S., & Brown, A. L. (1984). Reciprocal teaching of comprehension-fostering and comprehension-monitoring activities. *Cognition and Instruction, 1,* 117–175.

Paris, S. G., & Hamilton, E. E. (2009). The development of children's reading comprehension. In S. E. Israel & G. Duffy (Eds.), *Handbook of research on reading comprehension* (pp. 32–53). Mahwah, NJ: Erlbaum.

Paris, S. G., & Jacobs, J. (1984). The benefits of informed instruction for children's reading awareness and comprehension skills. *Child Development, 55,* 2083–2093.

Parris, S. R. & Block, C. C. (2007). The expertise of adolescent literacy teachers. *Journal of Adolescent & Adult Literacy, 50*(7), 582–598.

Porter, A., & Brophy, J. (1988). Synthesis of research on good teaching. *Educational Leadership, 45*(8), 74–85.

Prater, K. (2009). Reading comprehension and English language learners. In S. E. Israel & G. Duffy (Eds.), *Handbook of research on reading comprehension* (pp. 607–621). Mahwah, NJ: Erlbaum.

Pressley, M. (2006). *Reading instruction that works: The case for balanced teaching* (3rd ed.). New York: Guilford Press.

Pressley, M., & Afflerbach, P. (1995). *Verbal protocols of reading: The nature of constructively responsive reading.* Hillsdale, NJ: Erlbaum.

Pressley, M., Allington, R. L., Wharton-McDonald, R., Block, C. C., & Morrow, L. N. (2001). *Learning to read: Lessons from exemplary first grade classrooms.* New York: Guilford Press.

Pressley, M., Gaskings, I. W., Cunicelli, E. A., Burdick, N. J., Schaub-Matt, M., Lee, D. S., & Powell, N. (1991). Strategy instruction at Benchmark School: A faculty interview study. *Learning Disability Quarterly, 14,* 19–48.

RAND Reading Study Group. (2001). *Reading for understanding: Towards an R & D program in reading comprehension.* Washington, DC: RAND Education.

Raphael, T. E., & Au, K. H. (2005). QAR: Enhancing comprehension and test taking across grades and content areas. *The Reading Teacher, 59*(3), 206–221.

Reznitskaya, A., Anderson, R. C., Dong, T., Li, Y, Kim, I. & Kim, S. (2008). Learning to think well: Application of argument schema theory to literacy instruction.

In C. C. Block & S. R. Parris (Eds.), *Comprehension instruction: Research-based best practices* (2nd ed., pp.196–213). New York: Guilford Press.

Rose, M. L., & Block, C. C. (2010). *Changing the way we introduce books: Increasing student involvement to expand comprehension.* Unpublished manuscript, Texas Christian University.

Rosenblatt, L. M. (1978). *The reader, the text, the poem: The transactional theory of the literary work.* Carbondale: Southern Illinois University Press.

Rosenshine, B., & Meister, C. (1994). Reciprocal teaching: A review of the research. *Review of Educational Research, 66,* 181–221.

Ruddell, R. B. (1997). Researching the influential literacy teacher: Characteristics, beliefs, strategies, and new research directions. In C. K. Kinzer, K. A. Hinchman, & D. J. Leu (Eds.), *Inquiries in literacy theory and practice: 46th yearbook of the National Reading Conference* (pp. 37–53). Chicago: NRC.

Schmitt, M. C. (2005). Measuring students' awareness and control of strategic processes. In S. E. Israel, C. C. Block, K. L. Bauserman, & K. Kinnucan-Welsh (Eds.), *Metacognition in literacy learning: Theory, assessment, instruction and professional development* (pp. 315–335). Mahwah, NJ: Erlbaum.

Schmitt, M. C., & Hopkins, C. J. (1993). Metacognitive theory applied: Strategic reading instruction in the current generation of basal readers. *Reading Research and Instruction, 32,* 12–24.

Scholastic. (2010). *Scholastic Reading Bill of Rights.* New York: Scholastic, Inc.

Schraw, G. (1998). Promoting general metacognitive awareness. *Instructional Science, 26,* 113–125.

Slavin, R. E., Lake, C., Chambers, R., Cheung, A., & Davis, S. (2009). Effective reading programs for the elementary grades: A best-evidence synthesis. *Review of Educational Research, 79*(4), 1391–1466.

Smith, N. (1978). *History of reading instruction.* New York: World Book.

Smolkin, L. B., McTigue, E. M., & Donovan, C. A. (2008). Explanation and science text: Overcoming the comprehension challenges in nonfiction text for elementary students. In C. Block & S. Parris (Eds.), *Comprehension instruction: Research-based best practices* (2nd ed.). New York: Guilford Press.

Snow, C. E., Burns, M. S., & Griffin, P. (Eds.). (1998). *Preventing reading difficulties.* Washington, DC: National Academy Press.

Stahl, S. A., & Fairbanks, M. M. (1986). The effects of vocabulary instruction: A model-based meta-analysis. *Review of Educational Research, 56,* 72–110.

Swaab, T. Y., Baynes, K., & Knight, R. T. (2002). Separable effects of priming and imageability on word processing: An ERP study. *Cognitive Brain Research, 15*(1), 99–104.

Tangel, D., & Blachman, B. (1992). Effect of phoneme awareness instruction on kindergarten children's invented spelling. *Journal of Reading Behavior, 24,* 233–261.

Taylor, B. M. (1980). Children's memory for expository text after reading. *Reading Research Quarterly, 15,* 399–411.

Taylor, B., Pearson, P. D., Clark, K. F., & Wolpole, S. (1999). Effective schools/accomplished teachers. *Reading Teacher, 53*(2), 156–159.

Tharp, R. (1982). The effective instruction of comprehension: Results and description of the Kamehameha Early Education Program. *Reading Research Quarterly, 17*(4), 503–527.

Tyner, B. (2009). *Small-group reading instruction: A differentiated teaching model for beginning and struggling readers* (2nd ed.). Newark, DE: International Reading Association.

Van Dijk, T., & Kintsch, W. (1983). *Strategies of discourse comprehension.* New York: Academic Press.

Verhoeven, L. T. (1990). Acquisition of reading in a second language. *Reading Research Quarterly, 25*(2), 90–114.

Vygotsky, L. S. (1978). *Mind in society.* Cambridge: MIT Press.

Wharton-McDonald, R., Pressley, M., & Hampton, J. (1998). Literacy instruction in nine 1st grade class-rooms: Teacher characteristics and student achievement. *Elementary School Journal, 99,* 101–128.

Wilkinson, K. M. (2006). *Fast mapping and vocabulary expansion.* Worcester: University of Massachusetts Medical School, Eunice Kennedy Shriver Center.

Williams, J. P. (2008). Explicit instruction can help primary students learn to comprehend expository text. In C. C. Block & S. R. Parris (Eds.), *Comprehension instruction: Research-based best practices* (2nd ed., pp. 171–182). New York: Guilford Press.

Williams, J. P., Hall, K. M., Lauer, K. D., Stafford, K. B., DeSisto, I. A., & de Cani, J. S. (2005). Expository text comprehension in the primary grade classroom. *Journal of Educational Psychology, 94,* 235–248.

Willingham, D. T. (2006/2007, Winter). The usefulness of *brief* instruction in reading comprehension strategies. *American Federation of Teachers,* 39–45, 50.

Wisconsin Design for Reading Skill Development. (1976). *The Wisconsin design for reading skill development kit, grades K-12.* Madison: University of Wisconsin, Wisconsin Research Center for Cognitive Development.

Wittrock, M. C. (1974). Learning as a generative process. *Educational Psychologist, 11,* 87–95.

Woodward, M. M., & Talbert-Johnson, C. (2009). Reading intervention models: Challenges of classroom support and separated instruction. *Reading Teacher, 63*(3), 190–200.

Yuill, N., & Oakhill, J. (1991). *Children's problems in reading comprehension.* Cambridge, UK: Cambridge University Press.

Zinar, S. (2000). The relative contributions of word identification skill and comprehension-monitoring behavior to reading comprehension ability. *Contemporary Educational Psychology, 25,* 363–377.

CHAPTER 2

PROVEN AND PROMISING

The Eye of the Beholder?

Rollanda Estby O'Connor
University of California at Riverside

Cathy Collins Block's aim with her chapter is valuable: to provide a compact synthesis of research to help teachers pinpoint proven practices. The task of developing a best-evidence synthesis is to gather and evaluate available source material. My role with this response is to amend and expand this discussion of available evidence. While my views of excellent instruction often dovetail with Block's recommendations in "Proven and Promising Reading Instruction," my intent in this chapter is to consider evidence and points of view that at times contradict her conclusions or open additional evidence for consideration.

Teachers are familiar with the phrase, "Research says..." and unfortunately have learned to distrust it because it is used so frequently by textbook publishers and others who advocate a method or material that has not been field-tested rigorously. This distrust makes it all the more important for researchers who work toward implementing sound procedures in classrooms to ensure that the support they offer for recommendations is well ground-

Instructional Strategies for Improving Students' Learning, pages 43–52
Copyright © 2012 by Information Age Publishing

ed. In particular, if teachers or scholars review citations in a paper, each citation should offer direct evidence in support of the recommendation. Block organizes the research she reviews into practices with sufficient weight of evidence to be labeled "proven" and others with some, but less-weighty evidence, "promising." In many instances, my reading of the evidence suggests a reverse on which particular practices are strongly supported by multiple rigorous studies and which practices have limited support currently, despite their appeal. Throughout this chapter, I explore sources for areas where my recommendations differ from Block's: differing source material as evidence of effectiveness, differing interpretation of findings cited in Block's review, and what counts as evidence for effectiveness.

Every field of research has its own set of warrants for what "counts" as source material. Viewing practices from alternative perspectives (e.g., general education, special education, school psychology, educational psychology) can reveal new sources of evidence and account for differing conclusions. Researchers in each field consult and publish for different audiences, each with its own journals and outlets. Thus, when researchers disagree, the source of the difference could be what each researcher considers the gold standard for evidence. Researchers in one field do not necessarily read the journals in other fields, even when they are closely related. I write from a special education perspective, which uses peer-reviewed journals in special education or educational psychology as authority. Where book chapters and practitioner journals are cited in Block's review, it can be difficult for readers to find or evaluate the primary sources, and so I add evidence from special education journals to reframe recommendations.

In addition to evaluating different source material, we have differing interpretations for identical collections of evidence. One example is the *National Reading Panel Report of the Subgroups* (NRP, 2000), which we both respect. While Block contends that this source "found that phonemic awareness, phonics, comprehension, vocabulary, and fluency are the proven critical components to be taught," my understanding (reflected in the document's opening chapter) was that the panel merely used these categories organizationally. They selected these topics through their informed judgment to divide up the task of classifying and analyzing an enormous body of work and to determine the strength of evidence supporting various approaches to teaching children to read within each of these five categories. As Block suggests (and the NRP reports also), research of the past 15 years supports integrating activities for teaching phonemic awareness and phonics by contextualizing phonemic awareness with letters and sounds. This integration consistently generates stronger effects than either instructional focus in isolation (Ball & Blachman, 1991; Hatcher, Hulme, & Ellis, 1994; O'Connor, Jenkins, & Slocum, 1995). However, Block's claim that the NRP supports integrating phonemic awareness, letter sounds, and students drawing pictures to represent words is unfounded in this literature. In fact, none of the studies she cites in support of this "proven" practice included drawing pictures of words. I do not suggest that drawing pictures is a bad idea, just that this "proven" recommendation is not validated by the evidence cited in her chapter.

As additional examples of moving beyond the evidence, Block suggests that "even kindergartners can lead a reading group;" however, the Palincsar (1986) study she cites to support this assertion was conducted with first graders and their teachers. In this research, the first graders did not read the books; rather, the teacher read aloud to them and scaffolded the discussion. Block later suggests that kindergartners were able to achieve higher levels of achievement through metacognition and multiple strategies; however, the studies she cites to support this kindergarten recommendation used first and second graders as participants. Thus, I suggest that we know little about whether kindergartners are up to these tasks.

In first and second grades, Block suggests that we should attribute failures of the Reading First (RF) schools to students not taught to use comprehension and decoding skills interactively. In revisiting Gamse et al.'s (2009) study of the effect of RF, which Block cited for this point, I found no mention of failure to integrate instruction. In contrast, a major finding from that report was that teachers who spent more time on multiple reading components from the NRP (2000) generated higher reading comprehension scores. When tested individually, time spent on these dimensions of reading was statisticallly and positively related to reading achievement in grades 1 and 2. While the report shows that teachers in RF schools spent more time than those in control classes teaching each of the five components (including statistically more time teaching reading comprehension), analyses to show that teachers were not taught to use the components interactively were not conducted. For older students, a study by Calhoon, Sandow, and Hunter (2010) demonstrated that reading skills taught intensively in isolation generated stronger effects on reading comprehension than integrated skill instruction. It is possible that integrating comprehension and decoding skills is effective, but at present we lack evidence to support this assertion.

For second graders, Block describes reading two books back-to-back as a promising practice for early readers and builds an appealing case for the need for more expository text in the primary grades. While few would argue against more expository text earlier in school, the research she used to support this practice (Block, Parris, Reed, Whitely, & Cleveland, 2009) compared approaches for students in second through sixth grades and found that building schemata by reading two books on the same topic was less effective than other approaches for the second graders. In contrast to her recommendation, second and third graders made better progress in summarizing and retaining information with transactional learning (in which students read fictional text followed by group discussion) than by reading two expository books back-to-back. A statistically significant interaction showed that this approach was successful for the sixth graders in the study, but the findings did not support her recommendation for early readers.

As the range of cultures and language experiences grows in public schools, teachers and policymakers strive to employ the strongest instructional approaches to improve life outcomes for diverse students, and Block's attention to issues of culture and English Language Learners is welcome. Reading teachers find it intuitively appealing to use students' cultural contexts in their reading instruction, and as Block writes, "teachers reported not only to increase both [English Language Learners' (ELLs')] and monolinguals' reading abilities but to build stronger bridges between these students' lives and...schooled literacy." It may also be important to note that some of the sources cited as confirmation for linking students' cultural contexts to reading instruction (e.g., August & Shanahan, 2006) contradict Block's suggestion that doing so is a proven lesson characteristic; instead, they state in their recent work that "We were disappointed at the paucity of experimental evidence on how to teach literacy to English language learners and were quite tentative in our claims, based on so few studies" (August & Shanahan, 2010, p. 344). Thus, the source she cites as evidence for a proven practice found these recommendations to rest on tentative grounds. August and Shanahan's finding does not contradict notions of culturally responsive teaching, but it demonstrates the lack of research to confirm this practice as proven. Some studies have reported improved attitudes and participation of ELL students, which (although not assessed in these studies) may improve literacy outcomes over time. I believe, with Block, that teachers should do all they can to increase the relevance of instruction to students' lives; I also acknowledge that it is my opinion and not proven practice.

Perhaps a more important point for English Language Learners—omitted from Block's analysis—is that a growing body of meta-analyses has found that the same strong practices and instructional principles that have been validated with monolingual English-speaking children also benefit the literacy development of ELLs (Gersten et al., 2007; O'Connor, Bocian, Beebe-Frankenberger, & Linklater, 2010), particularly regarding code-related skills in early literacy (Lonigan & Shanahan, 2010). The concern in failing to report these consistent findings is that general "feel good" practices such as generating a language-rich environment and creating a culturally responsive classroom may take precedence over practices with a stronger research base of support. Also missing in Block's references on proven practices for ELLs is the incorporation of students' native language during instruction (Fung, Wilkinson, & Moore, 2002; Kamps et al., 2007; Klingner &

Vaughn, 1996). My concern is that instructional recommendations based on consistent findings have been overlooked, and that recommendations that may be promising are labeled as proven.

For example, teachers scaffolding students' learning is listed as a promising practice, but has a strong research base that spans many decades (Brophy & Good, 1986; Gersten, Baker, Haager, & Graves, 2005; Juel & Minden-Cupp, 1999; Klingner & Vaughn, 1996; Rupley, Blair, & Nichols, 2009). Although the research cited above relates to teacher scaffolding of student responses, some of this scaffolding can be managed by teaching peers to support each other during reading activities (Calhoon, Al Otaiba, Cihak, King, & Avalos, 2006; Rohrbeck, Ginsberg-Block, Fantuzzo, & Miller, 2003; Saenz, Fuchs, & Fuchs, 2005). Block revisits notions of scaffolding by peers in her discussion of ways to stimulate metacognition when she recommends her "Buddy Beside Me" as a reading approach. Although she cites no experimental studies to support her method of peer assistance, several teams of researchers have studied peer tutoring extensively over more than 20 years and deserve mention here, including the seminal work of Greenwood and colleagues with *Classwide Peer Tutoring* (CWPT; Delquadri, Greenwood, Whorton, Carta, & Hall, 1986; Greenwood, Delquadri, & Hall, 1989), and *Peer Assisted Learning Strategies* (PALS; Fuchs, Fuchs, Mathes, & Simmons, 1997; McMaster, Fuchs, & Fuchs, 2007). In these methods, teachers pair students to practice reading aloud to each other, with the expectation that peers will either be able to assist with word recognition and meanings of text when one partner has difficulty, or at least signal the teacher for occasional assistance during the time devoted to reading collaboratively. In arranging peer practice, these researchers sharply oppose Block's recommendation that students choose their partners. Instead, the researchers consistently recommend that teachers take care to avoid allowing peers to self-select partners because low-skilled children are less likely to be selected than average and good readers, which exacerbates difficulties with self-esteem and motivation in classes where children have mixed abilities.

For students in the mid-elementary grades, Block suggests the key approach to teaching vocabulary is to teach students to infer meanings. In the special education and struggling-reader literature, this approach is often the least effective, perhaps because students hear multiple incorrect responses before they hear or derive a correct inference, and it takes 12 or more exposures to a new word to know it well (McKeown, Beck, Omanson, & Pople, 1985). In reviews of vocabulary instruction (Bryant, Goodwin, Bryant, & Higgins, 2003; Jitendra, Edwards, Sacks, & Jacobson, 2004) mnemonic strategies (Levin, Levin, Glasman, & Nordwall, 1992; Mastropieri & Scruggs, 1998), semantic mapping (Levin et al., 1984; Margosein, Pascarella, & Pflaum, 1982; Scott & Nagy, 2004), and direct instruction (Jenkins, Matlock, & Slocum, 1989; Kame'enui, Carnine, & Freschi, 1982) were found to be most effective. These same strategies were vetted in the NRP's (2000) synthesis of vocabulary research through 1998. It is possible that these strategies are linked with their experimental evidence in Block and Mangieri's books (2004, 2006), but it is not possible to draw direct sources or review the evidence from the citations in the present chapter.

The strongest section of Block's chapter, in my view, is on reading comprehension, in which Block cites the researchers who tested the procedures along with prominent reviews, and generates a list of well-researched and viable strategies for increasing students' metacognition as they read. I would add Swanson, Hoskyn, and Lee's (1999) meta-analysis of interventions for students with learning disabilities, which also supports the strategies she recommends. Nevertheless, citing Bond and Dykstra's (1967) landmark study of strategies for first graders may be inappropriate evidence for instructional strategies in the upper elementary grades.

As Block moves into discussion of learning differences between Generation Yers and previous generations, I found myself again wondering about the evidence in the citations. Block cites Hahne, Eckstein, and Friederici (2004) as demonstration of brain differences of students across generations. However, those researchers compared the semantic process of younger with older children and adults, and found no differences between them. That is not to say that brain organization has not changed, just that the citations do not support a change. Block's 2008 study adds no clarity to understanding proven lesson features for older students, as it describes instituting hand motions in the primary grades.

The recommendations for firming up students' use of a taught strategy before teaching the next one has at least 30 years of history in the special education literature (for reviews, see Graham & Harris, 2009 and Schumaker & Deshler, 2009), as well as in syntheses of research on comprehension instruction. These may be better sources than a study of older adults with cortical degeneration (Morrison et al., 2004). The connection to Gen Yers is unclear because the notion of cumulative introduction of new strategies is not a new approach for this group of students, but is as old as special education in public schools.

The major difference between Block's and my views is "what counts as evidence." Citing carefully and specifically for a teacher audience is crucial so that teachers can validate and promote the use of better practices in schools. When teachers need to convince an administrator or department committee to change practices, they need more than a book of recommendations; they need the seminal sources that demonstrate the likely effects of the change they plan to implement and evidence that it is likely to work for the students they have in mind. In many instances, these seminal sources are lacking in Block's chapter, and many citations do not support the points she tries to make, even when the point itself is valid.

In all, two issues are important here: First, as Block advocates, the field has come a considerable distance in understanding how students learn to read and how teachers can improve their learning process. Second, to strengthen the connection between research and practice, researchers should ensure that the advice we give to teachers is not only founded in the research base, but that each reference we recommend supports the strategies and content that we advise.

As a last comment, I disagree with the notion of a "proven" practice in educational research. The Institute of Education Sciences currently demands analysis of what works for whom in reports of their funded projects. As a special educator, the notion of individual differences is paramount in instructional recommendations. We do not believe in magic bullets, but rather in approaches that work more frequently than others for students with particular characteristics. Moreover, the notion of a proven practice suggests we know all there is to know about it. In the same breath as some policy advocates insist that we know all there is to know about early intervention, large-scale studies of students' responsiveness to best practice intervention (RtI approaches) is demonstrating that we do not know how to reach all students. In other words, best practice does not mean proven. Research is not designed to prove a hypothesis, but rather to gather evidence supportive of one side over another.

I agree with Block's assertion that several directions for new research remain; however, I am not sure that the questions as she posed them can be answered. Researchers have examined the "How long does it take?" question with any number of reading skills, and the answer is a measure of individual differences in learning. More important, in my view, is for researchers to develop a range of strategies for teachers to employ when the "best evidence" strategy they began with is ineffective for particular learners and to study how instruction can be managed with the increasing range of need and ability in American schools.

REFERENCES

August, D., & Shanahan, T. (2006). *Developing literacy in second-language learners.* Mahwah, NJ: Lawrence Erlbaum.

August, D., & Shanahan, T. (2010). Response to a review and update on developing literacy in second-language learners: Report of the National Literacy panel on Language Minority Children and Youth. *Journal of Literacy Research, 42,* 341–348.

Ball, E. W., & Blachman, B. A. (1991). Does phoneme segmentation training in kindergarten make a difference in early word recognition and developmental spelling? *Reading Research Quarterly, 26,* 49–66.

Block, C. C., & Mangieri, J. N. (2004). *Powerful vocabulary for reading success and Word forward.* New York: Scholastic, Inc.

Block, C. C., & Mangieri, J. N. (2006). *Vocabulary enriched classrooms.* New York: Scholastic, Inc.

Block, C. C., Parris, S. R., Reed, K. L., Whiteley, C. S., & Cleveland, M. D. (2009). Instructional approaches that significantly increase reading achievmeent. *Journal of Educational Psychology, 101,* 262–281.

Block, C. C., Parris, S. R., & Whiteley, C.S. (2008). CpmS: Kinesthetic comprehension strategy. *The Reading Teacher, 61,* 460–472.

Bond, G. L., & Dykstra, R. (1967). The cooperative research program in first-grade reading instruction. *Reading Research Quarterly, 2,* 10–141.

Brophy, J., & Good, T. (1986). *Teacher behavior and student achievement.* In M. C. Wittrock (Ed.), *Handbook of research on teaching* (3rd ed., pp. 328–375). New York: Macmillan.

Bryant, D. P., Goodwin, M., Bryant, B. R., & Higgins, K. (2003). Vocabulary instruction for students with learning disabilities: A review of the research. *Learning Disability Quarterly, 26,* 117–128.

Calhoon, M. B., Al Otaiba, S., Cihak, D., King, A., & Avalos, A. C. (2007). Effects of a peer-mediated program on reading skill acquisition for two-way bilingual first grade classrooms. *Learning Disability Quarterly, 30,* 169–184.

Calhoon, M. B., Sandow, A., & Hunter, C. V. (2010). Reorganizing the instructional reading components: Could there be a better way to design remedial reading programs to maximize middle school students with reading disabilities' response to treatment? *Annals of Dyslexia, 60,* 57–85.

Delquadri, J. C., Greenwood, C. R., Whorton, D., Carta, J. J., & Hall, R. V. (1986). Classwide peer tutoring. *Exceptional Children, 52,* 535–542.

Fuchs, D., Fuchs, L. S, Mathes, P. G., & Simmons, D. C. (1997). Peer-assisted learning strategies: Making classrooms more responsive to diversity. *American Educational Research Journal, 34,* 174–206.

Fung, I. Y., Wilkinson, I. A. G., & Moore, D. W. (2002). L-1 assisted reciprocal teaching to improve ESL students' comprehension of English expository text. *Learning and Instruction, 13,* 1–31.

Gamse, B. C., Jacob, R. T., Horst, M., Boulay, B., Unlu, F., Bozzi, L., . . . Rosenblum, S. (2009). *Reading first impact study: Final report.* Washington, DC: U.S. Department of Education, Institute of Education Sciences.

Gersten, R., Baker, S. K., Haager, D., & Graves, A. W. (2005). Exploring the role of teacher quality in predicting reading outcomes for first-grade English learners: An observational study. *Remedial and Special Education, 26*(4), 197–206.

Gersten, R., Baker, S., Shanahan, T., Linan-Thompson, S., Collins, P., & Scarcella, R. (2007). *Effective literacy and English language instruction for English learners in the elementary school grades: A practice guide* (NCEE 2007-4011). Washington, DC: U.S. Department of Education, Institute of Education Sciences, National Center for Education Evaluation and Regional Assistance.

Graham, S., & Harris, K. R. (2009). Almost 30 years of writing research: Making sense of it all with The Wrath of Khan. *Learning Disabilities Research & Practice, 24,* 58–68.

Greenwood, C. R., Delquadri, J., & Hall, R. V. (1989). Longitudinal effects of class-wide peer tutoring. *Journal of Educational Psychology, 81,* 371–383.

Hahne, A., Eckstein, K., & Friederici, A. D. (2004). Brain signatures of syntactic and semantic processes during children's language development. *Journal of Cognitive Development, 16,* 1302–1318.

Hatcher, P., Hulme, C., & Ellis, A. (1994). Ameliorating early reading failure by integrating the teaching of reading and phonological skills: The phonological linkage hypothesis. *Child Development, 65,* 41–57.

Jenkins, J. R., Matlock, B., & Slocum, T. A. (1989). Two approaches to vocabulary instruction: The teaching of individual word meanings and practice in deriving word meanings from context. *Reading Research Quarterly, 24,* 215–235.

Jitendra, A. K., Edwards, L. L., Sacks, G., & Jacobson, L. A. (2004). What research says about vocabulary instruction for students with learning disabilities. *Exceptional Children, 70,* 299–322.

Juel, C., & Minden-Cupp, C. (1999). One down and 80,000 to go: Word recognition in the primary grades. *The Reading Teacher, 53*(4), 332–335.

Kame'enui, E. K., Carnine, D., & Freschi, R. (1982). Effects of text construction and instructional procedures for teaching word meanings on comprehension and recall. *Reading Research Quarterly, 17,* 367–388.

Kamps, D., Abbott, M., Greenwood, C., Arreaga-Mayer, C., Wills, H., Lonstaff, J., Culpepper, M., & Walton, C. (2007). Use of evidence-based, small-group reading instruction for English language learners in elementary grades: Secondary-tier intervention. *Learning Disability Quarterly, 30,* 153–168.

Klingner, J., & Vaughn, S. (1996). Reciprocal teaching of reading comprehension strategies for students with learning disabilities who use English as a second language. *Elementary School Journal, 96,* 275–293.

Levin, J. R., Johnson, D., Pittelman, S., Levin, K., Shriberg, L., Toms-Bronowski, S., & Hayes, B. (1984). A comparison of semantic- and mnemonic-based vocabulary-learning strategies. *Reading Psychology, 5*(1–2), 1–15.

Levin, J. R., Levin, M. E., Glasman, L. D., & Nordwall, M. B. (1992). Mnemonic vocabulary instruction: Additional effectiveness evidence. *Contemporary Educational Psychology, 17,* 156–174.

Lonigan, C. J., & Shanahan, T. (2010). Developing early literacy skills: Things we know we know and things we know we don't know. *Educational Researcher, 39,* 340–346.

Margosein, C. M., Pascarella, E. T., & Pflaum, S. W. (1982). The effects of instruction using semantic mapping on vocabulary and comprehension. *Journal of Early Adolescence, 2,* 185–194.

Mastropieri, M. A., & Scruggs, T. E. (1998). Enhancing school success with mnemonic strategies. *Intervention in School and Clinic, 33,* 201–208.

McKeown, M. G., Beck, I. L., Omanson, R. C., & Pople, M. T. (1985). The effects of long-term vocabulary instruction on reading comprehension: A replication. *Journal of Reading Behavior, 15,* 3–18.

McMaster, K. L., Fuchs, D., & Fuchs, L. (2007). Promises and limitations of Peer-Assisted Learning Strategies in reading. *Learning Disabilities: A Contemporary Journal, 5,* 97–112.

Morrison, R. G., Krawczyk, D. C., Holyoak, K. K., Hummel, J. E., Chow, T. W., Miller, B. L., & Knowlton, B. J. (2004). A neuro-computational model of analogical reasoning and its breakdown in frontal temporal lobar degeneration. *Journal of Cognitive Neuroscience, 16,* 260–271.

National Reading Panel. (2000). *Teaching children to read: An evidence-based assessment of the scientific research literature on reading and its implications for reading instruction.* Rockville, MD: NICHD Clearinghouse.

O'Connor, R. E., Bocian, K., Beebe-Frankenberger, M., & Linklater, D. (2010). Responsiveness of students with language difficulties to early intervention in reading. *Journal of Special Education, 43,* 220–235.

O'Connor, R. E., Jenkins, J. R., & Slocum, T. A. (1995). Transfer among phonological tasks in kindergarten: Essential instructional content. *Journal of Educational Psychology, 2,* 202–217.

Palincsar, A. S. (1986). The role of dialogue in providing scaffolded instruction. *Educational Psychologist, 21,* 73–98.

Rohrbeck, C. A., Ginsberg-Block, M. D., Fantuzzo, J. W., & Miller, T. R. (2003). Peer-assisted learning interventions with elementary school students: A meta-analytic review. *Journal of Educational Psychology, 95,* 240–257.

Rupley, W., Blair, T., & Nichols, W. (2009). Effective reading instruction for struggling readers: The role of direct/explicit teaching. *Reading & Writing Quarterly, 25,* 125–138.

Sáenz, L. M., Fuchs, L. S., & Fuchs, D. (2005). Peer-assisted learning strategies for English language learners with learning disabilities. *Exceptional Children, 71,* 231–247.

Scott, J. A., & Nagy, W. E. (2004). Developing word consciousness. In J. F. Baumann & E. A. Kame'enui (Eds.), *Vocabulary instruction: Research to practice* (pp. 201–217). New York: Guilford Press.

Schumaker, J. B., & Deshler, D. D. (2009). Adolescents with learning disabilities as writers: Are we selling them short? *Learning Disabilities Research & Practice, 24*(2), 81–92.

Swanson, H. L., Hoskyn, M., & Lee, C. (1999). *Interventions for students with learning disabilities: A meta-analysis of treatment outcomes.* New York: Guilford Press.

CHAPTER 3

REFLECTIONS ON WHAT'S PROVEN AND WHERE THE PROMISE LIES

Margaret G. McKeown

Cathy Collins Block presents an intriguing and productive framework for her discussion of proven and promising practices for literacy. The categories of content of instruction, strategies, lesson characteristics, and teacher actions allow for some important distinctions to be made and serve to draw focus to the complex aspects of the instructional scene. These features alone make Block's chapter a worthwhile read. But in addition, Block offers detailed accounts of a wide variety of practices, their positions in the field in terms of their research foundation and evidence base. In so doing, Block more than fulfills the purpose set for the chapter—"to provide compact syntheses of highly important facets of today's instructional programs" (p. 3).

My reading of Block's chapter is that the highest marks for proven practices are given to the teaching of comprehension strategies and to teacher actions. In my commentary, I will focus on those two areas. My perspective on strategies is somewhat different from Block's and ends up putting even more focus on the importance of teacher actions and also highlights the

Instructional Strategies for Improving Students' Learning, pages 53–63
Copyright © 2012 by Information Age Publishing

53

role of content in a different way. Block refers to "sufficient scientific basis" and "extensive empirical tests" (p. 24) about nine empirically validated comprehension strategies. However, much work in the area of strategies instruction, including work that I have conducted (McKeown, Beck, & Blake, 2009), suggests that answers about strategies instruction are not as clear as they might appear. The "sufficient scientific basis" needs to be considered in light of how effects in various studies were measured and to what the instructional intervention was compared. There are also questions about how strategies were instantiated in different studies. Results about a particular strategy may appear strong—until one delves into the separate studies and notices that how a particular strategy was described, taught, practiced, and tested and can differ greatly across studies.

HOW CLEAR IS THE EVIDENCE ON STRATEGIES?

Consider several of the studies that appear in the National Reading Panel (NRP) report (2000) as showing effects for comprehension monitoring. In Schmitt's study of metacomprehension (1988), students were taught to activate prior knowledge, set purposes, generate and answer prequestions, form hypotheses, verify or reject hypotheses, evaluate predictions, and summarize. Comprehension monitoring instruction in a study by Miller (1985) trained students to identify anomalous sentences by teaching them to ask themselves questions as they read, such as "Is there anything wrong with the story?" and to underline problems they found. Yet another study in the comprehension-monitoring category, by Babbs (1984), taught students to use cards containing monitoring questions and refer to cards as they read. Thus, not only do activities under comprehension monitoring vary widely, but studies of this strategy also include activities that represent other strategies, such as summarizing and asking questions. Results were assessed differently in each study as well, with Schmitt using a cloze task and Miller having students underline problems in passages. In Babbs' study, positive results were found when students used the cards, but effects did not transfer to the use of the strategies without the cards.

Under close examination, it seems that the literature on the success of strategies does not present a clear picture of what activities instantiate a particular strategy, what makes a particular strategy effective, or what it means for a strategy to be effective. As Rosenshine & Meister (1994) ask of the studies they reviewed on Reciprocal Teaching (RT): "What are cognitive changes that occur?" In the six studies in their review that tested students' ability to generate questions, RT students did better than control students on tests of comprehension, but for five of the six studies, there was no difference between RT and control in the quality of questions generated. So if question generation was not driving the results, what mechanisms were at work to make the intervention successful?

The starting point for discussion of how to develop students' comprehension seems a strong point of consensus in the field. Researchers acknowledge that successful readers take an active and strategic approach to reading. Readers are active by deliberately attending to what they are reading, and working to make sense of it as they proceed; they are strategic by keeping track of how the sense-making process is going and making revisions and repairs to the process when it is judged as not going well enough. The view of successful comprehension as active and strategic has been interpreted, for the most part, as meaning that young readers need to learn and practice specific strategies.

However, researchers who have taken a fine-grained look at strategies instruction seem to share a view that strategies *per se* may not be the root of success of strategy interventions. Among the researchers raising questions about strategies are some who have done seminal work on strategies instruction. Palincsar, David, Winn, and Stevens (1991) examined the quality of RT dialogues of several teachers and found that less successful teachers focused on delivering information about the strategy and involved children at only a surface level. The more successful teachers had a more flexible approach to strategy information and supported students at the idea level through linking them to new knowledge and the ongoing discussion. Palincsar (1986) concluded that talk that was more loosely structured and focused on making sense of text was preferable to an approach to RT that focused on the strategies themselves.

Brown and Campione (1998) expressed a similar concern, finding that some teachers implemented RT as "surface rituals of questioning, summarizing" in ways that were "divorced from the goal of reading for understanding" (p. 177, cited in Baker, 2002). Alexander and Murphy (1998) speak to this issue in noting that strategic efforts must shift as task demands and contexts change so that having students execute strategies in a rote way is a misconception of the nature of strategic processing.

Carver (1987) suggested that positive effects of strategies may be due to increased time spent reading and thinking about text rather than to the particulars of the strategies themselves. In a similar vein, Resnick posits that interactions around strategies may indicate a "psychological space" where powerful effects may occur, but that the effects may not be due to the application of strategies themselves (1987, p. 27). Graesser (2007) states that strategies "do not drive the comprehension engine" (p. 11), but rather the driver's seat is occupied by a bottom-up activation of text ideas and integration of those ideas. Willingham (2006/2007) makes a similar point, saying that reading strategies don't get reading comprehension done, but rather have a role in encouraging the reader to apply reading comprehension processes. In his view, strategies are likened to "tricks" that may serve to prompt students to apply comprehension processes, but they do not directly enhance those processes.

Willingham (2006/2007), however, does believe strategies can be useful to students. In contrast, Sinatra, Brown, and Reynolds (2002) voice a concern that strategies instruction may divert attention from comprehension. They suggest that comprehension instruction that supports students in approaching reading as problem solving may be more effective than explicitly teaching comprehension strategies. Similarly, Pearson and Fielding (1991) questioned the need for teaching students directly about strategies if student attention could be focused on understanding text content.

STRATEGIES VERSUS BEING STRATEGIC

Consider two distinct ways to look at the idea of becoming a strategic reader. One is through learning and applying specific strategies. The other is through attending, in the course of reading, to the process of building meaning from what a text says. The NRP seems to reflect these two approaches in summarizing findings on comprehension instruction: "Comprehension can be improved by teaching students to use specific cognitive strategies or to reason strategically when they encounter barriers to comprehension when reading" (2000, pp. 4–39). Discussions of NRP findings rarely take account of the "or" in that statement, to consider it as a suggestion of an alternative approach to strategies instruction. That is, students can be taught to "reason strategically" about text without resorting to specific strategies.

Teaching specific strategies seems to be considered as "direct instruction," while instructional focus on building meaning from text is considered indirect. But the goal of instruction is not the learning of the strategies; it is the ability to comprehend. There may be a more productive way to achieve equally powerful effects without the naming and practicing of the actual strategies. Instruction for comprehension, instead, can center on the comprehension process itself—by supporting students to identify important ideas as they read, carry those ideas forward in their reading, and make connections between those ideas and subsequent ideas throughout a text to build understanding. In this kind of approach, the focus is dealing with the content of what is read rather than applying strategies.

Developing comprehension by focusing on dealing with the content of what is read generally takes the form of discussion-based activities. In such discussions, students are invited to paraphrase and summarize the text, identify what is important, make connections within text and to their background knowledge, and cite evidence to support their responses. A teacher's open questions and use of students' responses creates the basic structure of discussion that guides students to attend to important ideas and events and how they connect: "What's going on?" "Why is that important?" "How does the author let you know...?" How does that connect?" How does that fit with...?" "What does that tell you?" "What do you mean by that?"

Discussion-based approaches include Instructional Conversations (Saunders & Goldenberg, 1999), Collaborative Reasoning (Chinn, Anderson, & Waggoner, 2001), Dialogic Instruction (Nystrand, 1997), Junior Great Books (Dennis & Moldof, 1983), and Questioning the Author (Beck & McKeown, 2006). Applebee, Langer, Nystrand, and Gamoran (2003) summarize such approaches as sharing "an emphasis on group discussion and problem solving...requiring evidence-based argument" (p. 693), and they cite substantial effects of these discussion-based approaches on students' comprehension and learning.

In a recent study, McKeown et al. (2009) compared strategies instruction with content-focused instruction. The 2-year study involved fifth-grade students who participated in lessons designed around the same set of texts for either a content or strategies approach. Content instruction focused student attention on the content of the text through open, meaning-based questions about the text (e.g., "What's going on here?" "How does all this connect with what we read earlier?"). In strategies instruction, students were taught specific procedures to guide their access to text during reading. Instruction focused on the following strategies: summarizing, predicting, drawing inferences, question generation, and comprehension monitoring. Assessments included comprehension of lesson texts, an analysis of lesson discourse, and two experimenter-designed assessments to measure transfer of knowledge. The results were consistent across the 2 years, with no differences on a recognition measure of lesson-text comprehension, but differences favoring the content instruction in recall of narrative text and in questions about expository text. For one of the transfer assessments, there was also a modest effect favoring the content students in text recall. Analyses of classroom discourse found substantial differences favoring the content condition in the amount of talk about the text (about 95% vs. about 70%) and length of student response (with content students' responses averaging two or three times the length of strategies students' responses across the 2 years of the study). The findings are not meant to be taken as definitive. The instantiation of strategies is only one example of what strategies instruction might look like, and other instantiations of content instruction are possible as well. Our selection of dependent measures was also limiting. What is measured naturally governs the effects that are shown, and there are limits to the effects that are feasible to measure. Specifically, the measurement of transfer was limited in that we measured instances of near transfer, which asked students to recall a text read in class following a set of lessons that provided scaffolding and gradual release of using the approach they had been experiencing. Clearly it would be desirable to measure further transfer; for example, what students could do if given a text to read completely on their own.

Despite the limitations, we believe the work has useful implications for research and practice. Although statistical differences between strategies and content conditions did not emerge on all measures, the differences in favor of the content condition showed a consistent pattern across the 2 years. The results indicate that an approach that allowed students to consider text meaning directly was feasible and at least as effective as pursuing meaning by going through strategies. This suggests that getting students to actively build meaning while reading does not necessitate knowledge and application of specific strategies, but rather it can be accomplished by focusing on text content in ways that promote attending to important ideas and establishing connections between them.

CONTENT VERSUS STRATEGIES FOR VOCABULARY

In Willingham's review of strategies (2006/2007), he states that he believes strategies can be useful to students, but he goes on to say that overall, he regards acquisition of a broad vocabulary and rich background knowledge as yielding greater benefits. That comment touches on another of Block's categories from the framework of her chapter: that of the content of instruction. I would like to draw attention to that aspect as it applies to vocabulary instruction. In her chapter, Block emphasized enhancing students' vocabulary development through the teaching of strategies.

My perspective is that instruction in vocabulary strategies, such as learning words from context or morphological analysis, will be productive only if the instruction is embedded within a rich, robust vocabulary program that engages students with words and their uses. Students need to think about and reflect on words and their uses, try out using them in their daily lives, and experience enough language that they can find evidence of the strategies they have been taught and know where they can be usefully applied. Vocabulary instruction also needs to capture students' interest and attention so that they will have language on their minds all the time! If the focus of instruction is on routines they need to apply, students are unlikely to devote enough of their cognitive resources to produce learning effects.

Learning words well enough to use them to make sense of text as one reads requires lots of experiences with the words. An understanding of a word's meaning accumulates as a learner meets the word in different contexts. These different contexts are necessary to provide the nuances of meaning that lead to a decontextualized representation of meaning—a representation that the reader can use to make sense of subsequent contexts containing the word (Nagy & Scott, 2000; Perfetti, 2007; Perfetti & Hart, 2002). A vocabulary program that offers students ample opportunities to encounter and manipulate word uses can amplify experiences with context and make them more productive.

Although it is the case that the bulk of a person's vocabulary is learned from printed context, it is also true that written language is not a reliable source for word meaning information (Beck, McKeown, & McCaslin, 1983; Nagy & Herman, 1987; Sternberg, 1987). Authors do not write in order to teach the meanings of words; they write to express ideas. Therefore, the extent to which a word's meaning is apparent from context is rather random, and thus the value of contextual analysis has its limits. Sometimes contexts are directive enough to allow a reader to glean the specific meaning of a word, but more often they promote the learning of some general property of the word (e.g., it applies to people or it has a negative connotation). Contexts can also occasionally be misdirective, seeming to indicate a meaning quite different from the word that is used (Beck et al., 1983). Consider that Nagy, Herman, and Anderson (1985) calculated that of every 100 unfamiliar words met in reading, about 5 of them would be learned. Compare the following sentences and consider the quality of information that a reader would have about each word if he or she were meeting it for the first time: "Martin walked into the meeting and noticed that everyone at the table looked *glum*." "Jasper and I had been excitedly looking forward to this trip for months and so we arrived at the bus early, *eager* to get on our way." For the first sentence, many possibilities might come to mind for the meaning of *glum*: Were the meeting members looking excited? relaxed? bored? angry? In the second sentence, however, it would likely be clear to the reader that *eager* signaled the characters' excited anticipation.

TEACHER ACTIONS

Turning now to Block's category of teacher actions as a key area of promising and proven practices, I completely concur with Block's decision to highlight this area. To my thinking, the "promise" in this area is that enhancing teachers' interactions around instruction has strong potential to be highly productive for student success, but the field seems still very much in the promissory phase. A major reason for the need for attention to teacher-student interactions is that current approaches to teaching and learning emphasize students' construction of their own knowledge, which takes place through interactions in the classroom with the teacher and other students.

This emphasis makes the teacher responsible for scaffolding, coaching, and monitoring student thinking and problem solving; a role that is vastly different from one that revolves around IRE (Initiation-Response-Evaluation) patterns of interaction, in which the teacher asks direct questions and students give brief, factual responses. If we expect teachers to support development of students' thinking and problem-solving skills, we need to develop techniques to aid teachers in that endeavor. We must help teachers attend to student contributions in the classroom in ways that key in on nascent thinking, and help teachers build patterns of responding that make use of student ideas and move student thinking forward.

For promising practices in the teacher actions domain, Block discusses the need for teachers to provide expanded explanations and elaborated feedback, stressing that feedback must go beyond telling students, "Your main idea and details were incorrect. Try again." I would concur, but add a caveat: although teachers do need to provide elaboration and explanation in their interactions with students, teachers also need to take care that in doing so they are not taking back from students the responsibility for doing the thinking. The need for teachers to explain and elaborate, and yet leave space for student thinking, is a key feature that makes the domain of teaching for higher-level thinking such a complex area. One approach to supporting teachers to develop their abilities in this domain involves having teachers interact with transcripts of lessons—their own and others'—to analyze teacher actions, and note the relationship of teacher actions and student responses (Correnti et al., in preparation; Kucan, 2009).

A CLOSING NOTE

A final note on perspectives of content versus strategies: I don't think that my position and Block's are all that different. Block's emphasis on the thinking processes in comprehension, as presented in her chapter, "The Thinking Process Approach to Comprehension Development" (2002), makes that clear. In that chapter, Block speaks of teaching comprehension not as a set of separate, segmented strategies, but as a set of ever-changing interactions of thinking processes. Her aim in a thinking process approach is to develop students' abilities to engage an effective set of thought processes at strategic points in a text to make rich, valid meanings. But in her chapter in this volume, my reading is that the emphasis on fluent processes is less clear. It has been my goal to move the emphasis back in the direction of processing content rather than applying strategies.

REFERENCES

Alexander, P. A., & Murphy, P. K. (1998). The research base for APA's learner-centered psychological principals. In N. M. Lambert & B. L. McCombs (Eds.), *How students learn: Reforming schools through learner-centered education* (pp. 25–60). Washington, DC: American Psychological Association.

Applebee, A. N., Langer, J. A., Nystrand, M., & Gamoran, A. (2003). Discussion-based approaches to developing understanding: Classroom instruction and student performance in middle and high school English. *American Educational Research Journal, 40*(3), 685–730.

Babbs, P. J. (1984, November). Monitoring cards help improve comprehension. *The Reading Teacher,* 200–204.

Baker, L. (2002). Metacognition in comprehension instruction. In C. C. Block & M. Pressley (Eds.), *Comprehension instruction: Research-based best practices* (pp. 77–95). New York: Guilford Press.

Beck, I. L., & McKeown, M. G. (2006). *Improving comprehension with Questioning the Author.* New York: Scholastic.

Beck, I. L., McKeown, M. G., & McCaslin, E. S. (1983). Vocabulary development: All contexts are not created equal. *The Elementary School Journal, 83,* 177–181.

Block, C. C. (2002). The thinking process approach to comprehension development. In C. C. Block, L. B. Gambrell, & M. Pressley (Eds.), *Improving comprehension instruction.* San Francisco: Jossey-Bass.

Brown, A. L., & Campione, J. C. (1998). Designing a community of young learners: Theoretical and practical lessons. In N. M. Lambert & B. L. McCombs (Eds.), *How students learn: Reforming schools through learner-centered education* (pp. 153–186). Washington, DC: American Psychological Association.

Carver, R. P. (1987). Should reading comprehension skills be taught? In J. E. Readance & R. S. Baldwin (Eds.), *Research in literacy: Merging perspectives* (36th yearbook of the National Reading Conference, pp. 115–126). Rochester, NY: National Reading Conference.

Chinn, C. A., Anderson, R. C., & Waggoner, M. A. (2001). Patterns of discourse in two kinds of literature discussion. *Reading Research Quarterly, 36*(4), 378–411.

Correnti, R., McKeown, M. G., Smith, M., Stein, M. K., Scherrer, J., & Ashley, K. (in preparation). *Classroom discussions in mathematics and language arts: Exploring the relationship between what teachers do and what students learn.*

Dennis, R., & Moldof, G. (1983). *A handbook on interpretive reading and discussion.* Chicago: Great Books Foundation.

Graesser, A. C. (2007). An introduction to strategic reading comprehension. In D. S. McNamara (Ed.), *Reading comprehension strategies: Theories, interventions, and technologies* (pp. 3–26). New York: Erlbaum.

Kucan, L. (2009). Engaging teachers in investigating their teaching as a linguistic enterprise: The case of comprehension instruction in the context of discussion. *Reading Psychology, 30,* 51–87.

McKeown, M. G., Beck, I. L., & Blake, R. G. K. (2009). Rethinking reading comprehension instruction: A comparison of instruction for strategies and content approaches. *Reading Research Quarterly, 44*(3), 218–253.

Miller, G. E. (1985). The effects of general and specific self-instruction training on children's comprehension monitoring performances during reading. *Reading Research Quarterly, 20*(5), 616–628.

Nagy, W. E., & Herman, P. A. (1987). Breadth and depth of vocabulary knowledge: Implications for acquisition and instruction. In M. G. McKeown & M. E. Curtis (Eds.), *The nature of vocabulary acquisition* (pp. 19–36). Hillsdale, NJ: Erlbaum.

Nagy, W. E., Herman, P. A., & Anderson, R. (1985). Learning words from context. *Reading Research Quarterly, 20,* 233–253.

Nagy, W. E., & Scott, J. A. (2000). Vocabulary processes. In M. L. Kamil, P. B. Mosenthal, P. David Pearson, & R. Barr (Eds.), *Handbook of reading research,* (Vol. 3, pp. 69–284). Mahwah, NJ: Erlbaum.

National Reading Panel. (2000). *Teaching children to read: An evidence-based assessment of the scientific literature on reading and its implications for reading instruction* (NIH Pub. No. 00-4754). Washington, DC: National Institutes of Health.

Nystrand, M. (1997). *Opening dialogue: Understanding the dynamics of language and learning in the English classroom.* New York: Teachers College Press.

Palincsar, A. S. (1986). The role of dialogue in providing scaffolded instruction. *Educational Psychologist, 21,* 73–98.

Palincsar, A. S., David, Y. M., Winn, J. A., & Stevens, D. D. (1991). Examining the context of strategy instruction. *Remedial and Special Education, 12,* 43–53.

Pearson, P. D., & Fielding, L. (1991). Comprehension instruction. In R. Barr, M. Kamil, P. Mosenthal, & P. D. Pearson (Eds.), *Handbook of reading research* (Vol. 2, pp. 815–860). New York: Longman.

Perfetti, C. A. (2007). Reading ability: Lexical quality to comprehension. *Scientific Studies of Reading, 11*(4), 357–383.

Perfetti, C. A., & Hart, L. (2002). The lexical quality hypothesis. In L. Verhoeven, C. Elbro, & P. Reitsma (Eds.), *Precursors of functional literacy* (pp. 189–213). Amsterdam/Philadelphia: John Benjamins.

Resnick, L. B. (1987). *Education and learning to think.* Washington, DC: National Academy Press.

Rosenshine, B., & Meister, C. (1994). Reciprocal teaching: A review of the research. *Review of Educational Research, 64*(4), 479–530.

Saunders, W. M., & Goldenberg, C. (1999). Effects of instructional conversations and literature logs on limited- and fluent-English-proficient students' story comprehension and thematic understanding. *Elementary School Journal, 99*(4), 279–301.

Schmitt, M. C. (1988). The effects of an elaborated directed reading activity on the metacomprehension skills of third graders. *National Reading Conference Yearbook, 37,* 167–181.

Sinatra, G. M., Brown, K. J., & Reynolds, R. (2002). Implications of cognitive resource allocation for comprehension strategies instruction. In C. C. Block & M. Pressley (Eds.), *Comprehension instruction: Research-based best practices* (pp. 62–76). New York: Guilford Press.

Sternberg, R. J. (1987). Most vocabulary is learned from context. In M. G. McKeown & M. E. Curtis (Eds.), *The nature of vocabulary acquisition* (pp. 89–105). Hillsdale, NJ: Lawrence Erlbaum and Associates.

Willingham, D. T. (2006/2007). How we learn: Ask the cognitive scientist. *American Educator*, 39–50.

CHAPTER 4

GOOD INTENTIONS AND UNEXPECTED CONSEQUENCES

The Case of Reading Fluency

James F. Baumann
University of Missouri–Columbia

Cathy Collins Block acknowledged that her "single chapter cannot propose to report every advancement that has been or is being made in reading instruction." Instead, she stated, that it was her "intent to provide compact syntheses of highly important facets of today's instructional programs" (p. 3). Given the breadth of her charge and space limitations, Block has done a remarkable job addressing critical aspects of both proven and promising evidence-based research on effective reading instruction. I appreciate, in particular, her focus on (a) using nonfiction texts when teaching young children, (b) employing culturally relevant pedagogy for teaching both minority and mainstream children, (c) providing multifaceted comprehension strategy instruction, (d) teaching word meanings to both enhance vocabulary and extend comprehension, and (e) capitalizing on what we know about the qualities of teachers who provide effective literacy instruction. Indeed, these foci address much of what the field has learned about effective reading instruction in the last 40 years.

Instructional Strategies for Improving Students' Learning, pages 65–77
Copyright © 2012 by Information Age Publishing

Block also acknowledged the importance of the contribution to the National Institute of Child Health and Human Development (NICHD) by the National Reading Panel (NRP), which was charged by Congress in 1997 "to assess the status of research-based knowledge, including the effectiveness of various approaches to teaching children to read" (NICHD, 2000a, p. 1-1). She stated accurately that the NRP's "analysis found that phonemic awareness, phonics, comprehension, vocabulary, and fluency are the proven critical components to be taught in early reading instruction" (p. 7).

One of Block's goals of her research synthesis was "to begin a discussion upon which chapter commentators could both amend and expand" (p. 4). In this commentary, I follow Block's overture by expanding on one aspect of "proven content." Specifically, I elaborate on the research on reading fluency, which she defines as "the ability to read with appropriate speed, accuracy, and phrasing so that the flow of English syntax can aid in determining meaning" (p. 6).

Research on reading fluency has expanded our understanding of what skillful, mature reading entails (Kuhn, Schwanenflugel, & Meisinger, 2010). Fluency research also has provided valuable insight into how to develop essential fluency abilities in both students who achieve normally in reading and those who experience difficulties learning to read (Pressley, Gaskins, & Fingeret, 2006; Torgesen & Hudson, 2006). Like many other advances in education sciences, however, the transition from research to practice on reading fluency has been fraught with honest misunderstandings and misinterpretations about how to enhance teachers' teaching and students' learning of this essential reading ability (cf. Allington, 2006; Cunningham, 2001; Pressley, 2006, ch. 5; Shanahan, 2006). Thus, I chronicle the research on reading fluency and the incumbent good intentions and unexpected consequences.

DEFINITIONS OF READING FLUENCY

There is not space here to recount the full history in American reading instruction of reading fluency—and its foundation in oral reading—and so I refer interested readers to other sources (Allington, 1984; Rasinski, 2006; Rasinski & Hoffman, 2003; Rasinski, Reutzel, Chard, & Linan-Thompson, 2011; Smith, 1934/2002). Let it suffice to say, however, that fluency has been defined and operationalized in reading curriculum and instruction in different ways at different times, from being an end itself (a skilled orator) to a means to an end (fluent silent reading). Although oral reading fluency was downplayed in elementary classrooms throughout much of the 20th century (Rasinski et al., 2011), there was resurgent interest in this "neglected reading goal" (Allington, 1983) in the latter part of the century

(Pinnell et al., 1995; Zuttell & Rasinski, 1991), culminating with the report of the NRP (NICHD, 2000a).

The NRP (NICHD, 2000b) defined reading fluency as the ability "to read orally with speed, accuracy, and proper expression" (p. 11). Recent definitions of reading fluency are more elaborate and typically substitute "automatic word recognition" for "speed" and "prosody" for "proper expression" (Kuhn & Stahl, 2003). *Automatic word recognition,* or simply *automaticity* (LaBerge & Samuels, 1974) includes speed, but goes beyond it. Drawing from Logan (1997), Kuhn et al. (2010, pp. 231–232) described automaticity in word reading as being effortless, autonomous, without conscious awareness, and rapid. *Prosody* involves using appropriate pitch, expression, intonation, stress, timing, and the chunking of words into meaningful phrases (Kuhn & Stahl, 2003, p. 5). Therefore, fluent reading is reasonably swift, automatic, and "sounds good," as demonstrated by a skilled orator or an elementary teacher who can read aloud to students in an expressive, engaging manner.

The NRP (NICHD, 2000b) concluded that "fluency is one of several critical factors necessary for reading comprehension" (p. 11). The experimental research literature up through the late 1990s that the panel reviewed demonstrated that instruction in repeated reading and guided oral reading—the prevalent techniques used at that time to promote fluency—had a positive impact on reading accuracy (mean effect size of $d = 0.55$), fluency (mean effect size of 0.44), and reading comprehension (mean effect size of 0.35), with an overall weighted effect size average of 0.41 on students' reading achievement. The experimental research literature since the release of the NRP has reinforced further the importance of fluency in promoting students' automatic word identification and text comprehension (e.g., Kuhn et al., 2006; Miller & Schwanenflugel, 2008; Rasinski et al., 2011; Schwanenflugel et al., 2006, 2009; Stahl, & Heubach, 2005).

It is important to note, however, that the relationship between and among dimensions of reading fluency and comprehension is complex (Fuchs, Fuchs, Hosp, & Jenkins, 2001). Although there is substantial evidence that automaticity has a direct effect on reading comprehension (Samuels, 2004), it still is not fully clear how prosody influences comprehension (Kuhn et al., 2010). Miller and Schwanenflugel (2008) reported that indices of prosody for children reading complex texts predicted their reading comprehension in later grades, but causality remained to be established. Most current models view fluency, and prosody in particular, as a bridge to reading comprehension (Chard, Pikulski, & McDonagh, 2006; Schwanenflugel & Ruston, 2008). Whether it's a one-way or two-way bridge (i.e., a bidirectional relationship), however, remains an open question (Kuhn et al., 2010).

Given the state of the current knowledge base, the most accurate, if not prudent, definition of fluency is the following one proffered by Kuhn et al. (2010):

> Fluency combines accuracy, automaticity, and oral reading prosody, which, taken together, facilitate the reader's construction of meaning. It is demonstrated during oral reading through ease of word recognition, appropriate pacing, phrasing, and intonation. It is a factor in both oral and silent reading that can limit or support comprehension. (p. 240)

FLUENCY RUN AMOK

Although research in the last decade has resulted in greater understanding of the three dimensions of fluency (accuracy, automaticity, and prosody), there has been an ongoing debate about the assessment of and instruction in fluency (Kuhn et al., 2010; Samuels, 2006a, 2006b). Specifically, concern has been expressed that some assessment tools have focused exclusively on accuracy and automaticity (that is, precision in oral reading), with little or no attention to prosody (Samuels, 2007). As a result, it has been argued that instructional practices in reading fluency have emphasized students' ability to read text rapidly and accurately but without prosody and full comprehension (Goodman, 2006).

Concerns over fluency assessment and instruction can be traced to the NRP report (NICHD, 2000a), which, as Block noted, identified reading fluency as one of five major components of skillful reading. The subsequent No Child Left Behind Act of 2001 that led to the Reading First initiative was grounded in the NRP report and required that fluency be assessed and taught in Reading First schools (Gamse, Jacob, Horst, Boulay, & Unlu, 2008). Thus, due to the NRP and accompanying educational policy, reading fluency attained a not heretofore position of prominence in elementary school reading curriculum.

Most fluency assessments used the metric of *correct words per minute* (CWPM), which was defined as the "total number of words read in 1 minute – [minus] the total number of miscues" (Miller & Groff, 2008, p. 137). Miscues were defined typically as "words read incorrectly, substitutions, skipped words, hesitations of more than 3 seconds, words read out of order, and words that are sounded out but not read as a whole word" (Good & Kaminski, 2011, p. 83). Fluency assessment tools that used CWPM were appealing in that they were quick to administer and produced reliable results that could be used to evaluate fluency growth over time (Riedel, 2007). However, the validity of fluency assessments, as we shall see, remained in question (Goodman, 2006; Samuels, 2006b).

The most widely used measure of oral reading fluency has been the Dynamic Indicators of Basic Early Literacy Skills (DIBELS) (Good & Kaminski, 2002). The current version of DIBELS, *DIBELS Next* (Good & Kaminski, 2011), includes five timed (1-minute) assessments, the first four of which assess initial sounds (First Sound Fluency), letter-name knowledge (Letter Naming Fluency), phonemic awareness (Phoneme Segmentation Fluency), and the alphabetic principle (Nonsense Word Fluency). Although researchers and writers have questioned whether it is appropriate to refer to abilities like letter naming and pseudoword reading as indices of fluency (Fuchs, Fuchs, & Compton, 2004), it is the fifth subtest, DIBELS Oral Reading Fluency (DORF), that generates CWPM scores and has been the most influential, if not controversial.

There is evidence that DORF is a good predictor of reading comprehension (Kim, Petscher, Schatschneider, & Foorman, 2010; Riedel, 2007; Roehrig, Petscher, Nettles, Hudson, & Torgesen, 2008; cf. Pressley, Hilden, & Shankland, 2006). Some reading researchers have argued, however, that DORF and other similar curriculum-based measurements (CBM) of oral reading fluency (e.g., Deno & Marsten, 2006) have redefined fluency as simply reading quickly, at the expense of prosody and understanding (Kuhn et al., 2010; Mathson, Allington, & Solic, 2006; Samuels, 2007).

As a result of reliance on CWPM assessments like DORF and other CBMs, the fluency curriculum has often involved speed-based activities that convey that to be fluent, one only needs to read quickly and accurately (Walker, Mokhtari, & Sargent, 2006). Kuhn et al. (2010) stated that "the current implementation of fluency instruction in many classrooms is often driven by assessments that build upon an incomplete conceptualization of the construct and can lead to both inappropriate instruction and a serious misconception of this essential characteristic of skilled reading" (p. 230). Samuels (2007) concurred: "The tests [DIBELS] have become a de facto curriculum in which the emphasis on speed convinces students that the goal in reading is to be able to read fast and that understanding is of secondary importance" (p. 563). Reading researchers and theorists have argued volubly (e.g., Kuhn et al., 2010) that prosody is an essential component of reading fluency, but in practice, many districts and schools continue to assess and instruct children's reading fluency using a CWPM orientation, with little attention to prosody and meaning construction (Gamse et al., 2008).

REASONS FOR OPTIMISM

In spite of common misunderstandings about what fluency entails and associated approaches for promoting it, there exists empirical support for several fluency instructional practices and programs that integrate prosody, accuracy, and rate in a balanced manner—and that also include attention to and instruction in reading comprehension (Stahl, 2008). Research-based approaches include Fluency-Oriented Reading Instruction (Stahl & Heubach, 2005), the Wide Reading Approach (e.g., Kuhn et al., 2006), the Fluency Development Lesson (Rasinski, Padak, Linek, & Sturtevant, 1994), the Oral Recitation Lesson and Shared Book Experience (Eldridge, Reutzel, & Hollingsworth, 1996; Reutzel & Hollingsworth, 1993), RAVE-O (Wolf & Katzir-Cohen, 2001), and others (see Kuhn & Schwanenflugel, 2008; Kuhn et al., 2010; Kuhn & Stahl, 2003; Rasinski, Blachowicz, & Lems, 2006; Samuels & Farstrup, 2006). Likewise, writers have developed a variety of techniques for assessing the multiple dimensions of reading fluency, including prosody (e.g., Caldwell, 2007; Johnston, 2006; Kuhn, 2007; McKenna & Stahl, 2008; Miller & Groff, 2008). Thus, teachers, supervisors, and administrators have ample empirically grounded instructional procedures and corresponding authentic assessment tools for implementing sound reading fluency programs.

INDEPENDENT READING AND READING ACHIEVEMENT

There is also reason for optimism from the growing literature on the relationship between independent reading and the development of overall reading ability (Hiebert, 2009), including fluency (Kuhn & Schwanenflugel, 2009). For instance, a meta-analysis of 49 experimental, quasi-experimental, and correlational studies (Lewis, 2002) revealed an overall "small" (Cohen, 1988) but statistically reliable correlation between students' exposure to reading and their reading achievement ($r = .010$ for fixed assumptions and $r = .192$ for random assumptions). For the eight studies that were true experiments, Lewis reported an overall "medium" (Cohen, 1988) effect size ($d = .422$) for reading exposure and achievement.

More recent studies have supported the potential positive impact of independent reading on reading fluency and comprehension. Reutzel, Fawson, and Smith (2008) reported that students who were provided a scaffolded independent silent reading program achieved at levels the same as students in a guided repeated oral reading program, an approach the NRP (NICHD, 2000a) identified as being effective. Extended research on fluency-oriented reading instruction and wide reading documented gains in excess of instructed controls on comprehension and fluency (Kuhn & Schwanenflugel, 2009). Kim and White (2008) reported that elementary students in a voluntary summer reading program who received book exposure with either oral reading scaffolding or scaffolding in oral reading and comprehension outperformed students in books-only and control groups.

It is important to consider the preceding findings in relation to the National Reading Panel's conclusion that there was not compelling "evidence supporting the effectiveness of encouraging independent silent reading as a means of improving reading achievement" (NICHD, 2000a, p. 3-3). The NRP's assertion has been challenged, however, on the basis that it was overly restrictive in study selection criteria and the types of dependent measures that the panel considered appropriate to document reading achievement (Cunningham, 2001; Garan, 2001; Garan & DeVoogd, 2008/2009; Hiebert & Martin, 2009; Krashan, 2004). The panel actually hedged on its own conclusion, stating that "these findings do not negate the positive influence that independent silent reading *may* have on reading fluency, nor do the findings negate the possibility that wide independent reading significantly influences vocabulary development and reading comprehension" (NICHD, 2000b, p. 13).

Finally, there are important lines of relevant research on the relationship between print exposure (through independent oral and silent reading or through read alouds) and a variety of reading abilities. For example, we know that reading aloud to youngsters (e.g., Elley, 1989; Senechal, 1997; Wasik, Bond, & Hindeman, 2006) and independent reading by upper-elementary and middle-grade students (e.g., Anderson, Wilson, & Fielding, 1988; Herman, Anderson, Pearson, & Nagy, 1987; Nagy, Anderson, & Herman, 1987; Nagy, Herman, & Anderson, 1985) are highly related to vocabulary and comprehension development (see Baumann, 2009). Likewise, longitudinal research conducted by Cunningham and Stanovich (1997, 1998, 2003) on the long-term effects of exposure to print (i.e., independent reading) document that "avid readers excel in most domains of verbal learning (2003, p. 669). Although these findings are correlational in nature (see Stanovich & Cunningham, 2004) and not restricted to fluency, there are consistently strong associations between exposure to written text and learners' literacy development.

CONCLUSION

Kamil, Afflerbach, Pearson, and Moje (2011) acknowledged that in the over 100 years since the publication of Edmund Burke Huey's (1908) treatise, *The Psychology and Pedagogy of Reading*, reading researchers have produced many reviews designed "to synthesize what it is that we know for certain about the conditions and practices under which we read and learn to read" (p. xiii). Cathy Collins Block's review of proven and promising practices in reading instruction provides one more excellent synthesis to add to the field's accumulating knowledge. As Block stated in her summary, "We know a lot about reading instruction and a lot about how to prevent reading failure. We are much closer to helping all students attain literacy success" (p. 32).

Indeed, the field is not without resources for assessing and teaching reading fluency in ways that address both the multiple dimensions of fluency and text comprehension, the ultimate goal of reading. Additionally, there exists both experimental and correlational research that points to the power of independent reading and other types of print exposure in the development of fluency and broader reading skill. The challenge remains for reading researchers to inform educational practitioners, curriculum developers, and policymakers about the multifaceted nature of reading fluency and the extant fluency tools that provide nuanced pedagogy and measurement of fluency. Only then will the good intentions of addressing fluency in elementary classrooms be matched with expected and desirable student outcomes.

REFERENCES

Allington, R. L. (1983). Fluency: The neglected goal of the reading program. *Reading Teacher, 36*, 556–561.

Allington, R. L. (1984) Oral reading. In P. D. Pearson (Ed.), *Handbook of reading research* (pp. 829–864). New York: Longman.

Allington, R. L. (2006). Fluency: Still waiting after all these years. In S. J. Samuels & A. E. Farstrup (Eds.), *What research has to say about fluency instruction* (pp. 94–105). Newark, DE: International Reading Association.

Anderson, R. C., Wilson, P., & Fielding, L. (1988). Growth in reading and how children spend their time outside of school. *Reading Research Quarterly, 23*, 285–303.

Baumann, J. F. (2009). Vocabulary and reading comprehension: The nexus of meaning. In S. E. Israel & G. G. Duffy (Eds.), *Handbook of research on reading comprehension* (pp. 323–346). New York: Routledge.

Caldwell, J. S. (2007). *Reading assessment: A primer for teachers and coaches* (2nd ed.). New York: Guilford.

Chard, D. J., Pikulski, J. J., & McDonagh, S. H. (2006). Fluency: The link between decoding and comprehension for struggling readers. In T. V. Rasinski, C. Blachowicz, & K. Lems, (Eds.), *Fluency instruction: Research-based best practices* (pp. 39–61). New York: Guilford.

Cohen, J. (1988). *Statistical power analysis of the behavioral sciences* (2nd ed). Hillsdale, NJ: Erlbaum.

Cunningham, A. E., & Stanovich, K. E. (1997). Early reading acquisition and its relation to reading experience and ability 10 years later. *Developmental Psychology, 33*, 934–945.

Cunningham, A. E., & Stanovich, K. E. (1998, Spring/Summer). What reading does for the mind. *American Educator, 8*–15.

Cunningham, A. E., & Stanovich, K. E. (2003). Reading matters: How reading engagement influences cognition. In J. Flood, D. Lapp, J. R. Squire, & J. Jensen, (Eds.), *Handbook of research on teaching the English language arts* (2nd ed., pp. 666–674). Mahwah, NJ: Lawrence Erlbaum.

Cunningham, J. W. (2001). Essay book review: The National Reading Panel Report. *Reading Research Quarterly, 36,* 326–345.

Deno, S. L., & Marston, D. (2006). Curriculum-based measurement of oral reading: An indicator of growth in fluency. In S. J. Samuels & A. E. Farstrup (Eds.), *What research has to say about fluency instruction* (pp. 179–203). Newark, DE: International Reading Association.

Eldridge, J. L., Reutzel, D. R., & Hollingsworth, P. M. (1996). Comparing the effectiveness of two oral reading practices: Round-robin reading and the shared book experience. *Journal of Literacy Research, 28,* 201–225.

Elley, W. B. (1989). Vocabulary acquisition from listening to stories. *Reading Research Quarterly, 24,* 174–187.

Fuchs, L. S., Fuchs, D., & Compton, D. L. (2004). Monitoring early reading development in first grade: Word identification fluency versus nonsense word fluency. *Exceptional Children, 71,* 7–21.

Fuchs, L. S., Fuchs, D., Hosp, M. K., & Jenkins, J. R. (2001). Oral reading fluency as an indicator of reading competence: A theoretical, empirical, and historical analysis. *Scientific Studies of Reading, 5*(3), 239–256.

Gamse, B. C., Jacob, R. T., Horst, M., Boulay, B., & Unlu, F. (2008). *Reading First Impact Study Final Report* (NCEE 2009-4038). Washington, DC: U.S. Department of Education, Institute of Education Sciences, National Center for Education Evaluation and Regional Assistance.

Garan, E. (2001). Beyond the smoke and mirrors: A critique of the National Reading Panel report on phonics. *Phi Delta Kappan, 82*(7), 500–506.

Garan, E. M., & DeVoogd, G. (2008/2009). The benefits of sustained silent reading: Scientific research and common sense converge. *Reading Teacher, 62,* 336–344.

Good, R. H., & Kaminski, R. A. (2002). *Dynamic indicators of basic early literacy skills* (6th ed.). Eugene, OR: Institute for the Development of Educational Achievement.

Good, R. H., & Kaminski, R. A. (Eds.). (2011). *DIBELS next assessment manual.* Eugene, OR: Dynamic Measurement Group.

Goodman, K. S. (2006). *The truth about DIBELS: What it is, what it does.* Portsmouth, NH: Heinemann.

Herman, P. A., Anderson, R. C., Pearson, P. D., & Nagy, W. E. (1987). Incidental acquisition of word meaning from expositions with varied text features. *Reading Research Quarterly, 22,* 263–284.

Hiebert, E. H. (Ed.). (2009). *Reading more, reading better.* New York: Guilford.

Hiebert, E. H., & Martin, L. A. (2009). Opportunity to read: A critical but neglected construct in reading instruction. In E. H. Hiebert (Ed.), *Reading more, reading better* (pp. 3–29). New York: Guilford.

Huey, E. B. (1908). *The psychology and pedagogy of reading: With a review of the history of reading and writing and of methods, texts, and hygiene in reading.* New York: Macmillan.

Johnston, S. (2006). The fluency assessment system: Improving oral reading fluency with technology. In T. V. Rasinski, C. Blachowicz, & K. Lems, (Eds.), *Fluency instruction: Research-based best practices* (pp. 123–140). New York: Guilford

Kamil, M. L., Afflerbach, P. P., Pearson, P. D., & Moje, E. B. (2011). Preface: Reading research in a changing era. In M. L. Kamil, P. D. Pearson, E. B. Moje, & P. Afflerbach (Eds.), *Handbook of reading research* (Vol. 4, pp. xiii–xxvi). Mahwah, NJ: Erlbaum.

Kim, J. S., & White, T. G. (2008). Scaffolding voluntary summer reading for children in grades 3 to 5: An experimental study. *Scientific Studies of Reading, 12,* 1–23.

Kim, Y., Petscher, Y., Schatschneider, C., & Foorman, B. (2010). Does growth rate in oral reading fluency matter in predicting reading comprehension achievement? *Journal of Educational Psychology, 102,* 652–667.

Krashen, S. D. (2004). *The power of reading: Insights from the research* (2nd ed.). Portsmouth, NH: Heinemann.

Kuhn, M. R. (2007). Effective oral reading assessment (or why round robin reading doesn't cut it). In J. R. Paratore & R. L. McCormack (Eds.), *Classroom literacy assessment: Making sense of what students know and do* (pp. 101–112). New York: Guilford.

Kuhn, M. R., & Schwanenflugel, P. J. (2008). (Eds.). *Fluency in the classroom.* New York: Guilford.

Kuhn, M. R., & Schwanenflugel, P. J. (2009). Time, engagement, and support: Lessons from a 4-year fluency intervention. In E. H. Hiebert (Ed.), *Reading more, reading better* (pp. 141–160). New York: Guilford.

Kuhn, M. R., Schwanenflugel, P. J., & Meisinger, B. (2010). Aligning theory and assessment of reading fluency: Automaticity, prosody, and definitions of fluency. *Reading Research Quarterly, 45,* 230–251.

Kuhn, M. R., Schwanenflugel, P. J., Morris, R. D., Morrow, L. M., Woo, D., Meisinger, B.,... Stahl, S. A. (2006). Teaching children to become fluent and automatic readers. *Journal of Literacy Research, 38*(4), 357–387.

Kuhn, M. R., & Stahl, S. A. (2003). Fluency: A review of developmental and remedial practices. *Journal of Educational Psychology, 95*(1), 3–21.

LaBerge, D., & Samuels, S. J. (1974). Toward a theory of automatic information processing in reading. *Cognitive Psychology, 6*(2), 293–323.

Lewis, M. (2002). *Read more—read better?: A meta-analysis of the literature on the relationship between exposure to reading and reading achievement.* Minneapolis: University of Minnesota.

Logan, G. D. (1997). Automaticity and reading: Perspectives from the instance theory of automaticity. *Reading & Writing Quarterly, 13,* 123–146.

Mathson, D. V., Allington, R. L., & Solic, K. L. (2006). Hijacking fluency and instructionally informative assessments. In T. Rasinski, C. Blachowicz, & K. Lems (Eds.), *Fluency instruction: Research-based best practices* (pp. 106–119). New York: Guilford.

McKenna, M. C., & Stahl, K. A. D. (2008). *Assessment for reading instruction* (2nd ed.). New York: Guilford.

Miller J., & Groff, C. A. (2008). Assessing reading fluency. In M. R. Kuhn & P. J. Schwanenflugel (Eds.), *Fluency in the classroom* (pp. 135–153). New York: Guilford.

Miller, J., & Schwanenflugel, P. J. (2008). A longitudinal study of the development of reading prosody as a dimension of oral reading fluency in early elementary school children. *Reading Research Quarterly, 43*(4), 336–354.

Nagy, W. E., Anderson, R. C., & Herman, P. A. (1987). Learning word meanings from context during normal reading. *American Educational Research Journal, 24,* 237–270.

Nagy, W. E., Herman, P. A., & Anderson, R. C. (1985). Learning words from context. *Reading Research Quarterly, 20,* 233–253.

National Institute of Child Health and Human Development. (2000a). *Report of the National Reading Panel. Teaching children to read: An evidence-based assessment of the scientific research literature on reading and its implications for reading instruction: Reports of the subgroups* (NIH Publication No. 00-4754). Washington, DC: U.S. Government Printing Office.

National Institute of Child Health and Human Development. (2000b). *Report of the National Reading Panel. Teaching children to read: An evidence-based assessment of the scientific research literature on reading and its implications for reading instruction* (NIH Publication No. 00-4769). Washington, DC: U.S. Government Printing Office.

No Child Left Behind (NCLB) Act of 2001, Pub. L. No. 107-110, § 115, Stat. 1425 (2002).

Pinnell, G. S., Pikulski, J. J., Wixson, K. K., Campbell, J. R., Gough, P. B., & Beatty, A. S. (1995). *Listening to children read aloud.* Washington, DC: U.S. Department of Education, Office of Educational Research and Improvement.

Pressley, M. (2006). *Reading instruction that works: The case for balanced teaching.* New York: Guilford.

Pressley, M., Gaskins, I. W., & Fingeret, L. (2006). Instruction and development of reading fluency in struggling readers. In S. J. Samuels & A. E. Farstrup (Eds.), *What research has to say about fluency instruction* (pp. 47–69). Newark, DE: International Reading Association.

Pressley, M., Hilden, K. R., & Shankland, R. K. (2006). *An evaluation of end-grade-3 Dynamic Indicators of Basic Early Literacy Skills (DIBELS): Speed reading without comprehension, predicting little.* East Lansing, MI: State University College of Education, Literacy Achievement Research Center (LARC).

Rasinski, T. V. (2006). A brief history of reading fluency. In S. J. Samuels & A. E. Farstrup (Eds.), *What research has to say about fluency instruction* (pp. 4–23). Newark, DE: International Reading Association.

Rasinski, T. V., Blachowicz, C., & Lems, K. (Eds.). (2006). *Fluency instruction: Research-based best practices.* New York: Guilford.

Rasinski, T. V., & Hoffman, J. V. (2003). Oral reading in the school literacy curriculum. *Reading Research Quarterly, 38,* 510–522.

Rasinski, T. V., Padak, N. D., Linek, W. L., & Sturtevant, E. (1994). Effects of fluency development on urban second-grade readers. *Journal of Educational Research, 87*(3), 158–165.

Rasinski, T. V., Reutzel, R., Chard, D., & Linan-Thompson, S. (2011). Reading fluency. In M. L. Kamil, P. D. Pearson, E. B. Moje, & P. Afflerbach (Eds.), *Handbook of reading research* (Vol. 4, pp. 286–319). Mahwah, NJ: Erlbaum.

Reutzel, D. R., Fawson, P. C., & Smith. J. A. (2008). Reconsidering silent sustained reading: An exploratory study of scaffolded silent reading. *Journal of Educational Research, 102,* 37–50.

Reutzel, D. R., & Hollingsworth, P. M. (1993). Effects of fluency training on second graders' reading comprehension. *Journal of Educational Research, 86,* 325–331.

Riedel, B. W. (2007). The relation between DIBELS, reading comprehension, and vocabulary in urban first-grade students. *Reading Research Quarterly, 42,* 546–567.

Roehrig, A. D., Petscher, Y., Nettles, S. M., Hudson, R. F., & Torgesen, J. K. (2008). Not just speed reading: Accuracy of the DIBELS oral reading fluency measure for predicting high-stakes third grade reading comprehension outcomes. *Journal of School Psychology, 46,* 343–366.

Samuels, S. J. (2004). Toward a theory of automatic information processing in reading, revisited. In R. B. Ruddell & N. J. Unrau (Eds.), *Theoretical models and processes* (pp. 1127–1148). Newark, DE: International Reading Association.

Samuels, S. J. (2006a). Reading fluency: Its past, present, and future. In T. Rasinski, C. Blachowicz, & K. Lems (Eds.), *Fluency instruction: Research-based best practices* (pp. 7–20). New York: Guilford.

Samuels, S. J. (2006b). Toward a model of reading fluency. In S. J. Samuels & A. E. Farstrup (Eds.), *What research has to say about fluency instruction* (pp. 24–46). Newark, DE: International Reading Association.

Samuels, S. J. (2007). The DIBELS tests: Is speed of barking at print what we mean by reading fluency? *Reading Research Quarterly, 42*(4), 563–566.

Samuels, S. J., & Farstrup, A. E. (Eds.). (2006). *What research has to say about fluency instruction.* Newark, DE: International Reading Association.

Schwanenflugel, P. J., Kuhn, M. R., Morris, R. D., Morrow, L. M., Meisinger, E. B., Woo, D. G., Quirk, M., & Sevcik, R. (2009). Insights into fluency instruction: Short- and long-term effects of two reading programs. *Literacy Research and Instruction, 48*(4), 318–336.

Schwanenflugel, P. J., Meisinger, E., Wisenbaker, J. M., Kuhn, M. R., Strauss, G. P., & Morris, R. D. (2006). Becoming a fluent and automatic reader in the early elementary school years. *Reading Research Quarterly, 41*(4), 496–522.

Schwanenflugel, P. J., & Ruston, H. P. (2008). Becoming a fluent reader: From theory to practice. In M. R. Kuhn & P. J. Schwanenflugel (Eds.), *Fluency in the classroom* (pp. 1–16). New York: Guilford.

Senechal, M. (1997). The differential effects of storybook reading on preschoolers' acquisition of expressive and receptive vocabulary. *Journal of Child Language, 24,* 123–138.

Shanahan, T. (2006). Developing fluency in the context of effective literacy instruction. In T. Rasinski, C. Blachowicz, & K. Lems (Eds.), *Fluency instruction: Research-based best practices* (pp. 21–38). New York: Guilford.

Smith, N. B. (1934/2002). *American reading instruction* [Special Edition]. Newark, DE: International Reading Association.

Stahl, K. A. D. (2008). Creating opportunities for comprehension instruction within fluency-oriented reading. In M. R. Kuhn & P. J. Schwanenflugel (Eds.), *Fluency in the classroom* (pp. 55–74). New York: Guilford.

Stahl, S. A., & Heubach, K. (2005). Fluency-oriented reading instruction. *Journal of Literacy Research, 37*(1), 25–60.

Stanovich, K. E., & Cunningham, A. E. (2004). Inferences from correlational data: Exploring associations with reading experience. In N. K. Duke & M. H. Mallette (Eds.), *Literacy research methodologies* (pp. 28–45). New York: Guilford.

Torgesen, J. K., & Hudson, R. F. (2006). Reading fluency: Critical issues for struggling readers. In S. J. Samuels & A. E. Farstrup (Eds.), *What research has to say about fluency instruction* (pp. 130–158). Newark, DE: International Reading Association.

Wasik, B. A., Bond, M. A., & Hindman, A. (2006). The effects of a language and literacy intervention on Head Start children and teachers. *Journal of Educational Psychology, 98,* 63–74.

Walker, B. J., Mokhtari, K., & Sargent, S. (2006). Hijacking fluency and instructionally informative assessments. In T. Rasinski, C. Blachowicz, & K. Lems (Eds.), *Fluency instruction: Research-based best practices* (pp. 86–105). New York: Guilford.

Wolf, M., & Katzir-Cohn, T. (2001). Reading fluency and its intervention. *Scientific Studies of Reading, 5*(3), 211–229.

Zuttell, J., & Rasinski, T. V. (1991). Training teachers to attend to their students' oral reading fluency. *Theory into Practice, 30,* 211–217.

CHAPTER 5

UNDERSTANDING READING RESEARCH FROM DIFFERENT SOCIOCULTURAL HISTORICAL CONTEXTS

Virginia W. Berninger
University of Washington

Block has provided a very interesting and useful review of recent approaches to teaching a variety of comprehension strategies. Even if not all in the field of reading might agree completely on her classification of exactly what is proven and what is promising, clearly she brings to the collective awareness a variety of evidence-based reading comprehension strategies. That alone is a contribution.

What I found most intriguing in this discussion of evidence-based reading comprehension strategies was the discussion of teaching reading to Generation Y students born from 1982 to 2001 (second paragraph under the section on "Proven Lesson Features"). It was not clear whether direct comparisons were made of teaching reading to Generation X children born before 1982 and teaching Generation Y born after 1982 or whether it was assumed that, because the culture has changed as a result of growing up

Instructional Strategies for Improving Students' Learning, pages 79–86
Copyright © 2012 by Information Age Publishing
All rights of reproduction in any form reserved.

with technology, what is found to be effective reading instruction in Generation X students is necessarily the result of the culture in which they are educated. Contemporary reading research may be introducing innovative, highly engaging approaches, which if tried in earlier generations, would also have been very effective.

I would advise caution in concluding, as Block did, that "today's students' brains have developmental differences, which contribute to these more specialized learning needs" (of Generation Y). Students' brains are modifiable based on experience, but they are also genetically and neurologically constrained to a large degree, as has been shown in much research (for recent review, see Berninger & Richards, 2010). There has been no documentation to my knowledge of major evolutionary changes in brain mechanisms over the past 50 years (see, for example, Geary, 2007). Given the strong evidence now available for nature-nurture interactions, there is also evidence that student brains can normalize in response to instruction. In some of these studies, strategies were used that had been validated in research in individuals born prior to 1982; they were again validated in brain research with individuals born after 1982, thus showing that the brain has not evolved to where different kinds of reading instruction are needed than in the past (Berninger & Wolf, 2009a, 2009b)! Clearly, a comprehensive review of evidence-based reading instruction needs to take into account research results for not only the generalized human mind but also for individual differences (biologically or experientially based) and alternative pathways in development (i.e., that there is more than one pathway to achieve the same reading outcome; for evidence, see Berninger & Abbott, 1992).

SOCIOCULTURAL FACTORS IN HISTORICAL CONTEXT

Thus, Block lays the groundwork for considering in future research whether the tried-and-true approaches for reading instruction may apply across the ever-evolving changes in the culture in which children grow up or whether they are specific to a given era. I thank her for helping me to realize that both research and teaching are always situated in the culture of the times in which we live at a particular moment in history.

As a result of considering how differences in culture at different points in history might affect what researchers and practitioners believe works in teaching reading, I considered, for the first time, what kind of changes I had observed in teaching reading and teaching teachers to teach reading over the past 45 years. In this commentary, I share some of these reflections, realizing that within- and across-generations, observers may vary in the kinds of experiences and perspectives they have. At the same time, I think it is helpful to bring diverse perspectives to the conversation. For example, I did not experience that only phonics in isolation was recommended before the 1960s, as Block suggests, or that only decoding should be taught in the early grades, and that comprehension should be delayed until the upper grades. I am not saying that some may not have believed this, but rather that not all held this view. I also do not think that Chall's (1979) message was to delay all reading comprehension instruction until the upper elementary grades. Indeed, learning to read includes not only word recognition but also reading comprehension. Chall's research showed the benefits of teaching phonics in the first three grades rather than in the upper grades. That does not rule out early reading comprehension instruction.

1960s

Many colleges offered undergraduate programs in teaching, with specialization in elementary or secondary education. As a psychology undergraduate in the mid-1960s who was interested in learning in general and reading in particular, I enrolled in two courses in a liberal arts college that trained many preservice teachers in the state. One course was on teaching reading and language arts in the general education classroom to students who learned easily, and another course was on teaching the same content to students who did not learn easily. In addition, I enrolled in a course in teaching children's literature. What I observed was that future teachers were prepared both conceptually about what reading is, based on research conducted prior to the 1960s, and practically for teaching reading (e.g., differentiated instruction for individual children who typically varied in initial skills at the beginning of the year and the rate at which they learned). Reading practices were based on research and not just beliefs.

Preservice teachers were prepared to teach systematically a variety of skills, ranging from decoding words using phonics to structural analysis of syllables and morphemes to vocabulary building to oral reading fluency to reading comprehension, in developmentally appropriate ways. All the skills covered by the National Reading Panel and more were covered in these courses. Both word recognition and reading comprehension were emphasized from first grade and thereafter. Believe or not, there was earlier research on reading, beginning with Huey (2008), and we learned the Directed Reading Activity (summarized for contemporary reading teachers in Table 7.2 of Berninger, 1994) for integrated reading instruction: background knowledge, vocabulary building, word identification strategies, purpose-setting questions to guide silent reading and oral rereading to answer a variety of questions designed to teach information extraction and summarization, inferential thinking, and other higher-order comprehension skills, and finally group and individual skill-building activities. Since then,

I have found that similar approaches work well with Generation Y students (e.g., Berninger & Wolf, 2009a, 2009b).

Moreover, it was emphasized that children would enter a grade at varying levels of reading skill. Teachers were encouraged to assess each student's instructional levels in word reading and passage reading at the beginning of the year to form reading groups of students with similar, if not identical, instructional levels. They were also encouraged to reassess during the year if any student seemed to be making relative gains or not making progress and to change their instructional group when warranted. Instructional levels and instructional groupings were explained similarly to how *zones of proximal development* (Vygotsky, 1978) and *differentiated instruction* (Tomlinson, 2001) are presented in contemporary preservice education courses.

Some attention was given to introducing students to the widely available textbooks in schools, which were organized for the most part to teach reading and language arts skills comprehensively and offered many practical suggestions for doing so. Some attention was given to handwriting and spelling, but composition was not given much attention until the junior high grades. (That, of course, has changed with the wide adoption of writers' workshop, thank goodness). However, teachers were also introduced to the best of children's literature, and they were encouraged to use it often in their teaching to foster love and enjoyment of both oral and written language.

I learned enough from these three courses to design, for the purpose of an honors thesis, a study of teaching an 8-year-old boy with dyslexia to read. Upon graduation from college, I enrolled in a graduate "psychology of reading" program at a university that, prior to national special education legislation and services, provided clinical assessment and treatment for children with reading disabilities whose parents (locally and from surrounding states) brought them to the university during the summer. The highly experienced faculty had developed, through research and over half a century of clinical experience, assessment protocols for identifying with graded passages instructional levels in word recognition in isolation and context, reading comprehension (both factual and inferential), and oral and silent reading rates. They had also developed protocols for teaching to the instructional needs of individual children based on the assessment results and monitoring their response to the instruction. Graduate students were given supervised practicum experience in assessing and teaching individual students referred by their parents to this clinic. Those instructed students typically improved, providing another kind of relevant evidence that the approach worked. Many graduate students who received this training went on to become trainers in preservice teacher education in that state or surrounding ones.

My education in what works in teaching reading was followed by teaching in a real public school through a special program that invited political activists in the civil rights movement, draft dodgers, or others interested in social justice to teach in the inner city. I had 50 third-generation welfare third graders in my first class (25 African American, 25 Puerto Rican), and I quickly learned that none of what I had learned about teaching reading from coursework, supervised clinical experience, or the Scott Foresman basal was working. Through trial and error, I learned that productive learning occurred only when the children first actively engaged in science experiments and then in writing and reading about them. Likewise, in teaching Generation Y children with dyslexia, our research has shown the benefits of hands-on, intellectually engaging activities and integrated writing-reading activities, but also coupled with special methods learned in my undergraduate and graduate school training during the 1960s based on research and practice before 1960 (Berninger & Wolf, 2009a, 2009b).

However, in that first year of teaching, there were competing systems variables with the research-based methods. Much of the time the principal was not in charge of the building, and the teachers were not in charge of their classrooms: Frequently the fire alarm was set off by various students, leading to frequent evacuations of the building; children threatened or succeeded in jumping out of windows until they were locked; children often injured each other; and gangs terrorized some students. Teachers were escorted by police to and from public transportation. Sometimes children died from infectious diseases, and we mourned their loss. Many children were hungry; there were no free and reduced-price lunches.

As an aside, I do worry that with all the pressure on schools now for teachers and students to be accountable, it may still be that schools with the highest achievement gap are those with the highest number of students who are still hungry. As one second grader told our research coordinator in a study showing how differentiated instruction can prevent reading problems (Berninger, Dunn, Lin, & Shimada, 2004), "My family is poor; sometimes there is food in the refrigerator and sometimes there is not. But my cousin is very poor; there is never food in the refrigerator where he lives." Now that there are free and reduced-price lunches, children sometimes cry when summer comes because access to food is uncertain until school reopens. Many other children, of course, do not even live in homes, but rather on the streets. Poverty can trump the best of evidence-based instruction in reading.

1970s to 1980s

The Civil Rights Movement of the 1960s gave birth to the Feminist Movement. Women now had options other than being a teacher, nurse, or secretary, and many pursued careers in business, medicine, law, and other professions. Those who remained in the teaching profession, women and men alike, began the continuing fight to make teaching a profession. As Barbara Wise astutely pointed out when given an award in 1990 for her numerous contributions to evidence-based effective teaching of students with dyslexia, the whole-language movement was just as much about the emerging voices for making teaching a profession, with professional autonomy as medicine, law, and psychology enjoy, as it was about teaching for meaning rather than decoding. However, not all researchers grasped that. During the 1970s, the 1960s Great Debate about how to teach reading gave rise to the Great War between the researchers (teach phonics) and the teachers (teach for meaning). Even the brain, which has a white fiber tract (arcuate fasciculus) connecting the back of the brain, where decoding begins, and the front of the brain, where reading comprehension culminates (Rilling et al., 2008), needs both decoding and comprehension to work together. Instructional research also supports the position that both word identification and comprehension should be taught from the beginning (Berninger et al., 2003; Berninger, Abbott, Vermeulen, & Fulton, 2006).

In my ongoing experience in teaching in suburban and rural schools, what I learned in undergraduate and graduate courses did work in classrooms where other system-level variables were operating in reasonably normal ways. In my PhD program in psychology (specialization in cognitive psychology and developmental psycholinguistics, with coursework in psychobiology) and subsequent clinical training and experience in clinical psychology and applied developmental neuropsychology, I learned that there were many variables (cognitive, linguistic, and sensory/motor in brain and experiential in homes and schools) that could interfere with both word recognition and reading comprehension in developing children and that require instructional attention.

1990s to the Present

National Reading Panel. The National Reading Panel's conclusions, which are well summarized in the Block article and consistent with what many teachers have known before and since the 1960s, are based on research in general education classrooms and not on research with students exhibiting learning differences (as discussed in Block's final section). Accumulating research is supporting the importance of additional skills such as orthographic and morphological awareness, which should also be taken into account (for review, see Berninger, Abbott, Nagy, & Carlisle, 2010).

What works. Research on effective ways to teach reading has expanded rapidly and so has the top-down approach of policymakers dictating to teachers at the local level. The hidden, unexamined assumption is that one approach will work for all, without adequate consideration of biologically based individual differences and individual differences in home literacy experiences and oral language spoken in the home, which also may affect what works with a given child. Also, the fact that Block's review shows that multiple approaches to comprehension instruction have been found to work is consistent with prior reports of alternative paths in acquiring written language, just as there are for oral language. Of greatest concern, the top-down What Works approach does not give professional respect to teachers, acknowledging that they are capable of reading and evaluating the research themselves and using their creative talents to implement reading instruction in artful and effective ways for the class at hand, both individually and as a group. So, despite all the research, we are left with the nagging question raised repeatedly by G. Reid Lyon (e.g., Lyon, 1991), who, in his testimony before the Committee on Labor and Human Resources, April 28, 1998, stated that "the real question is which children need what, how, for how long, with what type of teacher, and in what type of setting."

BIOLOGICALLY BASED INDIVIDUAL DIFFERENCES

The National Reading panel did not focus on students with specific learning disabilities or with other educational handicapping conditions such as developmental disabilities or neurogenetic disorders or brain injuries. Both genetic and neurological factors can interfere with reading development in children whose development is otherwise normal (for a review, see Berninger & Richards, 2010). Thus, instruction is not the only variable that can influence student learning outcomes, but is typically the only one taken into account in evaluating those outcomes, which are generally the result of individual differences within learners, instruction, and curriculum and instructional tools. Professional educators who are teacher leaders can model assessment-instruction that takes into account all relevant influences: In the least restrictive environment—the general education classroom—they can creatively adapt instruction for all students whose development falls within the normal range so that, despite their individual differences and possibly unique systems variables, students learn to read.

REFERENCES

Berninger, V. (1994). *Reading and writing acquisition. A developmental neuropsychological perspective.* Developmental Psychology Series (W. Jeffries, Ed.). Boulder, CO: Westview Press.

Berninger, V., & Abbott, R. (1992). Unit of analysis and constructive processes of the learner: Key concepts for educational neuropsychology. *Educational Psychologist, 27,* 223–242.

Berninger, V., Abbott, R., Nagy, W., & Carlisle, J. (2010). Growth in phonological, orthographic, and morphological awareness in grades 1 to 6. *Journal of Psycholinguistic Research, 39,* 141–163.

Berninger, V., Abbott, R., Vermeulen, K., & Fulton, C. (2006). Paths to reading comprehension in at-risk second grade readers. *Journal of Learning Disabilities, 39,* 334–351.

Berninger, V., Dunn, A., Lin, S., & Shimada, S. (2004). School evolution: Scientist-practitioner educators creating optimal learning environments for ALL students. *Journal of Learning Disabilities, 37,* 500–508.

Berninger, V., & Richards, T. (2010). Inter-relationships among behavioral markers, genes, brain, and treatment in dyslexia and dysgraphia. *Future Neurology, 5,* 597–617.

Berninger, V., Vermeulen, K., Abbott, R., McCutchen, D., Cotton, S., Cude, J., Dorn S., & Sharon, T. (2003). Comparison of three approaches to supplementary reading instruction for low achieving second grade readers. *Language, Speech, and Hearing Services in Schools, 34,* 101–116.

Berninger, V., & Wolf, B. (2009a). *Teaching students with dyslexia and dysgraphia: Lessons from teaching and science.* Baltimore: Paul H. Brookes.

Berninger, V., & Wolf, B. (2009b). *Helping students with dyslexia and dysgraphia make connections: Differentiated instruction lesson plans in reading and writing.* Baltimore: Paul H. Brookes.

Chall, J. (1979). The great debate 10 years later, with a modest proposal for research stages. In L. Resnick & P. Weaver (Eds.), *Theory and practice of early reading,* (Vol. 1, pp. 29–55). Hillsdale, NJ: Erlbaum.

Geary, D. C. (2007). Educating the evolved mind: Conceptual foundations for an evolutionary educational psychology. In J. S. Carlson & J. R. Levin (Eds.), *Educating the evolved mind: Conceptual foundations for an evolutionary educational psychology.* Charlotte, NC: Information Age.

Huey, H. (1908). *The psychology and pedagogy of reading.* New York: Macmillan.

Lyon, G. R. (1991). *Treatment interventions for children with learning disabilities.* Bethesda, MD: National Institute of Child Health and Human Development/NIH.

Rilling, J. K., Glasser, M. F., Preuss, T. M., Ma, X., Zhao, T., Hu, X., & Behrens, T. E. (2008). The evolution of the arcuate fasciculus revealed with comparative DTI. *Nature Neuroscience* DOI: 10.1038/nn2072

Tomlinson, C. (2001). *How to differentiate instruction in mixed-ability classrooms* (2nd ed.). Alexandria, VA: Association for Supervision and Curriculum Development.

Vygotsky, L. S. (1978). *Mind in society.* Cambridge. MIT Press.

CHAPTER 6

FROM PROVEN AND PROMISING READING INSTRUCTION TO PAVING NEW PATHS

Widening Highways, Crossing Borders, and Repairing Potholes

Cathy Collins Block
Texas Christian University

> *Criticisms [and accord] are the endeavors to find, to know, to love,*
> *to recommend, not only the best, but all the good, that has been known*
> *and taught and written in the world.*

—George Saintsbury, Preface, *Tom Jones,* Henry Fielding, 1749
(Bartlett, 1939, p. 1159)

I deeply respect each commentator as a person and scholar. Their remarkably fresh insights and masterful writings have advanced the field of reading instruction. I have divided my responses to their works into three sections: (a) the domains of knowledge upon which we agree (i.e., ways in which

Instructional Strategies for Improving Students' Learning, pages 87–104

we can widen our confidence in the directions we are traveling in reading instruction); (b) discussions of the new terrains that they entered into our conversation (the new borders they crossed and intersections within bodies of research that their commentaries highlighted); and (c) disparate interpretations among us that need attention before we too hastily move forward in our present research efforts (potholes in our knowledge base). In each section, I discuss the remarks of the four commentators in alphabetical order.

I particularly appreciated Jim Baumann's always-consummate thoroughness and in-depth discussion of reading fluency. His analysis of more than 80 references can provide educators, policymakers, and laypersons with a valuable, up-to-date synthesis of fluency research and practice. I am grateful for Virginia Berninger's long-standing career in educational neuropsychology and in creating optimal learning environments for special populations. She eloquently reminds us that future research must take the cognitive, linguistic, sensory/motor, and experiential variables into account, from the moment that reading instruction is designed until the instruments that evaluate its success have been created. I admire Margaret McKeown as the exquisite sophisticated craftswoman that she is. I appreciate her abilities to studiously and conscientiously present important domains of comprehension instruction and teacher actions with the creativity, passion, and freshness that characterize her immense body of research contributions to our field. I respect Rollanda O'Connor's attention to details and recommendations for scaffolding English Language Learners' literacy. I value her ability to provide new sources of evidence without entertaining the temptation to cling to one's own perspective; few can praise others while setting limitations upon those colleagues' works, but she did.

Taken together, these four essays reaffirm the advancements that have been made in early reading and comprehension instruction. I was uplifted to realize how often these commentaries reported common ground and covered new bodies of research. After reading my respected colleagues' essays, I judge that my initial chapter achieved its goal. It was designed (a) to begin a discussion upon which chapter commentators could both amend and expand; and (b) to assist educators, policymakers, parents, and laypersons to make more reliable educational decisions. Within and among the five reading-related chapters in this volume, many perspectives have been addressed. Situational interpretations and numerous points of commonality have been offered. First, I will highlight the commonalities in our writings as I perceived them.

Widening the Highways of Agreement

There is music even in the beauty, and the silent note, far sweeter than the sound of an instrument; for there is music wherever there is harmony, order or proportion.

—Sir Thomas Browne, *Religio Medici*, Part II, Section IX
(Bartlett, 1939, p. 320)

Widening the highway of agreement in reading instructional practices is defined as identifying points in the commentaries that were in accord with syntheses in my chapter. Such agreements could also be inferred when no critiques of individual syntheses were made, as the silences could be viewed as indicators that we are all likely traveling together in our interpretations. Even though each commentary made its own imprint on our understanding of reading instruction, our overall syntheses agree in many respects. When it is noted that I have never worked with any of the commentators on any research project, it makes this unity even more compelling. Despite our theoretical, empirical, and pedagogical differences, we agree (as explicitly explained by some authors and implicitly by others) that the highway that we are traveling in reading instruction is headed in the right direction in the following ways.

At the primary level:

1. The NRP's analysis found that phonemic awareness, phonics, comprehension, vocabulary, and fluency are the proven critical components to be taught in early reading instruction, and that more nonfictional texts and student selection of books (or electronic versions of them) should be used in reading instruction; and, as Berninger so aptly adds, this analysis needs to be extended to include research with "students exhibiting learning differences" (Berninger, ms. p. 10). (Type: Correct page number to be inserted when typeset.)
2. Work should continue to assist readers to initiate and monitor multiple comprehension strategies either in single lessons or, as McKeown notes, through added attention to problem-solving aids and discussion-based approaches.
3. Teaching early readers to use authorial writing patterns to learn new terms and to predict upcoming events and facts is proving to be effective.
4. Using multicultural content and students' own multicultural and linguistic resources as features in literacy lessons is valuable.
5. Work should continue to include scaffolds that increase students' active learning during whole class instruction.

6. Teachers can employ the behaviors identified in exemplary literacy teacher research to improve students' literacy.
7. Work to employ six domains of exemplary teacher competencies at distinct grade levels should continue.

At the upper elementary level:

1. Vocabulary strategies that unravel the complex relationships among students' abilities to discern word meanings, to comprehend, to read fluently, and to apply what is read to their unique sociocultural contexts should continue to be components of reading instruction.
2. When taught, higher-level thinking strategies of inference and meta-cognition increase students' reading abilities.
3. Individualizing comprehension instruction is effective, including generative fast mapping, generative learning, and helping students set their own purposes for reading.
4. Methods that match today's students' special learning needs are effective, realizing (as Berninger notes) that these methods might have worked equally well for prior generations, and that changes in human brain formation is not the cause for this need.
5. Delivering expanded explanations and elaborated feedback more effectively is an important teacher action, as is providing more enriching postreading discussions (as all commentators suggested).

Baumann, McKeown, and I agree that individual strategies and reading instruction must no longer be "an end itself (as becoming a skilled orator [or mastering a vocabulary or comprehension strategy]) to a means to an end (fluent silent reading [or strategic, problem solving while reading])" (Baumann, p. 67). Berninger, McKeown, and I agree that overemphasis on the "top-down What Works approach does not give professional respect to teachers, acknowledging that they are capable of ... using their creative talents to implement reading instruction in artful and effective ways for the class at hand, both individually and as a group" (Berninger, p. 85).

Berninger and I concur that future research must pay more attention to understanding how reading instruction is shaped by different sociocultural and historical contexts, and that research relative to teaching reading to Generation Y is "most intriguing" (Berninger, p. 79). I thank Berninger for her personal examples of how her (and all) learning is "always situated in the culture of the times in which we live at a particular moment in history" (Berninger, p. 80).

McKeown and I agree that vocabulary instruction must occur through a rich, continuous vocabulary program, and that much of today's practices rely too heavily on learning meanings through the use of context (McKeown, pp. 58–59). Research relative to the use of context analysis in my chapter reports its merits only in concert with syntax and first-syllable decoding for words that students see very frequently in books or in deducing the meaning of content-specific words when a full page of text is used as the context. I also thank McKeown's concurrence as to the importance of teacher actions in reading instruction. I particularly value her addition that teachers need to be responsible for scaffolding, coaching, and monitoring student thinking *and problem solving*" [emphasis added]; and that students need "the responsibility for doing the thinking... [and after teachers have explained and elaborated to] leave space for student thinking" (McKeown, p. 60).

I value O'Connor's agreement with the categories in my chapter, even though we do not fully agree as to which bodies of evidence are to be labeled as "proven" or "promising" reading practices. I judge that a part of our disagreement is definitional. I defined "proven practices" as those that have been "studied for several years and have provided evidence on many dependent measures that they reliably and validly play a part in improving students' literacy skills. The number of empirical studies that document their effects, as well as the variety of students with which they have proven their worth, is larger than those that exist for promising practices" (Block, p. 4). O'Connor states, "I disagree with the notion of a 'proven' practice in educational research. The Institute of Education Sciences currently demands analysis of what works for whom in reports of their funded projects. As a special educator, the notion of individual differences is paramount in instructional recommendations. We do not believe in magic bullets, but rather in approaches that work more frequently than others for students with particular characteristics. Moreover, the notion of a proven practice suggests we know all there is to know about it" (O'Connor, p. 49). However, O'Connor and I agree that "as the range of cultures and language experiences grows in public schools, teachers and policymakers [must] strive to employ the strongest instructional approaches to improve life outcomes for diverse students" (O'Connor, p. 46).

All commentators and I agreed that evaluations of reading instruction must be improved through future research. As noted in Baumann's commentary: "Kuhn et al. (2010) stated that 'the current implementation of fluency instruction [and I posit other domains of reading content] in many classrooms is often driven by assessments that build upon an incomplete conceptualization of the construct and can lead to...inappropriate instruction' (p. 230)" (Baumann, p. 69). McKeown adds that the 'sufficient scientific basis' needs to be considered in light of how effects in various studies were measured and to what the instructional intervention was compared" (McKeown, p. 54); and Berninger argues that "instruction is not the only variable that can influence student outcomes, but is typically the only one taken into account in evaluating those outcomes (Berninger, p. 85).

O'Connor and McKeown posit that past research and practice relied on reading assessments that evaluated its shallow aspects.

In summary, taken together, the works in this volume widen the highways of agreement in reading instruction. From my viewpoint, the research community agrees that the directions cited above can be traveled with relative confidence to improve reading instruction.

Crossing Borders

There is a tide in the affairs of men,
Which, taken at the flood, leads on to fortune;
Omitted, all the voyage of their life
Is bound in shallows and in miseries. (¥epi)

—William Shakespeare, *Julius Caesar*, Act III, Lines 213–217
(Bartlett, 1939, p. 851)

I concur with the quotation above that the time is right for reading practices to voyage into new domains of knowledge—to cross new borders so as to avoid a shallow interpretation of reading instruction. When I drive and savor the scenery, I notice subtle changes in terrain over a 4-hour trip. However, when I pass a marker denoting that I am entering a new state, I immediately look for the differences that must be present to characterize this newly crossed border. Crossing borders, in the context of this response, occurred when researchers describe how to apply data in my chapter in new ways; cited ways in which man-made boundaries in traditional research perspectives or instructional practices can be dissolved; or went beyond my points to demonstrate proven and promising applications of reading instruction in new domains of knowledge. Every commentator did so. They helped me to see more of the commonalities in our field rather than the often artificially imposed distinctions imposed on separate bodies of reading practices and research. Every commentator noted the complex interactive factors that are reading instruction at its best. These discussions are exceptionally well written and vital in that they shine light on different nuanced and contextualized views of how we can maximize what we presently judge to be effective reading instruction.

For example, Baumann expands our understanding of the intersections of reading fluency and other critical components in reading instruction. In crossing this border, he makes us vividly aware that we can no longer treat fluency, comprehension, and vocabulary instruction as distinct states of content. Methods must more frequently teach fluency in concert with other paths to literacy. Fluency instruction can no longer be left behind as a stepsister in our instructional scope and sequences; nor can it be dismissed in an out-of-hand fashion, as of course, young readers will become fluent as a necessary by-product of mastering the other critical domains of early reading instruction—vocabulary, phonics, phonemic awareness, and comprehension. As Baumann so expertly documents, to advance our field, we must continue to develop methods and assessments by which students learn to use their knowledge of words, comprehension of content, and fluent reading of the phrases and the rhythm of English to become more literate. As Baumann also notes, for too long, lessons in comprehension were taught one day, vocabulary the next, and reading fluency practiced at another time. Not only must we unite these states of knowledge in the manners in which they are taught, but teachers must assist students to become aware of when they are crossing borders by using one domain of their expertise to expand their other literacy components. Specifically, "[t]he experimental research literature since the release of the NRP has reinforced further the importance of fluency in promoting students' automatic word identification and text comprehension" (Baumann, p. 67). Baumann concludes, "The challenge remains for reading researchers to inform educational practitioners, curriculum developers, and policymakers about the multifaceted nature of reading fluency and the extant fluency tools that provide nuanced pedagogy and measurement of fluency" (Baumann, p. 72).

Baumann goes on to cross the border just as eloquently from instruction for readers who develop through normal instruction and special instruction for struggling readers. He states that the latter tends to emphasize decoding and "artificial" fluency word calling more frequently than the lessons provided for more able readers, which include more authentic discussions of content and depth of comprehension instruction. This raises the important question: Do struggling readers struggle because of our instruction? Baumann's crossing of this new border reminds researchers and practitioners that modifications in lesson features must meet individual student needs even more effectively when these needs are more numerous.

Berninger takes our conversations across the border into the sociocultural nature of reading instruction. Her comments hold proven and promising practices to the truth that individual students' backgrounds and diverse experiences interact with the instruction they are offered. Berninger's positions vividly describe the many ways that readers put their own imprint on what is taught, and that no person's interpretation of a text can ever be totally "correct" for all. What works in reading instruction must be placed in the context of how it worked for which types of students.

I also thank Berninger for vividly demonstrating that throughout the ages, the best teachers have created highly effective reading instruction, even in the face of pendulum swings within the educational research community. She masterfully concludes her discussion of this important crossing of borders by quoting G. Reid Lyon's (e.g., Lyon, 1991) testimony before the Committee on Labor and Human Resources, April 1998: "the real question is which children need what, how, for how long, with what type of teacher, and in what type of setting" (Berninger, p. 85). This point truly breaks down all artificial borders between content to be taught, instructional strategies to be used to convey this instruction, lesson features to employ, and actions that teachers should take as we move into the future of reading research and practice (i.e., the artificial, man-made borders that I created in my chapter). In this statement alone, Berninger captures the clarion call we must answer. As a united educational body, traveling among deeply rooted paths and long-standing research traditions, we must continuously view the merits of every practice by the degree to which it aids individual students.

McKeown takes our collective knowledge to be viewed from the borders surrounding the social nature of reading instruction. Her commentary documents that reading instruction is multifaceted and contextually based within the classroom situations in which this instruction occurs. She emphasizes the Vygotskian perspective of social situations that mediate learning, and that instruction must honor the role that teachers' and students' active actions have in learning.

I also deeply respect McKeown's crossing of another border. She wanted "to move the emphasis [in my chapter] back in the direction of processing content rather than applying strategies" (McKeown, p. 60). In my opinion, her commentary attained this goal. She and I completely concur that my divisions in the chapter did not do justice to the need for "fluent processes" as the ultimate objective of all reading instruction. For her thorough discussion of this need, I am grateful. May the educational community never again erect an artificial barrier between the need for teacher dominance and student internalization, but rather, as McKeown so eloquently states, may these two important instruction variables labor in concert as teachers work "to develop students' abilities to engage an effective set of thought processes at strategic points in a text to make rich, valid meanings" (McKeown, p. 60).

McKeown's emphasis is to extend the teaching of strategies better by assisting students to learn how to coordinate processes. I agree. My chapter emphasized the importance of pre-teaching strategies, while she merits the values of postreading discussion. I thank her for emphasizing that reading instruction, of any type, should never be reduced to the pre-teaching of one particular process (e.g., merely reminding students before they read to "think about a comprehension strategy that was just taught"). Rather, her outstanding research describes new means by which students can be taught how to relate multiple strategies together through *after-reading activities*. Alternatively, I describe methods that assist students to relate multiple strategies at specific points in a text at which they are needed *while they read,* such as how to sequence facts, recognize main ideas, relate main ideas vertically throughout a reading, verify connections within a text, and apply relevant data to their lives. Why not both? There just is not enough yet known about how to develop readers who monitor well and who, in turn, self-regulate their comprehension, vocabulary, decoding and fluency processes well. McKeown's excellent commentary makes us more keenly aware of the artificial border that has been created to limit the "view of successful comprehension as active and strategic [as being merely] interpreted, for the most part, as meaning that young readers need to learn and practice specific strategies" rather than to become "active by deliberately attending to what they are reading and working to make sense of it as they proceed; they are strategic by keeping track of how the sense-making process is going" (McKeown, p. 55).

I concur that the discussion-based approaches listed in McKeown's commentary have proven to increase students' comprehension and could be added as a new domain of research that is being used successfully in schools today. As McKeown reports, however, research to date has also not concluded whether such discussion-based approaches should supersede, precede, or follow instruction of the strategies listed in my chapter. Results of McKeown's discussion-based approaches "indicate that an approach that allowed students to consider text meaning directly was feasible and at least as effective as pursuing meaning by going through strategies" (McKeown, p. 58). I concur that pursuing meaning by going through strategies and through discussion approaches has proven effective. Research syntheses in my chapter have suggested that teaching students to predict/infer; monitor metacognitively; question, image, look-back, reread, and repair misunderstandings; find main ideas, summarize and draw conclusions; apply content to life; evaluate the merits in content read; and synthesize ideas have increased performances on a wide variety of reading achievement measures. My major goal in synthesizing this research was the same as McKeown's, to a large degree. We both intended to communicate that direct instruction of fewer, rather than more, comprehension strategies has proven to be more effective, especially in light of the concerns raised by Sinatra, Brown, and Reynolds (2002), Pearson and Fielding (1991) and McKeown's body of research.

O'Connor moves our discussion across the important border concerning special education. She contends that "[e]very field of research has its own set of warrants for what 'counts' as source material. Viewing practices from alternative perspectives (e.g., general education, special education, school psychology, educational psychology) can reveal new sources of evidence and account for differing conclusions" (O'Connor, p. 44). She asks us to examine more closely the man-made borders between special needs students' instruction and traditional, classroom reading instruction, and she posits that as student diversity increases, we must have more research to document what and how special students process instruction different-ly. We know from the research cited by Berninger and McKeown that the measures we use in this research are going to be empirically tempered by the culture in the instructional context, students' individual cultural under-standings, and the sociocultural nature within the classroom, pupil's home, and school environments.

In summary, the issues raised in my chapter and in all four commentar-ies reiterate the complexity of the topic being addressed. The research and practice of reading instruction cannot be boxed into simple ways of think-ing. The refreshing truth in all of these commentaries, from my viewpoint, is that in the future, large bodies of research are likely to unite to create a richer and more valid understanding of how to deliver and tailor highly suc-cessful reading instruction to meet each individual student's needs.

Repairing Potholes

> *Actions and counteractions, in the natural and political world,*
> *form the reciprocal struggle of discordant powers necessary to draw out*
> *the harmony of the universe.*
>
> —Edmond Burke, *Reflections on the Revolution in France,* 1790
> (Bartlett, 1939, p. 1283)

Repairing potholes represents points at which an individual commenta-tor's interpretations differ from mine, indicating that holes in our under-standings must be filled before we travel much further. My chapter limited its scope to "provide compact syntheses of highly important facets of to-day's instructional programs" (Block, p. 3). In the process of compacting the 164 studies reported in my essay, I could not elaborate on many distinct points within individual studies. In this section of my rejoinder, I provide more expanded explanation on individual points that were important to the commentators.

The editors of this volume sought to stimulate discussion, critique, and diverse commentaries concerning reading instruction. They succeeded in their attempt. I (and, I judge, all commentators) enhanced their perspec-tives through the "reciprocal struggle of discordant powers" (Burke, 1790). In the early elementary graders, there were differences between my and the commentators' research syntheses on the topic that I labeled, "Teach-ing the five domains of phonemic awareness, phonics, comprehension, vo-cabulary and fluency in early grades, and showing students how to apply them interactively." At the upper elementary level, there were alternative perspectives concerning the "teaching of nine research-based comprehension strategies; teaching comprehension and decoding strategies at exact points of need; and increasing student agency through the use of more student-led groups and scaffolds during whole-class instruction." In addition, I agree with Baumann that "[a]lthough there is substantial evidence that automaticity has a direct effect on reading comprehension (Samuels, 2004), it still is not fully clear how prosody influences comprehension (Kuhn et al., 2010)" (p. 67) This hole in our knowledge base must also be addressed. We can no longer view fluency and comprehension as separate avenues of instruction.

Baumann and McKeown posit the important question that reading exposure and its impact on reading achievement, fluency, and comprehension have not been answered. Research suggests that exposure alone has a "medium" effect (Lewis, 2002); others claim that more direct instruction is of greater value for literacy development (Block, Parris, Reed, Whiteley, & Cleveland, 2009). However, after reading Baumann's, McKeown's, and my chapters back-to-back-to-back, readers might more closely come to agree that *teacher supported or scaffolded* independent reading is important as well or even more important than either of the former dichotomous positions. McKeown and I did not disagree that just increasing the amount of time to spend reading without assisting students to apply what was read is a new direction that future reading instruction should take. We emphasize different ways to assist students. Her work has been very successful in showing us how to help students during and after reading, whereas more of my work has demonstrated how to assist students before and during reading.

Berninger asked for clarification as to whether "direct comparisons were made of teaching reading to Generation X children born before 1982 and teaching Generation Y born after 1982 or whether it was assumed that, because the culture has changed as a result of growing up with technology, what is found to be effective reading instruction in Generation X students is necessarily the result of the culture in which they are educated." (pp. 79–80). The proven lesson features that I describe on pages 26–28 had been used with earlier generations, but empirical tests of their resultant effects were not empirically tested. The point I wanted to make was that "creating methods that match today's students' special learning needs" has proven to have a statistically significant effect on students' subsequent reading abilities. I also wanted to emphasize that "since 1948, [with the creation of the Directed Reading Activity to which Berninger refers on p. 81], lessons have included features designed to meet individual student needs (Betts & Welch, 1948)" (Block, p. 26). We now have enough empirical evidence to continue research on features in reading lessons that address students' learning needs. The lesson features reported on pages 26–28 appear to meet the sociocultural needs, learning preferences, and more frequent mental processing pathways used by today's students. Berninger and I agree that creating methods that match Generation Y's special learning needs have proven to be effective, and that such methods might have been effective for prior generations, but research was not conducted to test this hypothesis. I also agree that other traditional approaches, such as those described by Berninger on pages 81–82, have proven to work well for today's students (Berninger & Wolf, 2009a, 2009b).

Berninger and I differ most in our interpretation of the newest brain research concerning Generation Y. We differ in our emphasis upon how much the neurological components in processing reading have been altered by genetic or cultural influences. These differences may have arisen, in part, by the differences in student populations upon which our syntheses are based. Berninger's extensive research has centered predominantly on how young children's and special needs populations' brain development interact with reading instruction. Most of the research cited in my chapter related to older, average readers' brain development. Although we agree that nurture affects reading development (see Block, p. 24 for a list of nine sociocultural realities or learning preferences that have been credited to nurture today's students), we differ in our understanding of degree. Nature nurtures us. Nurture determines our natures. Berninger "advise[s] caution in concluding, as Block did, that 'today's students' brains have developmental differences, which contribute to these more specialized learning needs'" (Berninger, p. 80). I agree with Berninger and advise extreme caution in concluding that Generation Y's brains have genetically and neurologically constrained developmental differences. I did not conclude that today's students' mental developmental differences were genetic or neurologically askew. My synthesis was designed to illustrate that neurological pathways that are used more frequently are stronger than those used less often and that today's students are processing information differently. I cited eight reasons why today's students appear to require "more specialized lesson modifications than previous generations" (Block, pp. 26–27). None of these reasons related to mental neurological differences that have evolved in the human brain since 1982. I also agree with Berninger that brain evolution is not the reason why lesson features have been altered to meet individual learning needs over the past 50 years. I agree with her conclusion that lesson features should be modified to address experientially based factors, such as those that I listed on pages 27 and 28.

Berringer and O'Connor agreed that "not all in the field of reading might agree completely on [Block's] classification of exactly what is proven and what is promising (Berninger, p. 79). I respect their positions, especially as they view the inability of our research base to "prove" that any instructional approach works 100% of the time for 100% of the students. For instance, what may have proven to work with the majority of gifted students would not even be viewed as a promising practice for students whose parents do not speak English at home.

McKeown's focus on comprehension strategies is "somewhat different from Block's and ends up putting even more focus on the importance of teacher actions and also highlights the role of content in a different way" (McKeown, pp. 53–54). We agree that research on strategy instruction has not used standardized tasks, interventions, or assessments to measure effects on students' reading achievement. This is a vital need for future research. McKeown and I agree but differ in comprehension instruction in that I emphasize the need for preloading, pre-reading supports, whereas she supports more postreading supports. Can we unite our views so that teachers do both more effectively? More research is needed before we can justify that time spent in one or the other is wasting the time that might be spent in more of only one or the other.

O'Connor interpreted my comments concerning the National Reading Panel (2000) in a manner that I did not intend. On page 7 I stated that "the National Reading (NRP) conducted a comprehensive review of 481 studies from 1980 to 1998 in peer-reviewed, scientific journals. . . . This analysis found that phonemic awareness, phonics, comprehension, vocabulary, and fluency are the proven critical components to be taught in early reading instruction." I went on to cite research conducted *after the NRP had completed their work* that "students must also be taught how to apply these components interactively" (e.g., Duke & Pearson, 2002, synthesize this body of research). I did not "claim that the NRP supports integrating phonemic awareness, letter sounds, and students drawing pictures to represent words" (O'Connor, pp. 44–45). I agree with her that the NRP did not make these statements, and I did not say in my chapter that they did.

O'Connor's commentary contended that I moved "beyond the evidence" (O'Connor, p. 45) when I stated that for 5- and 6-year-olds, specifically that they are able to "lead a reading group" and to use "metacognitive and multiple strategies." I understand why such an accusation could have been made for two reasons. First, in my synthesis of 164 research references, I could not cite every study that related to this and other points that I made within the text of my chapter due to space restraints. I addressed this limitation by referring readers to the tables that accompany each section of my text, as it was in these tables that I would cite as many relevant sources as possible to support each claim in each synthesis in the body of my chapter. O'Connor often focuses her critiques on the results of only one of the studies within the body of work that I reviewed. Second, O'Connor may examine evidence that I cited within a summary statement as validation for a section of that summary sentence for which it was not intended. For instance, in the two kindergarten references above, I stated on page 10: "Palincsar and Brown's work *has been extensively expanded* [emphasis added] to include nonfictional instructional settings (Palinscar, 2006), as well as more extensive teacher modeling and scaffolding, so that even kindergarteners can lead a reading group, use strategies without teacher prompting, and independently apply the strategies that were taught (Palincsar, 1986)." In this summary sentence, I intended to state that the initial Palincsar (1986) reciprocal teaching approach had been extensively expanded in the ways listed to apply the strategies cited in Palincsar (1986) in the manners that I described. The 12 citations for this extensive research appear in Table 1.1, with the following reporting studies in which kindergartners led small groups effectively: Cummins et al. (2005); and Block & Pressley, 2002). Similarly, on page 10 I made the statement that "Even kindergarteners can use multiple strategies, and through them, they were able to achieve higher levels of achievement than occurred for treated control groups (Brown, Pressley, Van Meter, & Schuder, 1996; Cummins, Stewart, & Block, 2005)." Contrary to O'Connor's contention, these citations document the effects of this form of reading instruction for kindergarten students, with the first citation reporting qualitative effects in the discussion and introductory sections of the study, and the second including quantitative data for kindergarten populations throughout the study. This explanation applies to the disparity between comments that Berninger and I made concerning the learning differences between Generation Y and previous generations (Berninger, pp. 79–80).

A different explanation may account for the discordance between O'Connor's and my commentary concerning the Reading First study. O'Connor read Gamse et al. (2009) and not Gamse et al. (2008), which was the source that I cited to support the claim I made. Another explanation can resolve O'Connor's dissonance with my synthesis of teaching multiple comprehension strategies in single lessons. The study she cited to refute my synthesis, Calhoon, Sandow, and Hunter (2010), involved middle school students who had been diagnosed with reading disabilities. In my chapter syntheses, I did not include research concerning reading instruction for middle school populations who also have reading difficulties. I would not dispute that reading instruction for early readers, as I presented, and the instruction offered by Calhoon et al. (2010) for older, remedial readers would contain different features.

On pages 45–46, O'Connor states that Block et al. (2009) did not provide data that reading two books on the same topic back-to-back was an effective instructional approach for second graders. Her evidence for this claim was the finding from one section of the 5 measures in a study that I conducted, where second graders' abilities to summarize and retain what they had read from a one-page story did not statistically increase through the use of this form of reading instruction. However, the reading of two books back-to-back was the method that was the most effective in building second graders' abilities to recognize main ideas, and was the second-most effective in building these students' abilities to retain details. It was also the only method to rank first or second in effectiveness in all five measures for second graders (Block et al., 2009). This study was not the only one to demonstrate the effects of this approach for early-grade instruction. The extensive research of John Guthrie and his team showed similar effects, (e.g., Guthrie et al., 2000), which I cited in the same paragraph in my study as the Block et al. (2009) study. Based on these data, I continue to maintain that this instructional practice can be labeled as promising.

As to the issue of whether or not multicultural content and students' own multicultural and linguistic resources should be used as lesson features is a proven or promising characteristic of highly effective reading instructional practices, O'Connor and I must respectfully disagree. I cited 12 studies recommending this practice. The 2006 report by August and Shanahan, *Developing Literacy in Second-Language Learners: Report of the National Literacy Panel on Language Minority Children and Youth*, was the study that O'Connor found to contradict my suggestion. I do not interpret this document or these researchers' subsequent response to a review of this National Literacy Panel Report to discredit the conclusions that I drew from these works and the works of other researchers cited in my chapter and summarized in Table 1.1. I praise O'Connor's expansion of research to document the need for building better lessons for English Language Learners. The studies she cited on pages 46–47 of her commentary are outstanding and should be considered as a part of future work in this area.

Although O'Connor cited two teams of researchers who oppose my recommendation that students should be allowed to choose their partners in paired reading sessions, those researchers and I agree that such choice must be tempered by teacher boundaries, a point that I made through this example on page 21: "If the lesson is designed so that the teacher selects the books that students are to read, pupils are allowed to select the partner with whom they will read the book." I also did not want to "suggest the key approach to teaching vocabulary is to teach students to infer meanings" (O'Connor, p. 47). Research suggests that inferring meanings is only one of 12 vocabulary-building strategies that I reported in my chapter. As I stated, inference has proven to be an effective strategy *only* for use in deducing the meaning of compound words and words with distinct prefixes and suffixes (when the meanings of these prefixes and suffixes were known by the reader. (For more information concerning this issue, see the section in my chapter titled: "Content for Upper Elementary Grades, Proven Content: Teaching Vocabulary Strategies that Unravel the Complex Relationship Between Students' Ability to Discern Word Meanings and their Ability to Comprehend.")

CONCLUSIONS

Although each of the commentators used their own theoretical perspective as the lens through which they drew their discussions, they did not allow their personal perspectives to act as blinders, to lead them to ignore aspects within other perspectives that are important. For that I thank them. We have come a long way in understanding how to create effective reading instruction, and we have many goals ahead of us. Every commentator identified immediate actions that we can take to widen our present instructional highways, cross new borders, and repair potholes in our theories and practices. As complicated as reading instruction is, the commentaries taken together struck me by the implications that perhaps it should be even more complicated. For instance, we must continue to learn what we can and cannot do with reliability for this type of student, under these conditions, with these sorts of efforts, restrained by these instruments, to reach these goals. So what should proven and promising reading instruction be the practice of, according to the authors in this book? We all agreed on at least the following answer:

1. We can increase the amount of instruction that is provided to children. This instruction can begin at least in the first grade and should continue through their school years.
2. There are many methods that can be used reliably, and we can work to encourage more educators to use them.
3. The directions for future research cited by every author in this volume are important. We must examine, in a scientific manner, the issues that they raise so as to enrich the literacy of even more students.
4. We have evolved in our understanding of effective reading instruction to the point where we know how to make productive use of a great many truths, often almost simultaneously.
5. Evaluations of reading instruction must be improved through future research.

A question remains: What do we do in the absence of clear evidence of what else we need to do to help students who are trying to improve their literacy through our present instructional actions? The good news is that advances have been made while this volume was in production and are continuously being made every day. The works presented in this volume point to the understanding that reading instruction will become a more complex, nuanced activity, and research tools are advancing to capture these interactions. We must trust that in the future, we will have more information so that we can more effectively teach every student to read and enjoy applying what they have learned throughout their lifetimes. When we do this, the joy of reading can become a more permanent pleasure and purposeful pursuit for countless generations to come.

Thank you, Jim, Margaret, Virginia, and Rollanda. I began by tossing a pebble into the water; you expanded this ripple into a wider field of understanding.

REFERENCES

August, D., & Shanahan, T. (2006). *Developing literacy in second-language learners.* Mahwah, NJ: Erlbaum.

Bartlett, J. (1939). Familiar quotations: A collection of passages, phrases and proverbs traced to their sources in ancient and modern literature (11th ed., Rev. ed., enlarged). Boston: Little Brown and Company.

Berninger, V., & Wolf, B. (2009a). *Teaching students with dyslexia and dysgraphia: Lessons from teaching and science.* Baltimore: Brookes.

Berninger, V., & Wolf, B. (2009b). *Helping students with dyslexia and dysgraphia make connections: Differentiated instruction lesson plans in reading and writing.* Baltimore: Brookes.

Betts, E. A., & Welch, C. M. (1948). *Betts basic readers.* New York: American Book.

Block, C. C., Parris, S. R., Reed, K. L, Whiteley, C. S., & Cleveland, M. D. (2009). Instructional approaches that significantly increase reading achievement. *Journal of Educational Psychology, 101,* 262–281.

Block, C. C., & Pressley, M. (Eds.). (2002). *Comprehension instruction: Research-based best practices.* New York: Guilford Press.

Brown, R., Pressley, M., Van Meter, P., & Schuder, T. (1996). A quasi-experimental validation of transactional strategies instruction with low-achieving second grade readers. *Journal of Educational Psychology, 88,* 18–37.

Calhoon, M. B., Sandow, A., & Hunter, C. V. (2010). Reorganizing the instructional reading components: Could there be a better way to design remedial reading programs to maximize middle school students with reading disabilities' response to treatment? *Annals of Dyslexia, 60,* 57–85.

Cummins, C., Stewart, M. T., & Block, C. C. (2005). Teaching several metacognitive strategies together increases students' independent metacognition. In S. E. Israel, C. C. Block, K. L. Bauserman, & K. Kinnucan-Welsh (Eds.), *Metacognition in literacy learning: Theory, assessment, instruction, and professional development* (pp. 277–295). Mahwah, NJ: Lawrence Erlbaum.

Gamse, B. C., Jacob, R. T., Horst, M., Boulay, B., Unlu, F., Bozzi, L., ... Rosenblum, S. (2009). *Reading first impact study: Final report, part 2.* Washington, DC: U.S. Department of Education, Institute of Education Sciences.

Gamse, B. C., Tepper-Jacob, R., Horst, M., Boulay, B., & Unlu, F. (2008). *Reading First impact study: Final report, part 1.* Washington, DC: U.S. Department of Education, Institute of Education Sciences.

Guthrie, J. T., Cox, K. E., Knowles, K. T., Buehl, M., Mazzoni, S. A., & Fasulo, L. (2000). Building toward coherent instruction. In L. Baker, M. J. Dreher, & J.

T. Guthrie (Eds.), *Engaging young readers: Promoting achievement and motivation* (pp. 209–236). New York: Guilford.

Kuhn, M. R., Schwanenflugel, P. K., & Meisinger, B. (2010). Aligning theory and assessment of reading fluency: Automaticity, prosody, and definitions of fluency. *Reading Research Quarterly, 45,* 230–251.

Lyon, G. R. (1991). *Treatment interventions for children with learning disabilities.* Bethesda, MD: National Institute of Child Health and Human Development/NIH.

Lewis, M. (2002). *Reading more—read better?: A meta-analysis of the literature on the relationship between exposure to reading and reading achievement.* Minneapolis: University of Minnesota.

National Reading Panel. (2000). *Teaching children to read: An evidence-based assessment of the scientific literature on reading and its implications for reading instruction* (NIH Pub. No. 00-4754). Washington, DC: National Institutes of Health.

Palincsar, A. S. (1986). The role of dialogue in providing scaffolded instruction. *Educational Psychologist, 21,* 73–98.

Palincsar, A. S. (2006, December). *Multiple strategy instruction at work in science classrooms.* Paper presented at the annual meeting of the National Reading Conference. Los Angeles, CA.

Pearson, P. D., & Fielding, L. (1991). Comprehension instruction. In R. Barr, M. Kamil, P. Mosenthal, & P. D. Pearson (Eds.), *Handbook of reading research* (Vol. 2, pp. 815–860). New York: Longman.

Samuels, S. J. (2004). Toward a theory of automatic information processing in reading, revisited. In R. B. Ruddell & N. J. Unrau (Eds.), *Theoretical models and processes* (pp. 1127–1148). Newark, DE: International Reading Association.

Sinatra, G. M., Brown, K. J., & Reynolds, R. (2002). Implications of cognitive resource allocation for comprehension strategies instruction. In C. C. Block & M. Pressley (Eds.), *Comprehension instruction: Research-based best practices* (pp. 62–76). New York: Guilford.

SECTION 2

MATHEMATICS INSTRUCTIONAL STRATEGIES

CHAPTER 7

LEARNING AND TEACHING EARLY AND ELEMENTARY MATHEMATICS

Douglas H. Clements and Julie Sarama
University at Buffalo, SUNY

Today's early childhood and elementary teachers work with more diverse students than ever before. Further, they have received little instructional support for the subject many are least prepared to teach—mathematics. Additional pressure to teach mathematics has emerged from recent research indicating that early mathematics learning is foundational for later academic success—possibly equal to or even more so than early learning of literacy.

Fortunately, recent research and development projects have also created and validated tools for teaching mathematics. In this chapter, we draw implications from research that can help early and elementary teachers both be more effective and find more enjoyment in teaching mathematics. We organize these lessons into three sections.

In "Learning Mathematics" we briefly ask, *How* do students learn mathematics? That is, what do we know about how students learn mathematical ideas and skills that can help guide curriculum development and teaching?

Instructional Strategies for Improving Students' Learning, pages 107–162
Copyright © 2012 by Information Age Publishing
All rights of reproduction in any form reserved.

In "Teaching Mathematics" we ask, *What* pedagogical strategies are supported by research? That is, what approaches to teaching are not only effective in helping students learn mathematics, but also in helping them *enjoy* mathematics and develop other important competences, such as self-regulation?

In "Learning to Teach Mathematics" we ask, What approaches to professional development are supported by research? That is, what should preservice and in-service teachers learn about the following three areas—mathematics, students' development of mathematics, and teaching mathematics? How might this professional development best occur?

LEARNING MATHEMATICS: HOW DO STUDENTS LEARN MATHEMATICS?

Recent documents that describe what mathematics should be taught and emphasized are subtly but significantly different from previous efforts. Both the *Curriculum Focal Points for Prekindergarten through Grade 8 Mathematics* (NCTM, 2006) and the *Common Core State Standards* (CCSSO/NGA, 2010) were based on research on children's learning as well as the structure of mathematics. As they learn about a mathematical topic, students progress through increasingly sophisticated *levels of thinking*. Teachers who understand both the mathematics and those levels of thinking are more effective. These levels form the core of a *learning trajectory*. As an example of how significant such research-based learning trajectories are, the authors of the *Common Core* started by writing brief learning trajectories for each major topic. These were used to determine what the sequence would be and were "cut" into grade-level-specific standards.

A learning trajectory has three parts: a goal, a developmental progression, and instructional activities. To attain a certain mathematical competence in a given topic or domain (the goal), students progress through several levels of thinking (the developmental progression), aided by tasks and experiences (the instructional activities) designed to build the mental actions-on-objects that enables thinking at each higher level (Clements & Sarama, 2004).

For example, the goal might be for young students to learn to be competent counters. The developmental progression describes a typical trajectory that students follow in developing understanding and skill in counting. The second column in Table 7.1 describes several levels of thinking in the counting-learning trajectory. The first column is the approximate age at which students achieve each level of thinking. They are present-day averages and *not* the goal; with good education, students often develop these levels earlier. The third column provides an example of students' behavior and thinking for each level.

TABLE 7.1 Samples from the Learning Trajectory for Counting

Age in years	Developmental Progression	Example Behavior	Instructional Tasks
1	**Chanter** *Verbal:* Chants "sing-song" or sometimes-indistinguishable number words.	Count for me. "one, two-twee, four, sev-...en, ten"	Repeated experience with the counting sequence in varied contexts.
2	**Reciter** *Verbal:* Verbally counts with separate words, not necessarily in the correct order.	Count for me. "one, two, three, four, six, seven."	Provide repeated, frequent experience with the counting sequence in varied contexts. *Count and Race:* Students verbally count along with the computer (up to 50) by adding cars to a racetrack one at a time. 
3	**Corresponder** Keeps one-to-one correspondence between counting words and objects (one word for each object), at least for small groups of objects laid in a line.	Counts: ☆ ☆ ☆ ☆ "1, 2, 3, 4" But may answer the question, "How many?" by re-counting the objects or naming any number word.	*Kitchen Counter:* Students click on objects one at a time while the numbers from 1 to 10 are counted aloud. For example, they click on pieces of food and a bite is taken out of each as it is counted. 

(continued)

TABLE 7.1 (continued)   Samples from the Learning Trajectory for Counting

Age in years	Developmental Progression	Example Behavior	Instructional Tasks
4	**Counter (Small Numbers)** Accurately counts objects in a line to 5 and answers the "how many" question with the last number counted. When objects are visible, and especially with small numbers, begins to understand cardinality.	Can you count these? ☆ ☆ ☆ ☆ "1, 2, 3, 4 . . . four!"	*How Many?* Tell students you have placed as many cubes (3, hidden) in your hand as you can hold. Ask them to count with you to see how many. Take out one at a time as you say the number word (so, when they say "2" they *see* two). Repeat the last counting number, "3," gesturing in a circular motion to all the cubes and say "That's how many there are in all." Challenge students to see how many they can hold during free time. 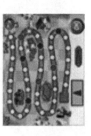
5	**Counter and Producer — (10+)** Counts and counts out objects accurately to 10, then beyond (to about 30). Keeps track of objects that have been counted, even in different arrangements. Gives next number (usually to 20s or 30s). Separates the decade and the ones part of a number word and begins to relate each part of a number word/numeral to the quantity to which it refers. Recognizes errors in others' counting *and* can eliminate most errors in own counting (point-object) if asked to try hard.	Counts a scattered group of 19 chips, keeping track by moving each one as they are counted.	*Counting Towers:* Students to stack as many cubes or coins as they can and count them to see how many they stacked. Students build a tower as high as they can, placing more coins, but not straightening coins already in the tower. The goal is to estimate and then count to find out how many coins are in your tallest tower. *Road Race:* Students identify numbers of sides (3, 4, or 5) on polygons and move forward a corresponding number of spaces on a game board

6 **Counter On Using Patterns** *Strategy*: Keeps track of a few counting acts, but only by using numerical pattern (spatial, auditory or rhythmic).

"How much is 3 more than 5?" Student feels 3 "beats" as (s)he counts, "5,... 6, 7, 8!"

How Many in the Box Now? Have the student count a small set of cubes. Put them in the box and close the lid. Ask the student how many cubes you are hiding. Then add 1 and ask again. When they answer, act incredulous, saying, "How do you *know* that? You can't even see them!" Have students explain their strategy, and counting with them to emphasize the auditory rhythm. Repeat, adding 1, 2, and even 3 as they succeed.

Counter On Keeping Track *Strategy*: Keeps track of counting acts numerically, first with objects, then by "counting counts." Counts up 1 to 4 *more* from a given number.

"How many is 3 more than 6?" "6...7 [puts up a finger], 8 [puts up another finger], 9 [puts up 3rd finger]. 9." "What is 8 take away 2?" "8...7 is one, and 6 is two. 6."

Easy as Pie: Students add two numerals to find a total number (sums of 1 through 10) and then move forward a corresponding number of spaces on a game board. The game encourages students to "count on" from the larger number (e.g., to add 3 + 4, they would count "4...5, 6, 7!").

7–8 **Counter Forward and Back** *Strategy*: Counts "counting words" (single sequence or skip counts) in either direction. Recognizes that decades sequence mirrors single-digit sequence.

Switches between sequence and composition views of multidigit numbers easily.

"What's 4 less than 63?" "62 is 1, 61 is 2, 60 is 3, 59 is 4, so 59." "What is 15 more than 28?" "2 tens and 1 ten is 3 tens. 38, 39, 40, and there's 3 more, 43."

Math-O-Scope: Students identify numbers (representing values that are 10 more, 10 less, 1 more, or 1 less than a target number) within the hundreds chart to reveal a hidden photograph.

The fourth, right-most, column in Table 7.1 provides an example instructional task, matched to each of the levels of thinking in the developmental progression. These tasks are designed to help students learn the ideas and skills needed to achieve that level of thinking. That is, as teachers, we can use these tasks to promote students' growth from one level to the next. More complete learning trajectories provide multiple illustrations of tasks for each level (e.g., see Clements & Sarama, 2009), but they are always only examples because many approaches are possible. There are many sources for learning trajectories, as well as several large projects designed to integrate them in the near future (D. M. Clarke et al., 2002; Clements & Sarama, 2009; Clements, Wilson, & Sarama, 2004; Confrey, Maloney, Nguyen, Mojica, & Myers, 2009; Fuson, 1992; Jones et al., 2001; Murata, 2004; Sarama & Clements, 2009a; Wright, Stanger, Stafford, & Martland, 2006).

TEACHING MATHEMATICS: WHAT PEDAGOGICAL STRATEGIES ARE SUPPORTED BY RESEARCH?

What does research say about the knowledge that teachers need to have to be effective in teaching? Knowledge of teaching can be categorized as content knowledge, general pedagogical knowledge, and pedagogical content knowledge (Shulman, 1986). Content knowledge is knowledge of the subject matter itself—mathematics, in this case. General pedagogical knowledge is knowledge of general teaching strategies that apply to many different subjects, such as classroom management and organization. Both are important, but inadequate without the third. Pedagogical content knowledge includes knowing the subject matter for *teaching*. It involves knowing how to represent and present concepts (through good illustrations, analogies, examples, explanation) from a particular subject such as mathematics, what makes concepts and skills difficult or easy to learn, how students understand and learn specific topics, and what teaching strategies affect the learning of certain topics. We have actually addressed this most difficult type of knowledge—pedagogical content knowledge—already. We believe that learning trajectories include the most important components of this type of knowledge. Teachers must possess all three types of knowledge to be effective instructors. Therefore, in this section, we discuss content and pedagogical knowledge before returning to pedagogical content knowledge.

Content Knowledge

The chapter on reading by Cathy Collins Block (this volume) does not emphasize content knowledge in that most of it is assumed. In mathematics, content knowledge cannot be assumed. In a survey, the vast majority of early childhood educators said they knew all the mathematics they needed to teach (Sarama, 2002). This appears reasonable because they know how to count and that is what they teach. Unfortunately, so many U.S. citizens have such a low level of understanding of mathematics that we often do not realize what we do not know. Even early childhood teachers, for example, do not understand the concepts and procedures that underlie counting nor how count connects to other areas of mathematics (Clements & Sarama, 2009; National Research Council, 2009). Teachers often believe they understand the mathematics they teach, which, even to the extent that this is true (even "simple" topics of mathematics are surprisingly deep), is inadequate. What educator would be satisfied if teachers of fourth grade could read only at a fourth grade level? Although beyond the scope of this chapter, there are many resources that can aid developing such content knowledge. All teachers should benefit by extending their knowledge of mathematics.

General Pedagogical Knowledge

General pedagogical knowledge involves such issues as classroom organization and management. The most general of these strategies are relevant to all teaching and not addressed here. Some pedagogical strategies, however, are particularly relevant to mathematics education. These suggestions, then, lie on the cusp between general and pedagogical content knowledge.

Our suggestions rely mainly on several recent reviews of research. For example, the NMAP's Instructional Practices group (author Clements was a member of this group) reviewed 10 "hot-button" issues. They provide useful information, which we include. But first a caveat: In learning from these and other reviews, educators must be aware of what we believe are false dichotomies that can impede progress. That is, although the results of these research reviews are useful, the dichotomies upon which many are based limit their usefulness, as do other dichotomies used in educational discussions. For example, one issue the NMAP investigated was whether instruction should be "student centered" or "teacher directed." Given the tendency of some to promote one approach over the other, our conclusion was important: "All-encompassing recommendations that instruction should be entirely 'student centered' or 'teacher directed' are not supported by research" (National Mathematics Advisory Panel, 2008, p. xxii). We agree, but add that the structure of the dichotomy restricted what could be learned about when, how, and how much to use each. Similar situations—what we would call false (or at least unfortunate) dichotomies include "emergent" versus "scripted" curricula, "direct" versus "inquiry" instruction, "traditional" versus "reform" curricula or teaching. With the false-dichotomy caveat in mind, what do the reviews teach us?

"Student centered" or *"teacher directed"*? The NMAP's review of these is-sues—a review that rejected using only one dichotomous approach or the other—identified one approach to collaboration as having evidence of ef-fectiveness. In *Peer-Assisted Learning Strategies* (PALS; http://kc.vanderbilt. edu/pals/), teachers identify students who require help on specific skills and others who might teach those skills. All pairs then study mathematics. These pairs and the specific skills change frequently, so that all students have the opportunity to be "coaches" and "players." The teacher circulates, observing and providing individual remedial lessons. Findings regarding this approach were promising, but not definitive. The clearest positive and statistically significant results were for low-achieving elementary students on computational measures. A similar, classwide peer tutoring program achieved substantial success (Greenwood, Delquadri, & Hall, 1989). This approach involves weekly pairing of the entire class into tutor-tutee pairs, with rewards for responding to the tasks. In one 4-year longitudinal study, low-SES schools were randomly assigned to experimental (classwide peer tutoring) and control (standard instructional program, including Chapter 1 services) conditions, and both were compared with high-SES schools us-ing the standard instructional program. The low-SES experimental group experienced statistically greater gains in mathematics (and literacy mea-sures) than did the low-SES control group, matching or exceeding national norms. There was no statistical difference in the gains of the low-SES ex-perimental and high-SES comparison students, although relative to the low-SES control group, the low-SES experimental group's advantage was less than that of the high-SES comparison group.

The NMAP did not find rigorous evaluations of other cooperative learn-ing strategies. However, broadening their review yields positive and con-sistent results: Cooperative learning strategies supported by research led to more positive academic and social outcomes than competitive or indi-vidualistic situations (Johnson & Johnson, 2009). In addition, research pro-vides several guidelines (see elaborate reviews in Johnson & Johnson, 2009; Nastasi & Clements, 1991). Elementary students need constructive group discussions, including presentations of different views, group engagement, solicitation and provision of explanations, and shared leadership (Wilkin-son, Martino, & Camilli, 1994).

A recommendation for an approach designed to enhance social skills, ef-fectance motivation, and higher-order thinking was based on an integration of the research (for the original studies and rationale for this synthesis, see Nastasi & Clements, 1991). This approach has the following characteristics (which may be limited to students in the upper primary grades and above).

- *Positive group interdependence.* "If you do well, I do well." Students in a group share the same goal and resources (e.g., one activity sheet for each pair of students). Each has a specific role to play, and these roles are rotated. Students talk together about the work, encouraging each other to learn.
- *Reciprocal sense-making.* "Build upon your partner's ideas." Students strive to understand and elaborate upon the viewpoints of their partners. They engage in a mutual process of making sense and understanding mathematics.
- *Cognitive conflict, then consensus.* "Two heads are better than one." Students learn by taking the perspective of their partners and trying to synthesize discrepant ideas to produce even better ideas. Each student is accountable for understanding the concepts.

These characteristics lead to the following responsibilities that the teacher must make clear:

- Work together, explaining fully to each other.
- Try to make sense of your partner's explanations.
- Ask specific questions when requesting help.
- Welcome conflicts of ideas, then work toward consensus. Partners must agree before writing down the final solution. Of course, they may agree just to "try out" the ideas of one partner.
- Encourage each other. When disagreeing, criticize ideas, not people.

Thus, the teacher plays a central role even in such (so-called) student-centered environments. In addition, explicit teacher-led instruction is equally important (especially for students at risk—an issue to which we will return). These two different instructional approaches, as well as some competitive and individual situations that are warranted by the educational goals (Johnson & Johnson, 2009), are complementary rather than at odds.

Meaningful teaching or "drill-and-kill"? This is another false, and perhaps especially damaging, dichotomy. Knowledge and skills often need to be practiced, including subitizing, counting strategies, arithmetic combinations ("facts"), geometric and measurement concepts and skills, mathematical processes, and so forth.

Fortunately, research has some clear guidelines. Substantial practice is required for learning certain knowledge and skills. The term *repeated experiencing* more accurately describes this practice than "drill-and-kill," because the former suggests many contexts and different types of activities, most of which do not have to be "drilled" (and none deadly) and because varying contexts support generalization and transfer (Baroody, 1999; Sarama & Clements, 2009a). Also, *distributed, spaced practice had been found to be better than massed* (all in one session, repetition of the same item over and over) *practice* (Cepeda, Pashler, Vul, Wixted, & Rohrer, 2006). Because we want such knowledge available quickly throughout the student's life, short, frequent practice sessions of facts and skills, the conceptual foundations of which have been well learned and understood, are recommended.

One large-scale study provides strong research support for ensuring that conceptual foundations and meaningful strategies are developed first. Textbooks in California in 2008 had to teach students to memorize all the facts in first grade, with little guidance for second grade. Researchers sampled teachers and students across nine elementary sites within four school districts in Southern California. Teachers completed surveys, and students were pretested and interviewed at the end of the year. Only 7% demonstrated adequate progress on basic facts (Henry & Brown, 2008). Two instructional practices were *negatively* related to basic-combinations retrieval: use of those California State-approved textbooks and timed tests. Flashcard use didn't hurt, but it didn't help either. Neither did extensive work on small sums. We can see that memorization without understanding or strategies is a bad idea. Some approaches were successful, such as using thinking strategies. For example, one of the most successful strategies was Break-Apart-to-Make-Ten (BAMT). For example, students would solve 8 + 7 by thinking, "I need 2 more to make a 10 out of 8. That leaves 5. 10 and 5 is 15."

In a later section, we illustrate how expert teachers develop students' competence with this strategy.

Skills or understanding? A similar false dichotomy is involved in the debate as to whether skills or conceptual understanding should be taught first. The National Panel concluded, "The curriculum must simultaneously develop conceptual understanding, computational fluency, and problem-solving skills." As an example, in a study by Blöte, van der Burg, & Klein (2001), second-grade classes were randomly assigned to one of two instructional programs. The first was a reform-based program based on Realistic Mathematics Education, in which students create and discuss their solution procedure. From the beginning of instruction, this program emphasized developing both conceptual understanding simultaneously with procedural skill, and flexible application of multiple strategies. These students scored statistically higher than those in a traditional textbook program that focused on mastery of procedures initially and varied application of strategies only toward the end of instruction. The reform-group students more often selected strategies related to the number properties of the problems and used strategies more adaptively, such as solving problems with an integer ending with the digit 8 by compensation strategies. That is, flexible problem solvers are those who can adapt their strategies to the number characteristics of the problem at hand. For example, using the "empty number line" to help record their computations, such students solved 62–

49 as 62–50 = 12, 12 + 1 = 13, but solved 62–44 as 44 + 6 = 50, 50 + 10 = 60, 60 + 2 = 62, and 6 + 10 + 2 = 18. Such flexible use indicates both conceptual understanding and procedural skill. The traditional group did not use the procedures flexibly, even after months of instruction in that program emphasized such flexible use. The reform group scored higher on three measures, showing superior conceptual understanding. Students in both groups developed conceptual understanding before achieving procedural skill, but the two domains were more interconnected for the reform group.

Other studies also suggest the wisdom of simultaneously promoting conceptual understanding, skill, and flexible thinking. In one study, low-SES, urban first and second graders learned to use the standard arithmetic algorithms skillfully and to understand them conceptually—when taught conceptually—by connecting place-value blocks and written representations (Fuson & Briars, 1990; no effect sizes, but assessments showed that second graders and high-ability first graders performed higher than third graders receiving traditional instruction). A far older, but important, study had similar conclusions. Early experiments involving 1,400 third graders showed that those taught mechanically were faster and more accurate on an immediate posttest, but those taught meaningfully were better able to explain why the algorithm worked, scored better on the retention test, and transferred their knowledge more successfully (Brownell & Moser, 1949; results differed in complex ways across four sites, with the researchers using Shen's formula for critical ratios for comparing differences). A third study similarly showed the benefits of conceptual instruction (Hiebert & Wearne, 1993). Of all children assigned to six second-grade classrooms, the top-scoring 60 were split between two above-average classrooms, and the others were (nearly) randomly assigned to the other four. Alternate instruction emphasizing conceptual understanding was implemented in one of the average (D) and one of the high-scoring classrooms (F). At the end of the year, classroom D scored about the same as classroom E, the initially above-average classroom (within 1/3 of a standard deviation for each of four assessments) and well above classrooms A, B, and C (about ½ to 1 standard deviations above). Thus, this instruction brought initially low-achieving students up to the level of their high-achieving peers. Classroom F outperformed classroom E, notably on place value (1.1. standard deviations higher) and story problems (.7 standard deviations higher). Each of these studies has limitations and recent expectations for hierarchical analyses and reporting of effect sizes missing, but the pattern is clear: Good conceptual and procedural instruction is superior to mechanical instruction in helping students achieve today's mathematical goals (Hiebert & Grouws, 2007).

Similarly, Pesek and Kirshner (2000) found that fifth graders who first received instruction only on procedures for calculating area and perimeter (Skemp's, 1976, "instrumental understanding") followed by instruction on understanding did not perform as well as those whose instruction focused on understanding throughout instruction ("relational understanding"; qualitative results were more convincing than quantitative, which, due to low power, missed statistical significance, $p = .059$, with an effect size of .33). In summary, studies show that the foundation of flexible and creative use of mathematical procedures is "conceptual understanding." Students' knowledge must connect procedures to ideas, to everyday experiences, to analogies, and to other skills and concepts (Baroody & Dowker, 2003).

Thus, we should teach students conceptually to help them build skills *and* ideas, helping them use skills adaptively. Students then have fluent and adaptive expertise rather than mere efficiency (Baroody, 2003): pose problems, make connections, and then work out these problems in ways that make the connections visible, playing both more and less active roles.

What Do We Do?: Beyond Dichotomies

A recent review agreed that most dichotomies describing ways of teaching mathematics were unhelpful (Hiebert & Grouws, 2007). Instead, it was important to recognize that different teaching methods are effective for different learning goals. If one's goal is mainly teaching *skills*, certain teaching strategies are effective. If one's goal is teaching for *conceptual understanding*, different teaching strategies will be effective.

Research suggests that for teaching skills only—that is, to promote instrumental learning—effective teaching is rapid-paced, includes teacher modeling with many teacher-directed product-type questions, and displays a smooth transition from demonstrations to substantial amounts of error-free practice (Hiebert & Grouws, 2007). Teachers must organize, pace, and present information to meet well-defined behavioral goals.

Instead, in teaching for conceptual understanding—relational understanding—effective teaching has two key features. The first is *attending explicitly to concepts*. That is, teachers clearly, and publicly, discuss and develop *connections* among mathematics facts, procedures, ideas (concepts), and processes. This may be one reason why both "student centered" and "teacher directed" teaching have some research support: If they explicitly attend to conceptual development, both approaches can be successful in developing high levels of student achievement. For example, a student-centered approach might have students connect written and manipulative (place-value block) strategies as they invented their own procedures for multi-digit addition and subtraction (Hiebert & Wearne, 1993). Low-achieving students engaged in those activities outperformed low-achieving students taught by a traditional textbook and matched the performance of high-achieving students taught from the textbook. In another example, teachers in another project similarly made careful connections between place-value blocks and written algorithms (Fuson & Briars, 1990). Virtually all students reached ceiling levels of performance, especially when explaining why and how regrouping works. Some classrooms used a teacher-directed approach, with careful demonstrations of the algorithms followed by class discussions. Others used small-group problem solving. Both were successful. The key seemed to be attending explicitly to concepts.

The second key feature of teaching for conceptual, or relational, understanding, is ensuring that *students struggle with important mathematics* (Hiebert & Grouws, 2007). That is, teachers motivate students to *work* to make sense of mathematics, to figure out mathematics—both solution strategies and connections between ideas and procedures that are the basis for conceptual understanding. Posing problems, making connections, and then working out these problems in ways that make the connections visible, with the teacher playing both more and less active roles, helps students develop relational understanding.

Effective teachers challenge students. They hold higher expectations of students than ineffective teachers (D. M. Clarke et al., 2002; Clements & Sarama, 2007b, 2008; Thomson, Rowe, Underwood, & Peck, 2005). They hold high expectations of *all* students (Askew, Brown, Rhodes, Wiliam, & Johnson, 1997).

Should teachers do a bit of teaching for instrumental learning and a bit of teaching for relational learning? At first glance, it would seem that the research indicates that teachers need to approach teaching skills and teaching concepts in different ways. However, there is one more critical finding.

Relational understanding, and teaching for it, appears to support skill development as effectively as teaching for skills only (Hiebert & Grouws, 2007). The studies that support the two key features of effective teaching for conceptual understanding also show that students develop skills as, or more effectively, than students in classrooms that focus teaching only on skill development.

This seems puzzling. Struggling with mathematics seems contradictory to the carefully guided, errorless performance of the skills-only teaching approaches. Why are skills also developed in classrooms that teach for relational understanding? When students learn meaningfully, the conceptual support for (and constraints on) procedures guide skill development. For example, if students understand and have a mental model for multidigit subtraction, they are less likely to make the errors of subtracting the "smaller from the larger" (e.g., mistakenly subtracting 4 from 8 in 354–718). Students are better able to adapt their skills to new situations. Their mathematical competence is broader. Research, in other words, supports the hierarchic interactionalism principle that *concepts and skills develop together and support each other.* Informally stated, teaching for relational understanding gives "teachers two for the price of one."

In the remainder of this section, we provide guidance from research on several other issues that may be less central and overarching, but are nonetheless important for effective teaching of mathematics.

How Should We Address Diverse Needs?

What students know when they enter school predicts their achievement in mathematics for years thereafter (see reviews in National Mathematics Advisory Panel, 2008; Sarama & Clements, 2009a). At every age, students who are considerably behind their peers need and deserve extra support for learning mathematics.

At the preschool level, a series of studies show that the *Building Blocks curriculum*[1] (Clements & Sarama, 2007a), built upon learning trajectories, *statistically and substantially increases the mathematics knowledge of low-SES preschool students.* Further, scale-up studies show that, with the proper systemic support, large positive effects can be achieved for entire urban school districts (Clements & Sarama, 2008; Sarama & Clements, 2009b).

Although a good early start is important, it is not sufficient. The early achievement gap between low-income and higher-income students progressively widens throughout their K–12 years (National Mathematics Advisory Panel, 2008; Sarama & Clements, 2009a). Therefore, we must build on these early efforts. Skeptics have disagreed with this position, arguing that it is not worth the effort if effects of early programs "fade." Although we need more research, we believe this negative point of view ignores the existing evidence. First, some studies do show lasting benefits for low-SES children. Second, programs that are continued into elementary school and that offer substantial exposure to early interventions have the most sustained long-term effects (Brooks-Gunn, 2003). Third, without such follow-through, it is simply not realistic to expect short-term early interventions to last indefinitely. This is especially so because most students at risk attend the lowest-quality schools. It would be surprising if these students did not gain less than their more advantaged peers year by year. Further, throughout school, the learning of groups traditionally underrepresented in mathematics fields can be improved by interventions that address social, affective, and motivational concerns (National Mathematics Advisory Panel, 2008). Social and intellectual support from peers and teachers is correlated with higher mathematics performance for all students, and such support is particularly important for many, especially African American and Hispanic students. Also important are interventions designed for students with learning difficulties and disabilities, a topic to which we now turn.

Students with special needs often do not fare well in mathematics. Such students can be classified into two categories: Students with mathematical difficulties (MD) are those who are struggling to learn math for any reason (even such reasons as lack of motivation; Berch & Mazzocco, 2007). As many as 35% to 40% of students may fall in that category. More severe are students with specific mathematics learning disabilities (MLD). They have a memory or cognitive deficit that interferes with their ability to learn math (Geary, 2004). About 6% to 7% of students have MLD (Berch & Mazzocco, 2007; Mazzocco & Myers, 2003). However, only 63% of those classified as MLD in kindergarten were still so classified in third grade (Mazzocco & Myers, 2003).

MLDs are assumed to have a genetic basis, but presently are defined by students' behaviors. However, experts are still debating what those behaviors are. One of the most consistent findings is that students with MLD have difficulty quickly retrieving basic arithmetic facts. This has been hypothesized to be due to an inability to store or retrieve facts and to impairments in visual-spatial representations. Limited working memory and speed of cognitive processing may be problems as early as kindergarten (Geary, Hoard, Byrd-Craven, Nugent, & Numtee, 2007).

Other possibilities include a lack of higher-order, or executive, control of verbal material, which may hamper learning basic arithmetic combinations or facts. As just one example, students with MLD might have difficulty inhibiting irrelevant associations, such as hearing 5 + 4 and saying "6" because it follows 5. As late as second grade, students with MLD may not fully understand counting and may not recognize errors in counting. They persist in using immature counting strategies throughout elementary school (Ostad, 1998). For example, some still count "one-by-one" on their fingers at end of the elementary grades. This may help explain their difficulty learning basic arithmetic combinations (Geary, Bow-Thomas, & Yao, 1992). However, other experts claim lack of specific competencies, such as in subitizing, are more important (Berch & Mazzocco, 2007). There is much in this domain that remains to be learned.

Until more is known, students should be labeled as MLD only with great caution and after good instruction has been provided. In the earliest years, such labeling will probably do more harm than good. Instead, high-quality instruction (preventative education) should be provided to all students. This should go beyond instruction that is regularly provided to students over months and years to provide dynamic, formative, assessments of the students' needs. Foundational abilities in subitizing, counting and counting strategies, simple arithmetic, and magnitude comparison are important. In later years, competencies in arithmetic combinations, place value, and word problem solving should also be ensured (Dowker, 2004).

Why *additional* instruction? As one example, in the primary years, students with MLD only (and those with a Reading Learning Disability as well, or MLD/RLD) performed worse than normally developing students in timed tests, but just as well in untimed tests. Thus, students who have MLD may simply only need extra time studying, and extra time to complete, calculation tasks. The use of a calculator and other computational aids would enable these students to concentrate on developing their otherwise good problem-solving skills (Jordan & Montani, 1997). Students with MLD/RLD may need more systematic remedial intervention aimed at problem conceptualization and the development of effective computational strategies, as well as strategies for efficient fact retrieval (Jordan & Montani, 1997)

Educators then need to determine whether students have benefited from good instruction. For example, some students identified as learning disabled leave remedial education (Geary, 1990). They may be developmentally delayed, but not formally classified as learning disabled. They were miseducated and mislabeled. Others may be developmentally different (true MLD) and in need of specialized instruction. Drill-and-practice only is not indicated. Counting on fingers, but using increasingly sophisticated strategies, would be encouraged. Educators should focus on essential areas such as components of "number sense" and "spatial sense." For example, some students with MLD may have difficulty maintaining one-to-one correspondence when counting or matching. They may need to physically grasp and move objects, as grasping is an earlier skill in development than is pointing (Lerner, 1997). They often understand counting as a rigid, mechanical activity (Geary, Hamson, & Hoard, 2000). These students also may count objects in small sets one-by-one for long after their peers are strategically subitizing these amounts. Emphasizing their ability to learn to subitize the smallest number, perhaps representing them on their fingers, may be helpful.

Historically, many have called for direct instruction in skills for students with MD or especially MLD. Direct Instruction (capitalized) has research support (Swanson & Hoskyn, 1998). It is a specific method that provides teachers with scripts for frequent interactions with students, clear feedback on the accuracy of students' work, and sequencing of problems so that important differences are brought to students' attention.

However, other approaches also are supported by research. They share characteristics with Direct Instruction, but these characteristics typically involve explicit, systematic instruction rather than highly teacher-directed lessons with specific instructions and demonstrations of procedures. For example, teachers may explain and demonstrate specific strategies, but they also encourage students to ask and answer questions and to think aloud about their reasoning. Thus, students play an active role. Further, following previous recommendations, instruction is not limited to memorization of simple skills, but includes computation, solving word problems, including solving problems that require the application of mathematics to novel situations. Including visual representations may make such explicit instruction even more effective. Further, educators should make sure that students are learning all foundational concepts and skills necessary for learning mathematics at their grade level (National Mathematics Advisory Panel, 2008). Such interventions should be in addition to other mathematics instruction.

Consider an example from the NMAP studies in which explicit instruction was provided to a second-grade MLD student who had not learned to "count on from larger" to solve addition problems (Tournaki, 2003).

> **Teacher:** When I get a problem, what do I do?
> **Student:** I read the problem: 5 plus 3 equals how many. Then I find the smaller number. [expected repetition of the rule]
> **Teacher:** (pointing to the smaller number) 3. Now I count the fingers. So how many fingers am I going to count?
> **Student:** 3. [and so forth . . .]

After a few problems, the teacher had students solve problems while thinking aloud, that is, repeating the steps and asking themselves the questions. Teachers always provided clear, immediate feedback when students made errors. The large effect size of this study (a standardized difference in means of 1.61 between students given explicit instruction and those given drill-and-practice) indicates the benefit of teaching a strategy, not just providing more practice, especially for LD students.

Other approaches that help students at risk for any number of reasons include the following:

- Use information about students' performance, and share this with students (supporting formative assessment, described previously, including differentiated activities).
- Provide clear, specific feedback to parents on their students' mathematics achievement.
- Use peers as tutors.
- Encourage students to verbalize their thinking or their strategies or even the explicit strategies that the teacher models.
- Explicitly teach strategies, not just "facts" or "skills." Encourage students to think aloud, and provide feedback from peers and the teacher. Highlight key aspects of each type of problem (not "keywords"). As one example, students with developmental delay who learned $n + 1$ tasks ($4 + 1$, $6 + 1$) discovered the "number-after-n" rule, after which students spontaneously invented counting-on (realizing, for example, that if $7 + 1$ is 8, $7 + 2$ is two count words after 7).

- Use high-quality, research-based software (Clements & Sarama, 2009).
- Target specific areas of need.
- Include individualized work, even for brief periods, as a component of such focused interventions (Dowker, 2004; Gersten et al., 2008).
- Consider small-group tutorial sessions, including the use of concrete objects, to promote conceptual learning (Fuchs et al., 2005; Zumeta, 2008).
- Focus on geometry and spatial sense as well (Clements & Sarama, 2009). Many students with special needs have quite different learning needs (Gervasoni, 2005; Gervasoni, Hadden, & Turkenburg, 2007). We need to individualize instruction.
- Further, it may not be necessary for students to master one domain (e.g., arithmetic) to meaningfully study another, such as geometry. For this reason, teaching with learning trajectories is the best way to address the needs of all students, especially those with special needs. Use of formative assessment, which is focused on later in this chapter, is a recommended strategy for putting learning trajectories to work, especially for students with any type of special needs.

There are many holes in resources to help students with special needs. There is no widely used measure to identify specific learning difficulties or disabilities in mathematics (Geary, 2004). Finally, however, the most important implication may be to prevent most learning difficulties by providing high-quality early and elementary childhood mathematics education for all students.

Gifted and talented students. Students who are gifted and talented similarly are not well served in many schools. Many are never identified. When they are noticed, they are rarely exposed to more sophisticated topics, even though they have advanced knowledge about and interest in them (Wadlington & Burns, 1993). They need to solve engaging, difficult problems in the domains of numbers, operations, geometry, and spatial sense. They need to be challenged to engage in high-level mathematical reasoning, including abstract reasoning.

Discussions and Connections

Effective teachers engage their students in discussions about mathematics and make greater use of open-ended questions than less effective teachers. They ask students, "Why?" and "How do you know?" They expect students to share strategies, explain their thinking, work together to solve problems, and listen to and understand one another. They help students summarize key ideas at the end of each lesson. They explicitly discuss connections between the properties and relationships of mathematics and connections between mathematical ideas and applications to everyday situations (Askew et al., 1997; Carpenter, Fennema, Franke, Levi, & Empson, 1999; Carpenter, Franke, Jacobs, Fennema, & Empson, 1998; D. M. Clarke et al., 2002; Clements & Sarama, 2007b, 2008; Cobb et al., 1991; Thomson et al., 2005).

Developing Positive Beliefs and Attitudes

As a culture, people in the United States have many negative attitudes and beliefs about mathematics. Indeed, all it takes to raise math anxiety in the approximately 17% of the population who exhibit such negativity is to show them this number (Ashcraft, 2006)!

One deeply embedded cultural belief is that achievement in mathematics depends mostly on native aptitude or ability. In contrast, people from other countries such as Japan believe that achievement comes from effort (Holloway, 1988). Even more disturbing, research shows that the U.S. belief hurts students and, further, that it is just not true. Students who believe— or are helped to understand—that they can learn if they try work on tasks longer and achieve better throughout their school careers than students who believe that one either "has it" (or "gets it") or does not (McLeod & Adams, 1989). This view often leads to failure and "learned helplessness" (McLeod & Adams, 1989; Weiner, 1986). Similarly, students who have mastery-oriented goals (i.e., students who try to learn and see the point of school to develop knowledge and skills) achieve more than students whose goals are directed toward high grades or outperforming others (Middleton & Spanias, 1999; National Mathematics Advisory Panel, 2008).

Fortunately, most young students have positive feelings about math and are motivated to explore numbers and shapes (Middleton & Spanias, 1999). After only a couple of years in typical schools, however, they begin to believe that "only some people have the ability to do math." Students who experience math as a sense-making activity will build positive feelings about math throughout their school careers.

Teachers can help by providing meaningful tasks that make sense to students and connect with their everyday interests and lives. The right degree of challenge and novelty can promote interest, and promoting and discussing skill improvement can promote a mastery orientation. Researchers have estimated that students should be successful about 70% of the time to maximize motivation (Middleton & Spanias, 1999).

Emotions play a significant role in problem solving, involving both joys and frustrations (McLeod & Adams, 1989). Based on Mandler's (1984) theory, the source of such emotion is the interruption of a schema. For example, if a plan is blocked, an emotion is generated, which might be negative or positive. If students realize they are incorrect, they may believe this warrants embarrassment, but one can change that by directly assuring students that trying and discussing, including making errors and being frustrated, are part of the learning process. Also, one can discuss how working hard to learn and figure out a problem can make you "feel good" (Cobb, Yackel, & Wood, 1989). In contrast, educators can hamper students' learning if they define success only as fast, correct responses and accuracy as following the teacher's example (Middleton & Spanias, 1999).

A common core of characteristics of learning environments enhances students' attitudes and beliefs about mathematics (Anghileri, 2004; Clements, Sarama, & DiBiase, 2004; Cobb, 1990; Cobb et al., 1989; Fennema et al., 1996; Hiebert, 1999; Kutscher, Linchevski, & Eisenman, 2002; McClain, Cobb, Gravemeijer, & Estes, 1999).

- Use problems that have meaning for students (both practical and mathematical).
- Expect that students will invent, explain, and critique their own solution strategies within a social context.
- Provide opportunities for both creative invention and practice.
- Encourage and support students progressing toward increasingly sophisticated and abstract mathematical methods and understandings, and in understanding and developing more efficient and elegant solution strategies.
- Help students see connections between various types of knowledge and topics, with the goal of having each student build a well-structured, coherent knowledge of mathematics.

"Concrete" Manipulatives for "Abstract" Ideas

Concrete manipulatives are commonly thought to help students learn mathematics. Teachers are thought to move students from "concrete to abstract" understanding. Research supports this position, but also adds several interesting twists. First the support: Students who use manipulatives in their mathematics classes often outperform those who do not (Driscoll, 1983; Suydam, 1986). For example, second graders randomly assigned to be taught with manipulatives achieved and retained significantly more on a place-value comprehension test than students assigned to be taught by conventional methods using algorithmic procedures and drill-and-practice (V. M. Johnson, 2000). A meta-analysis by Sowell (1989) reported moderate to large effect sizes for treatments of a year or more (Sowell, 1989; mean = .29 for broad objects and

1.86 for specific objectives). These benefits hold if the use of the manipulative makes sense for the lesson, across grade level, ability level, and topic.

However, manipulatives do not guarantee success. Students taught multiplication emphasizing understanding performed well whether they used manipulatives or symbols (Baroody, 1989; Clements, 1999). Further, the students randomly assigned to be taught with symbols scored higher on a near-transfer test involving different factors (Fennema, 1972). Manipulatives do not "carry" mathematical ideas. They may help in teaching concretely at first, but only if such concrete teaching emphasizes quantitative or spatial ideas.

Why might concrete manipulatives help? The answer has an interesting twist. Many would say because they are physical objects that students can grasp with their hands. This sensory characteristic makes manipulatives "real," connected with one's intuitively meaningful personal self, and therefore helpful. However, concepts cannot be "read off" manipulatives. That is, the physical objects may be manipulated without the concepts being illuminated. Concrete materials may help students build meaning, but the students must reflect on their actions with manipulatives. Said in another way, "understanding does not travel through the fingertips and up the arm" (Ball, 1992, p. 47). They need teachers who can reflect on their students' representations for mathematical ideas and help them develop increasingly sophisticated and mathematical representations. For additional theory and discussion of the benefits of manipulatives in early-learning environments, see Glenberg, Jaworski, Rischall, and Levin (2007).

Further, teachers of the intermediate grades talk of "concrete understanding," without referring to physical objects. They want students to see numbers as mental objects ("I can think of 43 + 26"). Thus, students have *Sensory-Concrete* knowledge when they need to *use* sensory material to make sense of an idea. *Integrated-Concrete* knowledge is knowledge that is *connected*. "Concrete" means "to grow together." Sidewalk concrete is strong due to the combination of separate particles in an interconnected mass. Integrated-Concrete thinking is strong due to the combination of many separate ideas in an interconnected structure of knowledge. Students do not learn numbers from objects or directly from adults. As Piaget's collaborator Hermine Sinclair (Sinclair, 1988, p. v) says, "numbers are *made* by students, not *found* (as they may find some pretty rocks, for example) or *accepted* from adults (as they may accept and use a toy). Students make numbers by connecting experiences with objects and with people. What makes ideas Integrated-Concrete is how "meaning-full"—connected to other ideas and situations—they are. Comparing the two levels of concrete knowledge, we see a shift in what the adjective "concrete" describes. *Sensory-Concrete* refers to knowledge that demands the support of concrete objects and students' knowledge of manipulating these objects. *Integrated-Concrete* refers to knowledge that is concrete at a higher level because it is connected to other knowledge, both physical knowledge that has been abstracted and thus distanced from concrete objects, and abstract knowledge of a variety of types.

Too often, teachers use manipulatives to "make math fun," where "manipulative math" and "real math" are seen as difference enterprises (Moyer, 2000). Justifications for their *instructional* role is often that they are concrete and thus understandable. Research offers guidelines to make manipulatives more effective.

- *Model with manipulatives.* Sensory-concrete support is useful if the manipulatives help students investigate and understand the mathematical structures and processes. For example, students benefited more from using (bendable) chenille sticks than pictures to make nontriangles into triangles (Martin, Lukong, & Reaves, 2007). They merely drew on top of the pictures, but they transformed the chenille sticks, engendering more learning.
- *Ensure manipulatives serve as symbols.* Students need to interpret the manipulative as representing a mathematical idea. For example, connecting work based on place-value blocks with verbal and representations of numbers and arithmetic can help build both concepts and skills successfully (Brownell & Moser, 1949; Fuson & Briars, 1990; Hiebert & Wearne, 1993).
- *Use drawings and symbols, moving away from manipulatives as soon as possible.* Students use manipulatives in second grade to do arithmetic, and they continue to do so even in fourth grade (Carr & Alexeev, 2011). That is a failure to move along the learning trajectory.

Technology: Computers and TV

Students frequently manipulate objects on the computer screen, and these are certainly not physical objects. What role might they play in mathematics education? We begin by directly considering computer manipulatives.

Computer manipulatives. Even if "concrete" is not just "physical," it may seem strange to consider computer pictures as valid manipulatives. However, research suggests that computer manipulatives can be just as meaningful to students (Clements, 1999). Further, such manipulatives may even be more manageable, "clean," flexible, and extensible than physical objects. For example, one group of young students learned number concepts with a computer environment in which they manipulated pictures of beans and sticks on the screen with a computer mouse. They selected and arranged beans, sticks, and number symbols. Compared to a physical bean-stick environment, this computer environment offered equal, and sometimes greater, control and flexibility to students (Char, 1989). The computer manipulatives were just as meaningful and easier to use for learning. In another study, students who used physical and computer manipulatives demonstrated a greater sophistication in classification and logical thinking than students who used only physical manipulatives (Olson, 1988). The reason might be traced to certain advantages of computer manipulatives.

Mathematical/psychological benefits. Perhaps the most powerful feature of computer software is that the actions possible with the software embody the processes we want students to develop and internalize as mental actions (Clements & Sarama, 2009; Sarama, Clements, & Vukelic, 1996).

- *Bringing mathematical ideas and processes to conscious awareness.* Most students solve physical puzzles by making intuitive movements. Using computer manipulatives brings those geometric motions to an explicit level of awareness (Sarama et al., 1996). They learn about flips, slides, and turns mathematically.
- *Encouraging and facilitating complete, precise explanations.* Compared to students using paper and pencil, students using computers work with more precision and exactness (Clements, Battista, & Sarama, 2001; Gallou-Dumiel, 1989; Johnson-Gentile, Clements, & Battista, 1994).
- *Supporting mental "actions on objects."* The flexibility of computer manipulatives allows them to mirror mental "actions on objects" better than physical manipulatives. For example, with physical base-ten blocks, students trade 1 hundred block for 10 tens. In contrast, students can decompose computer base-ten blocks, breaking 1 hundred into 10 tens. Such actions are more in line with the mental actions that we want students to learn.
- *Changing the very nature of the manipulative.* In a similar vein, computer manipulatives' flexibility allows students to explore geometric figures in ways not available with physical shape sets. For example, students can change the size of the computer shapes, altering all shapes or only some.
- *Linking the concrete and the symbolic with feedback.* Computers can link different representations, such as the number represented by the base-ten blocks being dynamically linked to symbols, both regular (105) and expanded (1 hundred and 5 ones) notation. When students add a hundred block, the symbols change automatically.
- *Recording and replaying students' actions.* Computers can record and replay *sequences* of students' actions on manipulatives. Students can replay, change, and view them, encouraging mathematical reflection.

Practical/pedagogical benefits of computer manipulatives. The following includes advantages that help students in a practical manner or that provide pedagogical opportunities for the teacher.

- *Providing another medium, one that can store and retrieve configurations.*
  Students can use as many manipulatives as they wish and store and return
  to their work.
- *Providing a manageable, clean, flexible manipulative.* For example, shapes
  can snap into correct position, and they stay where they are put.

Computers encourage students to make their knowledge explicit, which helps them build Integrated-Concrete knowledge.

With both physical and computer manipulatives, we should choose meaningful representations in which the objects and actions available to the student parallel the mathematical objects (ideas) and actions (processes or algorithms) we wish the students to learn. We then need to guide students in making connections between these representations.

Computer-assisted instruction (CAI). CAI is structured software that teaches or provides practice. Practice software can help young students develop competence in such skills as counting and sorting (Clements & Nastasi, 1993), as well as addition combinations (Fuchs et al., 2006). Some reviews conclude that the use of CAI—tutorials, drill-and-practice, or some combination—has been particularly successful in mathematics for young students, especially in compensatory education (Lavin & Sanders, 1983). For example, a synthesis of multiple randomized experiments by Ragosta, Holland, and Jamison (1981) yielded mathematics effect sizes ranging from .36 for one-year studies to .72 for three-year studies on the CTBS computation test and from .80 for one-year studies to 1.23 for three-year studies on a curriculum-specific tests. (Ragosta et al., 1981; note that results on concepts and applications were mixed, consistent with the drill-and-practice nature of the software used).

In another meta-analysis by Niemiec and Walberg (1985), the average effect size for the primary grades in one meta-analysis was .81, compared to .27 for intermediate and .32 for upper grades (7–8). Average effect sizes for exceptional students ranged from .83 for students who were emotionally disturbed to 1.43 for those who were visually impaired. About 10 minutes per day proved sufficient for statistically significant gains; 20 minutes was even better. Such an approach is successful with all students, with substantial gains reported for students from low-resource communities (Primavera, Wiederlight, & DiGiacomo, 2001). Computer drill-and-practice can be helpful for all students who need to develop automaticity, but especially for those who have MD or MLD. However, this must come at the right point in the learning trajectory. Drill does *not* help students who deploy more immature counting strategies; they must understand the concepts and even know the arithmetical fact (although they may remember it slowly) before drill is useful (Hasselbring, Goin, & Bransford, 1988). Many CAI systems also employ computer-managed instruction (CMI), in which computers keep track of students' progress and help individualize the instruction they receive.

Computer games. Properly chosen, computer games may also be effective. Kraus (1981) reported that second graders randomly assigned to an average of 1 hour of interaction with a computer game over a 2-week period responded correctly to twice as many items on an addition facts speed test as did students in a randomized control group. Preschoolers benefit from a wide variety of on-computer as well as off-computer games (Clements & Sarama, 2008).

Logo and turtle geometry. In turtle geometry, students program the computer, often beginning by directing a robot, or onscreen "turtle," to draw geometric shapes. Many students can draw shapes with pencil and paper. But to draw shapes using Logo commands, they must analyze the visual aspects of the figure and its movements in drawing it. Writing a sequence of Logo commands, or a procedure, to draw a figure "allows, or obliges, the student to externalize intuitive expectations. When the intuition is translated into a program it becomes more obtrusive and more accessible to reflection" (Papert, 1980, p. 145). That is, students must analyze the spatial aspects of the shape and reflect on how they can build it from components. Students have shown greater explicit awareness of the properties of shapes and the meaning of measurements after working with the turtle (Clements & Nastasi, 1993). They learn about measurement of length (Campbell, 1987; Clements, Battista, Sarama, Swaminathan, & McMillen, 1997; Sarama, 1995) and angle (Browning, 1991; Clements & Battista, 1989; du Boulay, 1986; Frazier, 1987; Kieran, 1986; Kieran & Hillel, 1990; Olive, Lankenau, & Scally, 1986). One microgenetic study confirmed that students transform physical and mental action into concepts of turn and angle in combined off- and on-computer experiences (Clements & Burns, 2000). Students synthesized and integrated two schemes—"turn as body movement" and "turn as number" (Clements, Battista, Sarama, & Swaminathan, 1996). They used a process of psychological curtailment in which students gradually replace full rotations of their bodies with smaller rotations of an arm, hand, or finger, and eventually internalized these actions as mental imagery.

Logo is not easy to teach or to learn. However, as one student declared, "This picture was very hard and it took me 1 hour and 20 minutes to do it, but it had to be done. I liked doing it." (Carmichael, Burnett, Higginson, Moore, & Pollard, 1985, p. 90). Moreover, when the Logo environment is gradually and systematically introduced to the students, and when the interface is age-appropriate, even elementary students learn to control the turtle and benefit (Allen, Watson, & Howard, 1993; Brinkley & Watson, 1987/1988; Clements, 1983/1984; Cohen & Geva, 1989; Howard, Watson, & Allen, 1993; Stone, 1996; Watson et al., 1992). They transfer their knowledge to other areas, such as map-reading tasks and interpreting right and left rotation of objects. They reflect on mathematics and their own problem solving. For example, first-grader Ryan wanted to turn the turtle to point into his rectangle. He asked the teacher, "What's half of 90?" After she responded, he typed RT [right turn] 45. "Oh, I went the wrong way." He said nothing, keeping his eyes on the screen. "Try LEFT 90," he said at last. This inverse operation produced exactly the desired effect (Kull, 1986). A major evaluation of a Logo-based geometry curriculum across grades K–6 revealed that Logo students scored statistically higher than matched comparison students on a general geometry achievement test, with Logo students' gains about double those of the comparison students (Clements et al., 2001). In most successful efforts, the teacher guides student work and encourages students to reflect on their work and connect it to specific mathematical concepts and processes.

TV. There is even more debate in the early childhood field about the influences (positive and especially negative) of television. There is an extensive literature (see Clements & Nastasi, 1993). The following summarizes key findings:

- Educational TV such as Sesame Street, Blue's Clues, Square One, and Cyberchase have positive effects on learning and continues to be updated in content and pedagogy.
- Longitudinal studies show that high school students who watched educational television have higher grades than those who did not. This is probably due to the early learning model—learning leads to success in the first grades of school, which leads to positive motivation, perceptions of teachers of competence, placement in higher-ability groups, receiving more attention, and thus continuous success in school.
- Students' learning is increased when adults mediate the students' use of TV (as well as other media). Parents might watch educational TV with their children and discuss what is viewed. They might involve the child in active engagement with the material, following suggestions from the show or creating their own. Interactive books can actually increase the amount of time that parents read with their students.
- Providing parents with print materials or in-person workshops on how to follow up on media is helpful and maybe even necessary.

One disturbing result is that high-SES preschoolers understand the mathematical ideas presented on Sesame Street better than their low-SES counterparts. Also, the better the vocabulary and math understanding the student has, the better that student can comprehend the mathematics presented on the screen (Morgenlander, 2005). Another finding, that "the rich get richer"—high-SES, more educationally advantaged children understand and learn more than low-SES children—presents a challenge to educators and the society as a whole.

Formative Assessment

Of the 10 instructional practices the National Mathematics Advisory Panel (2008) researched, only a few had an adequate number of rigorous studies supporting them. One of the most strongly supported was teachers' use of formative assessment. Formative assessment is the ongoing monitoring of student learning to inform instruction. Teachers might monitor both the class as a whole and individuals in the class.

Although the NMAP's rigorous studies included students only as young as the upper primary grades, other studies confirm that regular assessment and individualization are key to effective early math education (Shepard, 2005; Thomson et al., 2005). Teachers should observe students' answers and also their strategies, asking themselves the following questions (Shepard, 2005):

- What is the key error?
- What is the probable reason the student made this error?
- How can I guide the student to avoid this error in the future?

Formative assessment is a general pedagogical strategy. However, to use it well in mathematics, one needs pedagogical content knowledge, a category to which we now turn.

PEDAGOGICAL CONTENT KNOWLEDGE

Content knowledge and general pedagogical knowledge are essential, but they are inadequate without pedagogical content knowledge. For example, the effective general strategy of formative assessment is of no use to teachers unless they can assess "where students are" in learning a mathematical topic and how and where to move them to the next level. This is why we believe that learning trajectories are the core component of useful pedagogical content knowledge in mathematics. The developmental progressions of learning trajectories give teachers a tool to understand the levels of thinking at which their students are operating. They also provide direction concerning the *next* level of thinking that students should learn. Further, the matched instructional tasks provide guidance as to the type of educational activity that would support that learning and help explain why those activities would be particularly effective. Such knowledge helps teachers be more effective professionals.

Learning trajectories promote the learning of skills and concepts together. This is often the most effective approach. For example, acquiring skills before developing understanding can lead to learning difficulties (Baroody, 2004a, 2004b; Fuson, 2004; Kilpatrick, Swafford, & Findell, 2001; Sophian, 2004; Steffe, 2004). Further, effective curricula and teaching often build on students' thinking, provide opportunities for both invention and practice, and ask students to explain their various strategies (Hiebert, 1999). Such programs facilitate conceptual growth and higher-order thinking without sacrificing the learning of skills. Effective teachers also consistently integrate real-world situations, problem solving, and mathematical content (Fuson, 2004). Making connections to real-life situations also enhances students' knowledge and positive beliefs about mathematics (Perlmutter, Bloom, Rose, & Rogers, 1997).

The instructional tasks in learning trajectories are, of course, not the only way to teach students to achieve the levels of thinking. In some cases, there is research evidence that certain tasks or teaching trajectories are especially effective. For example, recall that students develop the critical cardinality concept of the Counter (Small Numbers) level of the counting learning trajectory by connecting subitizing and counting. Notice how the simple activity listed in Table 7.1, "How Many?" builds, connects, and applies these competencies. Many other activities could be used, but research suggests that activities that similarly connect students' counting and subitizing will be particularly effective.

Similarly, in teaching students the "Counter On Using Patterns" level, the *How Many in the Box Now?* activity connects competencies from earlier levels of the counting trajectory (e.g., counting up starting at any number) to other subitizing abilities (*rhythmic* subitizing) to the new activity of counting-on to solve arithmetic problems. Research has shown that these competencies, well developed and then educed by the teacher, are particularly effective in supporting the learning of meaningful counting-on.

In other cases, instructional tasks are simply illustrations of the kind of activity that would be appropriate to reach that level of thinking. The highest level in Table 7.1, for example, provides a worthwhile activity, but it is simply one of numerous problems that teachers might present. Teachers need to use a variety of pedagogical strategies in teaching the content, such as presenting the tasks, guiding students in completing them, and orchestrating discussions and extensions.

As another illustration, consider a well-researched learning trajectory for a different topic: the composition and decomposition of geometric shapes (adapted from Clements & Sarama, 2009; Sarama & Clements, 2009a; see Table 7.2). From a lack of competence in composing geometric shapes (Pre-Composer), students gain abilities to combine shapes—initially through trial and error (e.g., Picture Maker) and gradually by attributes—into pictures, and finally to synthesize combinations of shapes into new shapes (composite shapes). For example, consider the Picture Maker level in Table 7.2. Unlike earlier levels, students concatenate shapes to form a

TABLE 7.2 Samples from a Learning Trajectory for Composition and Decomposition of Geometric Shapes

Age	Developmental Progression	Example Behavior	Instructional Tasks
2–3	**Piece Assembler:** Makes pictures in which each shape represents a unique role (e.g., one shape for each body part) and shapes touch.	Make a picture	In the first "Pattern Block Puzzles" tasks, each shape is not only outlined, but touches other shapes only at a point, making the matching as easy as possible. Students merely match pattern blocks to the outlines.
			Pattern Block Puzzles
		Solve a puzzle Fills simple puzzles such as those at the right using trial and error.	Then, the puzzles moved to those that combine shapes by matching their sides, but still mainly serve separate roles. **Pattern Block Puzzles**

(continued)

TABLE 7.2 (continued) Samples from a Learning Trajectory for Composition and Decomposition of Geometric Shapes

Age	Developmental Progression	Example Behavior	Instructional	Tasks
4	**Picture Maker:** Puts several shapes together to make one part of a picture (e.g., two shapes for one arm). Uses trial and error and does not anticipate creation of new geometric shape. Chooses shapes using "general shape" or side length.	Make a picture 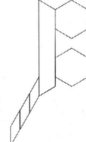 Solve a puzzle Fills easy puzzles that suggest the placement of each shape (but note to the far right that the student is trying to put a square in the puzzle where its right angles will not fit—this remains a level of "trial and error" strategies).	The "Pattern Block Puzzles" at this level start with those where several shapes are combined to make one "part," but internal lines are still available.	Later puzzles in the sequence require combining shapes to fill one or more regions without the guidance of internal line segments. 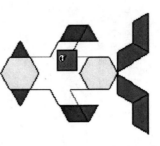

(*continued*)

Simple Decomposer:
Decomposes ("takes apart" into smaller shapes) simple shapes that have obvious clues as to their decomposition.

Given hexagons, break them apart to make a picture such as the following.

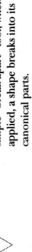

"Super Shape 1" is like "Piece Puzzler" with an essential difference. Students have only one shape in the shape palette and they must decompose that "super" (superordinate) shape and then recompose those pieces to complete the puzzle. The tool they use for decomposition is a simple "break apart" tool; when applied, a shape breaks into its canonical parts.

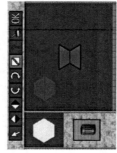

TABLE 7.2 (cont.) Samples from a Learning Trajectory for Composition and Decomposition of Geometric Shapes

Age	Developmental Progression	Example Behavior	Instructional	Tasks
5	**Shape Composer:** Composes shapes with anticipation ("I know what will fit!"). Chooses shapes using angles as well as side lengths. Rotation and flipping are used intentionally to select and place shapes.	Make a picture  Solve a puzzle Solves puzzles using side and angle recognition and matching are correct	The "Pattern Block Puzzles" and "Piece Puzzler" activities have no internal guidelines and larger areas; therefore, students must compose shapes accurately.  Pattern Block Puzzles	
6	**Substitution Composer:** Makes new shapes out of smaller shapes and uses trial and error to substitute groups of shapes for other shapes to create new shapes in different ways.	Make a picture with intentional substitutions 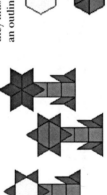	At this level, students solve "Pattern Block Puzzles" in which they must substitute shapes to fill an outline in different ways. 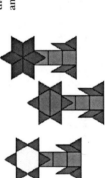	"Piece Puzzler" tasks are similar; the new task here is to solve the same puzzle in several different ways.

| 7 | Shape Decomposer with Imagery: Decomposes shapes flexibly using independently generated imagery. | Given hexagons, can break one or more apart to make shapes such as these. 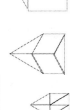 | In "Super Shape 6," students again have only one shape in the shape palette, and they must decompose that shape and then recompose those pieces to complete the puzzle. The tool they use for decomposition is a "scissors" tool, in which they must specify two points to make a "cut." Therefore, their decompositions must be more intentional and anticipatory. 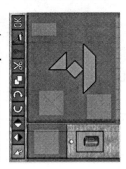 |

(continued)

TABLE 7.2 (cont.) Samples from a Learning Trajectory for Composition and Decomposition of Geometric Shapes

Age	Developmental Progression	Example Behavior	Instructional Tasks
8	**Shape Composer-Units of Units:** Builds and *applies* units (shapes made from other shapes). For example, in constructing spatial patterns, extend patterning activity to create a tiling with a new unit shape—a unit of unit shapes that they recognize and consciously construct.	Builds a large structure by making a combination of pattern blocks over and over and then fitting them together.	In this "Tetrominoes" task, the student must repeatedly build and repeat superordinate units. That is, as in the illustration here, the student repeatedly built "Ts" out of four squares, used 4 Ts to build squares, and used squares to tile a rectangle. 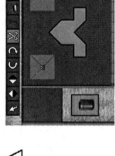
	Shape Decomposer with Units of Units: Decomposes shapes flexibly using independently generated imagery and planned decompositions of shapes that themselves are decompositions.	Given only squares, can break them apart—*and then break the resulting shapes apparent again*—to make shapes such as these.	In "Super Shape 7," students get only the exact number of "super shapes" they need to complete the puzzle. Again, multiple applications of the scissors tool is required. 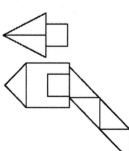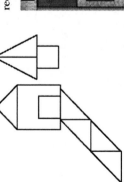

component of a picture. In the top picture in that row, a student made arms and legs from several contiguous rhombi. However, students do not conceptualize their creations (parallelograms) as geometric shapes. The puzzle task pictured at the bottom of the middle column for that row illustrates a student incorrectly choosing a square because the student is using only one component of the shape—in this case, side length. The student eventually finds this does not work, and completes the puzzle, but only by trial and error.

A main instructional task, and motivating activity, requires students to solve outline puzzles with shapes off and on the computer (Sales, 1994; Sarama et al., 1996). The objects are shapes and composite shapes, and the actions include creating, duplicating, positioning (with geometric motions), combining, and decomposing both individual shapes (units) and composite shapes (units of units). The characteristics of the tasks require actions on these objects corresponding to each level in the learning trajectory. For example, puzzles to develop the Shape Composer level of thinking have larger areas than earlier puzzles, with no guidelines inside the puzzle outlines. Students must develop the ability to recognize side lengths, angles, and shapes, and they must compose shapes with anticipatory imagery to solve such puzzles accurately and in a reasonable time period.

Ample opportunity for student-led, student-designed, open-ended projects are included in each set of activities. For example, students create their own puzzles and solve each others' both on and off computer.

Decomposition is also developed in this learning trajectory. The highest levels combine decompostion and (re)composition. Recall that ages are approximate. Without high-quality educational experiences, most adults struggle to complete the tasks at the highest levels of Table 7.2.

Arithmetic

Recall the study of textbooks in California that showed the importance of teaching concepts and meaningful strategies for basic arithmetic facts (Henry & Brown, 2008). The previously discussed Break-Apart-to-Make-Tens (BAMT) strategy was found to be particularly effective. Some Japanese teachers are masters of teaching this strategy (Murata & Fuson, 2006). The sequence of instructional activities they use illustrate a part of research-based adding and subtracting learning trajectories (extensive trajectories can be found in Clements & Sarama, 2009; Fuson, 1992; Sarama & Clements, 2009a; Verschaffel, Greer, & De Corte, 2007).

Before lessons on BAMT, students worked on several related learning trajectories. They developed solid knowledge of numerals and counting (i.e., moving along the counting learning trajectory). This includes the number structure for teen numbers as 10 + another number, which is more straightforward in Asian languages than English ("13" is "10 and 3"—note that U.S. teachers must be particularly attentive to this competence). They learn to solve addition and subtraction of numbers with totals less than 10, often chunking numbers into 5 (e.g., 7 as 5-plus-2) and using visual models.

With these levels of thinking established, students develop several levels of thinking within the composition/decomposition developmental progression. For example, they work on "break-apart partners" of numbers less than or equal to 10. They solve addition and subtraction problems involving teen numbers using the 10s structure ($10 + 2 = 12$; $18 - 8 = 10$), and addition and subtraction with three addends using 10s (e.g., $4 + 6 + 3 = 10 + 3 = 13$ and $15 - 5 - 9 = 10 - 9 = 1$).

Teachers then introduce problems such as $8 + 6$. They first elicit, value, and discuss student-invented strategies and encourage students to use these strategies to solve a variety of problems. Only then do they move the class to the use of BAMT. They provide supports to connect visual and symbolic representations of quantities. For example, for $9 + 4$, they show 9 counters (or fingers) and 4 counters, then move 1 from the 4 to make a group of 10. Next, they highlight the 3 left. Then students are reminded that the 9 and 1 made 10. Last, students see 10 counters and 3 counters and think 10-3, or count on "10-1, 10-2, 10-3." Later, representational drawings serve this role, in a sequence such as shown in Figure 7.1.

Teachers spend many lessons on ensuring students' understanding and skill using the BAMT strategy. Students are asked why the strategy works and what its advantages are. Extensive repeated experiencing (distributed practice) is used to develop fluency.

Arithmetic algorithms. Although presentation of a complete learning trajectory for arithmetic is beyond the scope of this chapter, findings regarding multidigit addition and subtraction address a "hot button" issue: the teaching of algorithms. Some argue that the teaching and learning of al-

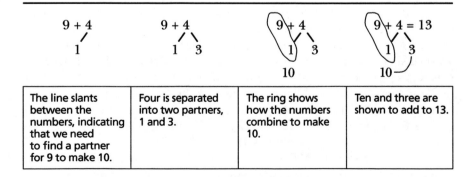

| The line slants between the numbers, indicating that we need to find a partner for 9 to make 10. | Four is separated into two partners, 1 and 3. | The ring shows how the numbers combine to make 10. | Ten and three are shown to add to 13. |

Figure 7.1 Teaching BAMT.

gorithms has been neglected, and direct instruction and massive practice are necessary. Others have argued, with supporting evidence, that standard algorithms are actually harmful to students (see Kamii & Dominick, 1998, for their own statement and a review of other researchers with similar conclusions). Algorithms achieve efficiency by separating the place value of numbers from their composition. Because teachers often directly teach the standard algorithm regardless of their students' developmental progressions in counting strategies, some students treat the standard algorithm as a meaningless but prescribed procedure unconnected to their understandings of counting and other number concepts and processes (Biddlecomb & Carr, 2011; see also Kamii & Dominick, 1997, 1998).

In contrast, studies indicate that curricula and teaching that emphasize both conceptual understanding simultaneously with procedural skill and flexible application of multiple strategies, lead to equivalent skill, but more fluent, flexible use of such skills, as well as superior conceptual understanding, compared to approaches that initially emphasize mastery of procedures (Fuson & Kwon, 1992; National Mathematics Advisory Panel, 2008). For example, Hiebert and Wearne (1996) followed a randomly selected group of primary-grade students for 3 years as they learned arithmetic. Some of the classrooms received conventional instruction, and others received alternative instruction on place value and arithmetic emphasizing conceptual understanding. Mainly, students invented their own strategies for solving multidigit addition and subtraction problems and explained them to their peers. Class discussions focused on why the nonstandard algorithms worked or not. Qualitative and descriptive analyses of interviews revealed that the students who demonstrated conceptual understanding were more likely than their peers to invent new procedures and modify old ones to solve new problems. The alternative instruction was more effective than conventional instruction in developing both skill and concepts and especially in linking them, a difference that grew from first to third grade (and was statistically significant at a $p > .01$ level only in third grade; Hiebert & Wearne, 1996).

Thus, explicit teaching of arithmetic does not have to lead to learning problems—but it may if it emphasized only prescribed procedures. Teaching that develops number concepts, counting and compositional strategies, and skills with respect to students' level in the learning trajectory benefit students. This teaching must not neglect the connections between the development of place-value understandings and the procedures for doing multidigit arithmetic. Students' knowledge of these are correlated, and conceptual knowledge predicts not only concurrent but future procedural skill (Hiebert & Wearne, 1996). Also, better instruction, designed to emphasize concepts of place value, leads to greater increases in both conceptual and procedural knowledge, relative to instruction that deemphasizes concepts or that leaves a gap between the two types of knowledge (Verschaffel et al., 2007).

Research supports the notion that inventing one's own procedures is often a good first phase in ensuring these advantages (Carpenter, Ansell, Franke, Fennema, & Weisbeck, 1993; Carpenter & Moser, 1984; Fennema, Carpenter, & Franke, 1997; Kamii & Dominick, 1997, 1998). As a specific example, a 3-year longitudinal study of students' multidigit number concepts and operations in grades 1–3 showed that about 90% of all students used invented procedures to solve multidigit addition and subtraction problems (Carpenter et al., 1998). Students who used invented strategies before they learned standard algorithms demonstrated better knowledge of base-ten number concepts and were more successful in extending their knowledge to new situations than were students who initially learned standard algorithms.

Some authors contend that students' invention at this level is not the critical feature, but rather the sense making (conceptual understanding and work on challenging problems) in which students engage, whether or not they invent, adapt, or copy the method (Fuson, 2009). As we discussed previously, sense making is probably the essence. However, most research indicates that initial student invention develops multiple interconnecting concepts, skills, and problem solving. This does not mean that students must invent every procedure but that conceptual development, adaptive reasoning, and skills are developed simultaneously, and that initial student invention may be a particularly effective way of achieving these goals.

As one example, the Dutch more recently promoted the use of the "empty number line" as a support for "jump" strategy (Beishuizen, 1993). The number line is "empty" in that it is not a measurement/ruler model but simply keeps the order of numbers and the size of "jumps" recorded, as is shown in Figure 7.2.

There are many arguments about whether to teach *the* standard algorithms. Too often, such arguments have generated more heat than light, for several reasons. First, there is no single standard algorithm. Many different ones have been used in the United States and around the world. All are valid (Kilpatrick et al., 2001). Second, what are taken as different "standard" algorithms by teachers and laypeople are often not viewed as different by

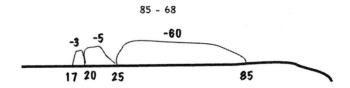

Figure 7.2 The empty number line supporting arithmetic.

mathematicians, some of whom might consider them simply modifications (often in the way in which numbers are recorded) of general place-value based algorithms.

The classic study by Brownell and Moser (1949) described previously compared the benefits of teaching either meaningfully or mechanically the decomposition and equal addends subtraction algorithms. The meaningful (or conceptual) approach used manipulatives for grouping, expanded notation, connections between representations, and delaying the written algorithm until the meanings were established. The mechanical approach taught the algorithm step-by-step and used the saved time for practice. On the immediate posttest, the mechanical group scored higher on speed and accuracy. On retention and transfer, however, the meaningful approach group's scores were greater. The meaningful approach was better for the decomposition method or for students who had already learned an algorithm. The main message is that for retention, transfer, and understanding, meaningful teaching was superior (Brownell & Moser, 1949). Research from cognitive psychology in general supports the use of conceptually based approaches, especially high-quality models that are complete, concise, coherent, concrete (often visual), conceptual, and correct (Mayer, 1989).

If teachers are helped to understand students' thinking, studies show that they help students invent and use adaptive calculation strategies (e.g., Carpenter et al., 1998). Further, if students invent their own strategies first, they have fewer errors than do students who were taught algorithms from the start.

Finally, a consistent result is that conceptually based instruction supports mathematical proficiency (Carpenter et al., 1998; Fuson & Briars, 1990; Fuson et al., 1997; Resnick, 1992; Verschaffel et al., 2007). In one study, most of the students who developed conceptual knowledge either first or simultaneously with procedural knowledge could invent new solution procedures or use their knowledge adaptively, whereas those who learned procedures first could not. They relied on conventional procedures and, more frequently, on "buggy" procedures than those receiving nontraditional instruction. This nontraditional instruction encouraged students to develop their own procedures and to make sense of others' procedures. Thus, conceptual knowledge facilitates procedure selection, procedure monitoring, and transfer. Also, once again, students' invented strategies are a good starting point (Hiebert & Wearne, 1996). In contrast, students taught in conventional classrooms, focusing on the mastery of (only) the standard paper-and-pencil algorithms for solving multidigit additions and subtractions, more frequently use erroneous, or "buggy," procedures and make more systematic errors than do students instructed in nonconventional classrooms (Hiebert & Wearne, 1996).

In another study, second-grade classes were randomly assigned to one of two instructional programs (Blöte et al., 2001). The first was a reformed-based program based on the Dutch Realistic Mathematics Education, in which students invent and discuss their solution procedure. From the beginning of instruction, this program emphasizes developing conceptual understanding simultaneously with procedural skill, as well as flexible application of multiple strategies. These students outperformed those in a traditional textbook program that focused on mastery of procedures initially and varied application of strategies only toward the end of instruction. The reform group students more often selected strategies related to the number properties of the problems and used strategies more adaptively, such as solving problems with "8" or "9" in the one's place with compensation strategies. That is, these were flexible problem solvers who adapted their strategies to the number characteristics of the problem at hand. For example, they solved $62 - 49$ as $62 - 50 = 12$, $12 + 1 = 13$, but solved $62 - 44$ as $44 + 6 = 50$, $50 + 10 = 60$, $60 + 2 = 62$, and $6 + 10 + 2 = 18$. Such flexible strategy use indicates both conceptual understanding and procedural skill. The traditional group did not use the procedures flexibly, even after months of instruction in that program emphasized such flexible use. The reform group scored higher on three measures (all $p < .01$), showing superior conceptual understanding. Students in both groups developed conceptual understanding before achieving procedural skill, but the two domains were more interconnected for the reform group (Blöte et al., 2001).

A third study with intermediate-grade (fourth and fifth grade) students indicated that conceptual instruction led to increased conceptual understanding and to generation and transfer of a correct procedure. Procedural instruction led to increased conceptual understanding and to adoption, but only limited transfer, of the instructed procedure (Rittle-Johnson & Alibali, 1999; with $p < .05$ on each). On the transfer tasks, only 13% of the children in the procedural-instruction group attempted to apply a correct procedure to all tasks, compared to 59% of the children in the conceptual instruction group. Moreover, 29% of these children used more than one correct procedure, compared to no one in the procedural-instruction group.

As we previously stated, at the point of learning traditional algorithms, relatively simple modifications can make them more accessible to students. One successful modification is shown in Figure 7.3. Notice that regrouping everywhere first helps students concentrate just on the need to regroup and the regrouping itself. Once that has been completed, then the subtraction operations are performed one after the other. Not having to "switch" between the two processes allows better focus on each one.

$4\,5\,6$ $-1\,6\,7$	$3^1 4$ $4\,\cancel{5}^1 6$ $-1\,6\,7$	$3^1 4$ $4\,\cancel{5}^1 6$ $-1\,6\,7$ $\overline{2\,8\,9}$
	Regroup everywhere needed.	Subtract everywhere.

Figure 7.3 A useful modification of the U.S. algorithm (Fuson, 2009).

LEARNING TO TEACH MATHEMATICS: WHAT APPROACHES TO PROFESSIONAL DEVELOPMENT ARE SUPPORTED BY RESEARCH?

Teachers make a difference. They remain the most important factor in students' learning of mathematics. Professional development can make a difference for teachers. However, across the grades, what we know with certainty about professional development is slim. There are indications that certification alone is not a reliable predictor of high-quality teaching (National Mathematics Advisory Panel, 2008). This is probably due to the wide variety of certification programs and the low quality of too many of them. More direct measures of what teachers know about mathematics and the learning and teaching of mathematics *do* predict the quality of their teaching (National Mathematics Advisory Panel, 2008). For example, first and third graders' math achievement gains were statistically related to their teachers' mathematics content knowledge for teaching (Hill, Rowan, & Ball, 2005). For example, students gained roughly 2.25 points on an achievement test (or about .5 to .67 of a month of additional growth) for every standard deviation increase in teachers' mathematics content knowledge.

What Does Not Work

Few teachers receive professional development designed to develop the kind of knowledge we have described in this chapter, especially knowledge of mathematics content and learning trajectories. The average was 8.3 hours of professional development on how to teach mathematics and 5.2 hours on the "in-depth study" over a year (Birman et al., 2007). For early-childhood teachers, the amount is even less, usually zero. Ignoring professional development in mathematics does not work. As obvious as that sounds, it is common practice in the United States.

Further, many professional development efforts that are attempted do not work well (adapted from Sarama & DiBiase, 2004). One common ineffective format is the 1-day workshop. This is simply inadequate "dosage." Frequently, such workshops also focus on topics selected not by the teachers, but by others. Indeed, 2/3 of teachers report they have no say in what or how they learn on the job (Darling-Hammond, 1998). Such training does not address teachers' concerns. Another ineffective format involves teachers and groups that are not from the same site, limiting social support. Finally, there is too often a lack of conceptual basis for the programs or strategies that are the topic of the training, much less their implementation (Fullan, 1982).

What Does Work

A focus on teachers' behaviors has less positive effect than a focus on teachers' knowledge of the subject, on the curriculum, and on how students learn the subject (Carpenter, Fennema, Peterson, & Carey, 1988; Kennedy, 1998; Peterson, Carpenter, & Fennema, 1989). Successful professional development projects emphasize research on students' learning, made meaningful to teachers (Sarama, 2002). Most do this in the context of curriculum and reflection upon that curriculum. Most also involve collaborative efforts that involve extensive interactions among teachers and university professors, with some providing substantial modeling and mentoring in classrooms. Most integrate research and theory, connecting it closely to teachers' practice. Those who provide intensive, sustained, and content-focused professional development succeed in helping students learn mathematics (Birman et al., 2007). The average total time was over 50 hours of professional development.

Prospective, or preservice, teachers appear to benefit from the same emphasis: how students learn mathematics (Philipp et al., 2007). Research also supports an approach of encouraging sharing, risk taking, and learning from and with peers. This approach prepares participants to teach a specific curriculum and developing teachers' knowledge and beliefs that the curriculum is appropriate and its goals are valued and attainable. It situates work in the classroom, formatively evaluating teachers' fidelity of implementation and providing feedback and support from coaches in real time (D. Clarke, 1994; Garet, Porter, Desimone, Birman, & Yoon, 2001; Hall & Hord, 2001; Schoen, Cebulla, Finn, & Fi, 2003).

Success with our *Building Blocks and TRIAD (scale-up) projects is arguably largely attributable to the focus on learning trajectories* (Clements & Sarama, 2008). Several other projects also report success with variations of that approach (Bright, Bowman, & Vacc, 1997; Wright, Martland, Stafford, &

Stanger, 2002). All of these projects included far more extensive and intensive professional development than the usual one-shot workshop, ranging from 5 to 14 full days.

Successful projects have similar characteristics (Bobis et al., 2005; Clements & Sarama, 2008; Clements, Sarama, Spitler, Lange, & Wolfe, 2011; Sarama, Clements, Starkey, Klein, & Wakeley, 2008). First, they have research-based frameworks, including the use of developmental progressions of learning trajectories. Second, teachers learn about mathematics and the teaching and learning of early mathematics—in these cases, especially by conducting one-to-one interviews of students. Third, ongoing, reflective, professional development should be conducted schoolwide (Bobis et al., 2005). Related research reports emphasized the combination of workshops, in-school support, and modeling (Thomas & Tagg, 2004; Young-Loveridge, 2004).

Other reviews suggest that soliciting teachers' commitment to participating actively; allowing time for planning, reflection, and feedback; recognizing that change is gradual, difficult, and often painful; and providing for support from peers (D. Clarke, 1994) is most effective. Across several studies, including the TRIAD/*Building Blocks* work, there is a sign that targeted coaching and mentoring is an essential piece (Certo, 2005; Clements & Sarama, 2008). Coaching reminds teachers that the project is a priority, that a commitment has been made to it, and that somebody cares about them (Hord, Rutherford, Huling-Austin, & Hall, 1987). Research indicates that when staff development includes ongoing coaching, classroom innovations continue at a 90% level after external funding ceases (Copley, 2004; Costa & Garmston, 1994; Nettles, 1993).

In brief, we recommend that those who are planning professional development in early and elementary mathematics consider the following guidelines:

- Address both knowledge of and beliefs about mathematics and mathematics education.
- Develop knowledge and beliefs regarding specific subject-matter content, including deep conceptual knowledge of the mathematics they are to teach, as well as the processes of mathematics.
- Respond to each individual's background, experiences, and current context or role.
- Instruction should be extensive, ongoing, reflective, and sustained.
- Actively involve teachers in observation, experimentation, and mentoring.
- Focus on common actions and problems of practice, which, as much as possible, should be situated in the classroom.
- Focus on making small changes guided by a consistent, coherent, grand vision.

- Ground experiences in particular curriculum materials and allow teachers to learn and reflect on that curriculum, implement it, and discuss their implementation.
- Consider approaches such as research lessons and case-based teacher education.
- Focus on students' mathematical thinking and learning, including learning trajectories.
- Include strategies for developing higher-order thinking and for working with special populations.
- Address equity and diversity concerns.
- Involve interaction, networking, and sharing with peers/colleagues.
- Include a variety of approaches.
- Use the early childhood professional career lattice as a means of encouraging professional development at all levels.
- Ensure the support of administration for professional development to promote sustained and wide-scale reform.
- Consider school-university partnerships, especially collaborative efforts involving extensive interactions among teachers and university professors.
- Sustain efforts to connect theory, research, and practice.
- *Investigate the use of nontraditional* publications, including trade publications, direct mailing, and *distance learning for communications.*
- Provide participants with high-quality mathematics curriculum materials and ensure that participants receive adequate experience to use the materials effectively.
- Address economic, institutional, and regulatory barriers.

ACKNOWLEDGMENT

This chapter was based upon work supported in part by the Institute of Education Sciences (U.S. Dept. of Education) under Grant No. R305K05157. Work on the research was also supported in part by the National Science Foundation under Grant No. DRL-1019925. Any opinions, findings, and conclusions or recommendations expressed in this material are those of the authors and do not necessarily reflect the views of the funding agencies, Learning and Teaching Early and Elementary Mathematics.

NOTE

1. This curriculum has been published by the authors, who thus have a vested interest in the results. An external auditor oversaw the research design, data

collection, and analysis, and other researchers independently confirmed findings and procedures of all evaluations.

REFERENCES

Allen, J., Watson, J. A., & Howard, J. R. (1993). The impact of cognitive styles on the problem solving strategies used by preschool minority children in Logo microworlds. *Journal of Computing in Childhood Education, 4,* 203–217.

Anghileri, J. (2004). Disciplined calculators or flexible problem solvers? In M. J. Høines & A. B. Fuglestad (Eds.), *Proceedings of the 28th conference of the International Group for the Psychology in Mathematics Education* (Vol. 1, pp. 41–46). Bergen, Norway: Bergen University College.

Ashcraft, M. H. (2006, November). *Math performance, working memory, and math anxiety; Some possible directions for neural functioning work.* Paper presented at the the Neural Basis of Mathematical Development, Nashville, TN.

Askew, M., Brown, M., Rhodes, V., Wiliam, D., & Johnson, D. (1997). Effective teachers of numeracy in UK primary schools: Teachers' beliefs, practices, and children's learning. In M. Van den Heuvel-Panhuizen (Ed.), *Proceedings of the 21st conference of the International Group for the Psychology of Mathematics Education* (Vol. 2, pp. 25–32). Utrecht, The Netherlands: Freudenthal Institute.

Ball, D. L. (1992). Magical hopes: Manipulatives and the reform of math education. *American Educator, 16*(2), 14, 16–18, 46–47.

Baroody, A. J. (1989). Manipulatives don't come with guarantees. *Arithmetic Teacher, 37*(2), 4–5.

Baroody, A. J. (1999). The development of basic counting, number, and arithmetic knowledge among children classified as mentally handicapped. In L. M. Glidden (Ed.), *International review of research in mental retardation* (Vol. 22, pp. 51–103). New York: Academic Press.

Baroody, A. J. (2003). The development of adaptive expertise and flexibility: The integration of conceptual and procedural knowledge. In A. J. Baroody & A. Dowker (Eds.), *The development of arithmetic concepts and skills: Constructing adaptive expertise* (pp. 1–33). Mahwah, NJ: Lawrence Erlbaum Associates.

Baroody, A. J. (2004a). The developmental bases for early childhood number and operations standards. In D. H. Clements, J. Sarama, & A.-M. DiBiase (Eds.), *Engaging young children in mathematics: Standards for early childhood mathematics education* (pp. 173–219). Mahwah, NJ: Lawrence Erlbaum Associates.

Baroody, A. J. (2004b). The role of psychological research in the development of early childhood mathematics standards. In D. H. Clements, J. Sarama, & A.-M. DiBiase (Eds.), *Engaging young children in mathematics: Standards for early childhood mathematics education* (pp. 149–172). Mahwah, NJ: Lawrence Erlbaum Associates.

Baroody, A. J., & Dowker, A. (2003). *The development of arithmetic concepts and skills: Constructing adaptive expertise.* Mahwah, NJ: Lawrence Erlbaum Associates.

Beishuizen, M. (1993). Mental strategies and materials or models for addition and subtraction up to 100 in Dutch second grades. *Journal for Research in Mathematics Education, 24,* 294–323.

Berch, D. B., & Mazzocco, M. M. M. (Eds.). (2007). *Why is math so hard for some children? The nature and origins of mathematical learning difficulties and disabilities.* Baltimore: Paul H. Brookes.

Biddlecomb, B., & Carr, M. (2011). Counting schemes and strategies: Evidence from exploratory factor analysis. *International Journal of Science and Mathematics Education, 9,* 1–24.

Birman, B. F., LeFloch, K. C., Klekotka, A., Ludwig, M., Taylor, J., Walters, K.,... O'Day, J. (2007). *State and local implementation of the No Child Left Behind Act, Volume II—Teacher quality under NCLB: Interim report.* Washington, DC: U.S. Department of Education, Office of Planning, Evaluation and Policy Development, Policy and Program Studies Service.

Blöte, A. W., van der Burg, E., & Klein, A. S. (2001). Students' flexibility in solving two-digit addition and subtraction problems: Instruction effects. *Journal of Educational Psychology, 93,* 627–638.

Bobis, J., Clarke, B. A., Clarke, D. M., Gill, T., Wright, R. J., Young-Loveridge, J. M., & Gould, P. (2005). Supporting teachers in the development of young children's mathematical thinking: Three large scale cases. *Mathematics Education Research Journal, 16*(3), 27–57.

Bright, G. W., Bowman, A. H., & Vacc, N. N. (1997). Teachers' frameworks for understanding children's mathematical thinking. In E. Pehkonen (Ed.), *Proceedings of the 21st conference of the International Group for the Psychology of Mathematics Education* (Vol. 2, pp. 105–112). Lahti, Finland: University of Helsinki.

Brinkley, V. M., & Watson, J. A. (1987/1988). Logo and young children: Are quadrant effects part of initial Logo mastery? *Journal of Educational Technology Systems, 19,* 75–86.

Brooks-Gunn, J. (2003). Do you believe in magic? What we can expect from early childhood intervention programs. *Social Policy Report, 17*(1), 1, 3–14.

Brownell, W. A., & Moser, H. E. (1949). *Meaningful vs. mechanical learning: A study in grade III subtraction.* Durham, NC: Duke University Press.

Browning, C. A. (1991). Reflections on using Lego TC Logo in an elementary classroom. In E. Calabrese (Ed.), *Proceedings of the third European Logo Conference* (pp. 173–185). Parma, Italy: Associazione Scuola e Informatica.

Campbell, P. F. (1987). *Measuring distance: Children's use of number and unit. Final report submitted to the National Institute of Mental Health under the ADAMHA Small Grant Award Program.* Grant No. MSMA 1 R03 MH423435-01. College Park: University of Maryland.

Carmichael, H. W., Burnett, J. D., Higginson, W. C., Moore, B. G., & Pollard, P. J. (1985). *Computers, children and classrooms: A multisite evaluation of the creative use of microcomputers by elementary school children.* Toronto, Ontario, Canada: Ministry of Education.

Carpenter, T. P., Ansell, E., Franke, M. L., Fennema, E. H., & Weisbeck, L. (1993). Models of problem solving: A study of kindergarten children's problem-solving processes. *Journal for Research in Mathematics Education, 24,* 428–441.

Carpenter, T. P., Fennema, E. H., Franke, M. L., Levi, L., & Empson, S. B. (1999). *Children's mathematics: Cognitively guided instruction.* Portsmouth, NH: Heinemann.

Carpenter, T. P., Fennema, E. H., Peterson, P. L., & Carey, D. A. (1988). Teacher's pedagogical content knowledge of students' problem solving in elementary arithmetic. *Journal for Research in Mathematics Education, 19,* 385–401.

Carpenter, T. P., Franke, M. L., Jacobs, V. R., Fennema, E. H., & Empson, S. B. (1998). A longitudinal study of invention and understanding in children's multidigit addition and subtraction. *Journal for Research in Mathematics Education, 29,* 3–20.

Carpenter, T. P., & Moser, J. M. (1984). The acquisition of addition and subtraction concepts in grades one through three. *Journal for Research in Mathematics Education, 15,* 179–202.

Carr, M., & Alexeev, N. (2011). Developmental trajectories of mathematic strategies: Influence of fluency, accuracy and gender. *Journal of Educational Psychology, 103,* 617–631.

CCSSO/NGA. (2010). *Common Core state standards for mathematics.* Washington, DC: Council of Chief State School Officers and the National Governors Association Center for Best Practices.

Cepeda, N. J., Pashler, H., Vul, E., Wixted, J. T., & Rohrer, D. (2006). Distributed practice in verbal recall tasks: A review and quantitative synthesis. *Psychological Bulletin, 132,* 354–380.

Certo, J. L. (2005). Support, challenge, and the two-way street: Perceptions of a beginning second-grade teacher and her quality mentor. *Journal of Early Childhood Teacher Education, 26,* 3–21.

Char, C. A. (1989). *Computer graphic feltboards: New software approaches for young children's mathematical exploration.* San Francisco: American Educational Research Association.

Clarke, D. (1994). Ten key principles from research for the professional development of mathematics teachers. In D. B. Aichele & A. F. Coxford (Eds.), *Professional development for teachers of mathematics* (pp. 37–48). Reston, VA: National Council of Teachers of Mathematics.

Clarke, D. M., Cheeseman, J., Gervasoni, A., Gronn, D., Horne, M., McDonough, A.,... Sullivan, P. (2002). *Early Numeracy Research Project final report.* Department of Education, Employment and Training, the Catholic Education Office (Melbourne), and the Association of Independent Schools Victoria.

Clements, D. H. (1983/1984). Supporting young children's Logo programming. *The Computing Teacher, 11*(5), 24–30.

Clements, D. H. (1999). "Concrete" manipulatives, concrete ideas. *Contemporary Issues in Early Childhood, 1*(1), 45–60.

Clements, D. H., & Battista, M. T. (1989). Learning of geometric concepts in a Logo environment. *Journal for Research in Mathematics Education, 20,* 450–467.

Clements, D. H., Battista, M. T., & Sarama, J. (2001). Logo and geometry. *Journal for Research in Mathematics Education Monograph Series, 10.*

Clements, D. H., Battista, M. T., Sarama, J., & Swaminathan, S. (1996). Development of turn and turn measurement concepts in a computer-based instructional unit. *Educational Studies in Mathematics, 30,* 313–337.

Clements, D. H., Battista, M. T., Sarama, J., Swaminathan, S., & McMillen, S. (1997). Students' development of length measurement concepts in a Logo-based unit on geometric paths. *Journal for Research in Mathematics Education, 28*(1), 70–95.

Clements, D. H., & Burns, B. A. (2000). Students' development of strategies for turn and angle measure. *Educational Studies in Mathematics, 41,* 31–45.

Clements, D. H., & Nastasi, B. K. (1993). Electronic media and early childhood education. In B. Spodek (Ed.), *Handbook of research on the education of young children* (pp. 251–275). New York: Macmillan.

Clements, D. H., & Sarama, J. (2004). Learning trajectories in mathematics education. *Mathematical Thinking and Learning, 6,* 81–89.

Clements, D. H., & Sarama, J. (2007a). *Building Blocks—SRA Real Math Teacher's Edition, Grade PreK.* Columbus, OH: SRA/McGraw-Hill.

Clements, D. H., & Sarama, J. (2007b). Effects of a preschool mathematics curriculum: Summative research on the *Building Blocks* project. *Journal for Research in Mathematics Education, 38,* 136–163.

Clements, D. H., & Sarama, J. (2008). Experimental evaluation of the effects of a research-based preschool mathematics curriculum. *American Educational Research Journal, 45,* 443–494.

Clements, D. H., & Sarama, J. (2009). *Learning and teaching early math: The learning trajectories approach.* New York: Routledge.

Clements, D. H., Sarama, J., & DiBiase, A.-M. (2004). *Engaging young children in mathematics: Standards for early childhood mathematics education.* Mahwah, NJ: Lawrence Erlbaum Associates.

Clements, D. H., Sarama, J., Spitler, M. E., Lange, A. A., & Wolfe, C. B. (2011). Mathematics learned by young children in an intervention based on learning trajectories: A large-scale cluster randomized trial. *Journal for Research in Mathematics Education, 42*(2), 127–166.

Clements, D. H., Wilson, D. C., & Sarama, J. (2004). Young children's composition of geometric figures: A learning trajectory. *Mathematical Thinking and Learning, 6,* 163–184.

Cobb, P. (1990). A constructivist perspective on information-processing theories of mathematical activity. *International Journal of Educational Research, 14,* 67–92.

Cobb, P., Wood, T., Yackel, E., Nicholls, J., Wheatley, G. H., Trigatti, B., & Perlwitz, M. (1991). Assessment of a problem-centered second-grade mathematics project. *Journal for Research in Mathematics Education, 22*(1), 3–29.

Cobb, P., Yackel, E., & Wood, T. (1989). Young children's emotional acts during mathematical problem solving. In D. B. McLeod & V. M. Adams (Eds.), *Affect and mathematical problem solving: A new perspective* (pp. 117–148). New York: Springer-Verlag.

Cohen, R., & Geva, E. (1989). Designing Logo-like environments for young children: The interaction between theory and practice. *Journal of Educational Computing Research, 5,* 349–377.

Confrey, J., Maloney, A., Nguyen, K., Mojica, G., & Myers, M. (2009). *Equipartitioning/splitting as a foundation of rational number reasoning using learning trajectories.* Paper presented at the proceedings of the 33rd conference of the International Group for the Psychology in Mathematics Education.

Copley, J. V. (2004). The early childhood collaborative: A professional development model to communicate and implement the standards. In D. H. Clements, J. Sarama, & A.-M. DiBiase (Eds.), *Engaging young children in mathematics: Stan-*

dards for early childhood mathematics education (pp. 401–414). Mahwah, NJ: Lawrence Erlbaum Associates.

Costa, A., & Garmston, R. (1994). *The art of cognitive coaching: Supervision for intelligent teaching. Training syllabus.* Sacramento, CA: Institute for Intelligent Behavior.

Darling-Hammond, L. (1998). Teachers and teaching: Testing policy hypotheses from a national commission report. *Educational Researcher, 27,* 5–15.

Dowker, A. (2004). *What works for children with mathematical difficulties?* (Research Report No. 554). Nottingham, UK: University of Oxford/DfES Publications.

Driscoll, M. J. (1983). *Research within reach: Elementary school mathematics and reading.* St. Louis, MO: CEMREL, Inc.

du Boulay, B. (1986). Part II: Logo confessions. In R. Lawler, B. du Boulay, M. Hughes, & H. Macleod (Eds.), *Cognition and computers: Studies in learning* (pp. 81–178). Chichester, UK: Ellis Horwood Limited.

Fennema, E. H. (1972). The relative effectiveness of a symbolic and a concrete model in learning a selected mathematics principle. *Journal for Research in Mathematics Education, 3,* 233–238.

Fennema, E. H., Carpenter, T. P., & Franke, M. L. (1997). Cognitively guided instruction. In S. N. Friel & G. W. Bright (Eds.), *Reflecting on our work: NSF teacher enhancement in K–6 mathematics* (pp. 193–196). Lanham, MD: University Press of America.

Fennema, E. H., Carpenter, T. P., Franke, M. L., Levi, L., Jacobs, V. R., & Empson, S. B. (1996). A longitudinal study of learning to use children's thinking in mathematics instruction. *Journal for Research in Mathematics Education, 27,* 403–434.

Frazier, M. K. (1987). *The effects of Logo on angle estimation skills of 7th graders.* Unpublished master's thesis, Wichita State University.

Fuchs, L. S., Compton, D. L., Fuchs, D., Paulson, K., Bryant, J. D., & Hamlett, C. L. (2005). The prevention, identification, and cognitive determinants of math difficulty. *Journal of Educational Psychology, 97,* 493–513.

Fuchs, L. S., Fuchs, D., Hamlett, C. L., Powell, S. R., Capizzi, A. M., & Seethaler, P. M. (2006). The effects of computer-assisted instruction on number combination skill in at-risk first graders. *Journal of Learning Disabilities, 39,* 467–475.

Fullan, M. G. (1982). *The meaning of educational change.* New York: Teachers College Press.

Fuson, K. C. (1992). Research on learning and teaching addition and subtraction of whole numbers. In G. Leinhardt, R. Putman, & R. A. Hattrup (Eds.), *Handbook of research on mathematics teaching and learning* (pp. 53-187). Mahwah, NJ: Lawrence Erlbaum Associates.

Fuson, K. C. (2004). Pre-K to grade 2 goals and standards: Achieving 21st century mastery for all. In D. H. Clements, J. Sarama, & A.-M. DiBiase (Eds.), *Engaging young children in mathematics: Standards for early childhood mathematics education* (pp. 105–148). Mahwah, NJ: Lawrence Erlbaum Associates.

Fuson, K. C. (2009). *Mathematically-desirable and accessible whole-number algorithms: Achieving understanding and fluency for all students.* Manuscript submitted for publication.

Fuson, K. C., & Briars, D. J. (1990). Using a base-ten blocks learning/teaching approach for first- and second-grade place-value and multidigit addition and subtraction. *Journal for Research in Mathematics Education, 21,* 180–206.

Fuson, K. C., & Kwon, Y. (1992). Korean childen's understanding of multidigit addition and subtraction. *Child Development, 63,* 491–506.

Fuson, K. C., Wearne, D., Hiebert, J. C., Murray, H. G., Human, P. G., Olivier, A. I., . . . Fennema, E. (1997). Children's conceptual structures for multidigit numbers and methods of multidigit addition and subtraction. *Journal for Research in Mathematics Education, 28,* 130–162.

Gallou-Dumiel, E. (1989). Reflections, point symmetry and Logo. In C. A. Maher, G. A. Goldin, & R. B. Davis (Eds.), *Proceedings of the eleventh annual meeting, North American Chapter of the International Group for the Psychology of Mathematics Education* (pp. 149–157). New Brunswick, NJ: Rutgers University.

Garet, M. S., Porter, A. C., Desimone, L., Birman, B. F., & Yoon, K. S. (2001). What makes professional development effective? Results from a national sample of teachers. *American Educational Research Journal, 38,* 915–945.

Geary, D. C. (1990). A componential analysis of an early learning deficit in mathematics. *Journal of Experimental Child Psychology, 49,* 363–383.

Geary, D. C. (2004). Mathematics and learning disabilities. *Journal of Learning Disabilities, 37,* 4–15.

Geary, D. C., Bow-Thomas, C. C., & Yao, Y. (1992). Counting knowledge and skill in cognitive addition: A comparison of normal and mathematically disabled children. *Journal of Experimental Child Psychology, 54,* 372–391.

Geary, D. C., Hamson, C. O., & Hoard, M. K. (2000). Numerical and arithmetical cognition: A longitudinal study of process and concept deficits in children with learning disability. *Journal of Experimental Child Psychology, 77,* 236–263.

Geary, D. C., Hoard, M. K., Byrd-Craven, J., Nugent, L., & Numtee, C. (2007). Cognitive mechanisms underlying achievement deficits in children with mathematical learning disability. *Child Development, 78,* 1343–1359.

Gersten, R., Chard, D. J., Jayanthi, M., Baker, M. S., Morpy, S. K., & Flojo, J. R. (2008). *Teaching mathematics to students with learning disabilities: A meta-analysis of the intervention research.* Portsmouth, NH: RMC Research Corporation, Center on Instruction.

Gervasoni, A. (2005). The diverse learning needs of children who were selected for an intervention program. In H. L. Chick & J. L. Vincent (Eds.), *Proceedings of the 29th conference of the International Group for the Psychology in Mathematics Education* (Vol. 3, pp. 33–40). Melbourne, AU: PME.

Gervasoni, A., Hadden, T., & Turkenburg, K. (2007). Exploring the number knowledge of children to inform the development of a professional learning plan for teachers in the Ballarat Diocese as a means of building community capacity. In J. Watson & K. Beswick (Eds.), *Mathematics: Essential research, essential practice (Proceedings of the 30th annual conference of the Mathematics Education Research Group of Australasia)* (Vol. 3, pp. 305–314). Hobart, Australia: MERGA.

Glenberg, A. M., Jaworski, B., Rischall, M., & Levin, J. R. (2007). What brains are for: Action, meaning, and reading comprehension. In D. S. McNamara (Ed.), *Reading comprehension strategies: Theories, interventions, and technologies* (pp. 221–240). New York: Lawrence Erlbaum Associates.

Greenwood, C. R., Delquadri, J. C., & Hall, R. V. (1989). Longitudinal effects of classwide peer tutoring. *Journal of Educational Psychology, 81,* 371–383.

Hall, G. E., & Hord, S. M. (2001). *Implementing change: Patterns, principles, and potholes.* Boston: Allyn and Bacon.

Hasselbring, T. S., Goin, L. I., & Bransford, J. (1988). Developing math automaticity in learning handicapped children: The role of computerized drill and practice. *Focus on Exceptional Children, 20*(6), 1–7.

Henry, V. J., & Brown, R. S. (2008). First-grade basic facts: An investigation into teaching and learning of an accelerated, high-demand memorization standard. *Journal for Research in Mathematics Education, 39,* 153–183.

Hiebert, J. C. (1999). Relationships between research and the NCTM standards. *Journal for Research in Mathematics Education, 30,* 3–19.

Hiebert, J. C., & Grouws, D. A. (2007). The effects of classroom mathematics teaching on students' learning. In F. K. Lester, Jr. (Ed.), *Second handbook of research on mathematics teaching and learning* (Vol. 1, pp. 371–404). New York: Information Age Publishing.

Hiebert, J. C., & Wearne, D. (1993). Instructional tasks, classroom discourse, and students' learning in second-grade classrooms. *American Educational Research Journal, 30,* 393–425.

Hiebert, J. C., & Wearne, D. (1996). Instruction, understanding, and skill in multidigit addition and subtraction. *Cognition and Instruction, 14,* 251–283.

Hill, H. C., Rowan, B., & Ball, D. L. (2005). Effects of teachers' mathematical knowledge for teaching on student achievement. *American Educational Research Journal, 42,* 371–406.

Holloway, S. C. (1988). Concepts of ability and effort in Japan and the United States. *Review of Educational Research, 58,* 327–345.

Hord, S., Rutherford, W., Huling-Austin, L., & Hall, G. (1987). *Taking charge of change.* Alexandria, VA: Association for Supervision and Curriculum Development.

Howard, J. R., Watson, J. A., & Allen, J. (1993). Cognitive style and the selection of Logo problem-solving strategies by young black children. *Journal of Educational Computing Research, 9,* 339–354.

Johnson, D. W., & Johnson, R. T. (2009). An educational psychology success story: Social interdependence theory and cooperative learning. *Educational Researcher, 38*(5), 365–379.

Johnson, V. M. (2000). *An investigation of the effects of instructional strategies on conceptual understanding of young children in mathematics.* Paper presented at the American Educational Research Association, New Orleans, LA.

Johnson-Gentile, K., Clements, D. H., & Battista, M. T. (1994). The effects of computer and noncomputer environments on students' conceptualizations of geometric motions. *Journal of Educational Computing Research, 11,* 121–140.

Jones, G. A., Langrall, C. W., Thorton, C. A., Mooney, E. S., Wares, A., Jones, M. R., . . . Nisbet, S. (2001). Using students' statistical thinking to inform instruction. *Journal of Mathematical Behavior, 20,* 109–144.

Jordan, N. C., & Montani, T. O. (1997). Cognitive arithmetic and problem solving: A comparison of children with specific and general mathematics difficulties. *Journal of Learning Disabilities, 30,* 624–634.

Kamii, C., & Dominick, A. (1997). To teach or not to teach algorithms. *Journal of Mathematical Behavior, 16,* 51–61.

Kamii, C., & Dominick, A. (1998). The harmful effects of algorithms in grades 1–4. In L. J. Morrow & M. J. Kenney (Eds.), *The teaching and learning of algorithms in school mathematics* (pp. 130–140). Reston, VA: National Council of Teachers of Mathematics.

Kennedy, M. (1998). *Form and substance of inservice teacher education* (Research Monograph No. 13). Madison, WI: National Institute for Science Education, University of Wisconsin-Madison.

Kieran, C. (1986). Logo and the notion of angle among fourth and sixth grade children. In C. Hoyles & L. Burton (Eds.), *Proceedings of the 10th annual meeting of the International Group for Psychology in Mathematics Education* (pp. 99–104). London: City University.

Kieran, C., & Hillel, J. (1990). "It's tough when you have to make the triangles angles": Insights from a computer-based geometry environment. *Journal of Mathematical Behavior, 9,* 99–127.

Kilpatrick, J., Swafford, J., & Findell, B. (2001). *Adding it up: Helping children learn mathematics.* Washington, DC: National Academy Press.

Kraus, W. H. (1981). Using a computer game to reinforce skills in addition basic facts in second grade. *Journal for Research in Mathematics Education, 12,* 152–155.

Kull, J. A. (1986). Learning and Logo. In P. F. Campbell & G. G. Fein (Eds.), *Young children and microcomputers* (pp. 103–130). Englewood Cliffs, NJ: Prentice-Hall.

Kutscher, B., Linchevski, L., & Eisenman, T. (2002). From the lotto game to subtracting two-digit numbers in first-graders. In A. D. Cockburn & E. Nardi (Eds.), *Proceedings of the 26th conference of the International Group for Psychology in Mathematics Education* (Vol. 3, pp. 249–256).

Lavin, R. J., & Sanders, J. E. (1983). *Longitudinal evaluation of the C/A/I Computer Assisted Instruction Title 1 Project: 1979–82:* Chelmsford, MA: Merrimack Education Center.

Lerner, J. (1997). *Learning disabilities.* Boston: Houghton Mifflin Company.

Mandler, G. (1984). *Mind and body: Psychology of emotion and stress.* New York: Norton.

Martin, T., Lukong, A., & Reaves, R. (2007). The role of manipulatives in arithmetic and geometry tasks. *Journal of Education and Human Development, 1*(1).

Mayer, R. E. (1989). Models for understanding. *Review of Educational Research, 59,* 43–64.

Mazzocco, M. M. M., & Myers, G. F. (2003). Complexities in identifying and defining mathematics learning disability in the primary school-age years. *Annals of Dyslexia, 53,* 218–253.

McClain, K., Cobb, P., Gravemeijer, K. P. E., & Estes, B. (1999). Developing mathematical reasoning within the context of measurement. In L. V. Stiff & F. R. Curcio (Eds.), *Developing mathematical reasoning in grades K–12* (pp. 93–106). Reston, VA: National Council of Teachers of Mathematics.

McLeod, D. B., & Adams, V. M. (Eds.). (1989). *Affect and mathematical problem solving.* New York: Springer-Verlag.

Middleton, J. A., & Spanias, P. (1999). Motivation for achievement in mathematics: Findings, generalizations, and criticisms of the research. *Journal for Research in Mathematics Education, 30,* 65–88.

Morgenlander, M. (2005). *Preschoolers' understanding of mathematics presented on Sesame Street.* Paper presented at the American Educational Research Association, New Orleans, LA.

Moyer, P. S. (2000). Are we having fun yet? Using manipulatives to teach "real math." *Educational Studies in Mathematics, 47,* 175–197.

Murata, A. (2004). Paths to learning ten-structured understanding of teen sums: Addition solution methods of Japanese grade 1 students. *Cognition and Instruction, 22,* 185–218.

Murata, A., & Fuson, K. C. (2006). Teaching as assisting individual constructive paths within an interdependent class learning zone: Japanese first graders learning to add using 10. *Journal for Research in Mathematics Education, 37,* 421–456.

Nastasi, B. K., & Clements, D. H. (1991). Research on cooperative learning: Implications for practice. *School Psychology Review, 20,* 110–131.

National Mathematics Advisory Panel. (2008). *Foundations for success: The final report of the National Mathematics Advisory Panel.* Washington DC: U.S. Department of Education, Office of Planning, Evaluation and Policy Development.

National Research Council. (2009). *Mathematics in early childhood: Learning paths toward excellence and equity.* Washington, DC: National Academy Press.

NCTM. (2006). *Curriculum focal points for prekindergarten through grade 8 mathematics: A quest for coherence.* Reston, VA: National Council of Teachers of Mathematics.

Nettles, S. M. (1993). Coaching in community settings. *Equity and Choice, 9*(2), 35–37.

Niemiec, R. P., & Walberg, H. J. (1985). Computers and achievement in the elementary schools. *Journal of Educational Computing Research, 1*(4), 435–440.

Olive, J., Lankenau, C. A., & Scally, S. P. (1986). *Teaching and understanding geometric relationships through Logo: Phase II. Interim Report: The Atlanta–Emory Logo Project.* Altanta, GA: Emory University.

Olson, J. K. (1988, August). *Microcomputers make manipulatives meaningful.* Paper presented at the International Congress of Mathematics Education, Budapest, Hungary.

Ostad, S. A. (1998). Subtraction strategies in developmental perspective: A comparison of mathematically normal and mathematically disabled children. In A. Olivier & K. Newstead (Eds.), *Proceedings of the 22nd conference for the International Group for Psychology in Mathematics Education* (Vol. 3, pp. 311–318). Stellenbosch, South Africa: University of Stellenbosch.

Papert, S. (1980). *Mindstorms: Children, computers, and powerful ideas.* New York: Basic Books.

Perlmutter, J., Bloom, L., Rose, T., & Rogers, A. (1997). Who uses math? Primary children's perceptions of the uses of mathematics. *Journal of Research in Childhood Education, 12*(1), 58–70.

Pesek, D. D., & Kirshner, D. (2000). Interference of instrumental instruction in subsequent relational learning. *Journal for Research in Mathematics Education, 31,* 524–540.

Peterson, P. L., Carpenter, T. P., & Fennema, E. H. (1989). Teachers' knowledge of students' knowledge in mathematics problem solving: Correlational and case analyses. *Journal of Educational Psychology, 81,* 558–569.

Philipp, R. A., Ambrose, R., Lamb, L. L. C., Sowder, J. T., Schappelle, B. P., Sowder, L., . . . Chauvot, J. (2007). Effects of early field experiences on the mathematical content knowledge and beliefs of prospective elementary school teachers: An experimental study. *Journal for Research in Mathematics Education, 38,* 438–476.

Primavera, J., Wiederlight, P. P., & DiGiacomo, T. M. (2001, August). *Technology access for low-income preschoolers: Bridging the digital divide.* Paper presented at the American Psychological Association, San Francisco.

Ragosta, M., Holland, P., & Jamison, D. T. (1981). *Computer-assisted instruction and compensatory education: The ETS/LAUSD study.* Princeton, NJ: Educational Testing Service.

Resnick, L. B. (1992). From protoquantities to operators: Building mathematical competence on a foundation of everyday knowledge. In G. Leinhardt, R. Putman, & R. A. Hattrup (Eds.), *Analysis of arithmetic for mathematics teaching* (pp. 373–429). Hillsdale, NJ: Lawrence Erlbaum Associates.

Rittle-Johnson, B., & Alibali, M. W. (1999). Conceptual and procedural knowledge of mathematics: Does one lead to the other? *Journal of Educational Psychology, 91,* 175–189.

Sales, C. (1994). *A constructivist instructional project on developing geometric problem solving abilities using pattern blocks and tangrams with young children.* Unpublished master's thesis, University of Northern Iowa, Cedar Falls, IA.

Sarama, J. (1995). *Redesigning Logo: The turtle metaphor in mathematics education.* Unpublished doctoral dissertation, State University of New York at Buffalo.

Sarama, J. (2002). Listening to teachers: Planning for professional development. *Teaching Children Mathematics, 9,* 36–39.

Sarama, J., & Clements, D. H. (2009a). *Early childhood mathematics education research: Learning trajectories for young children.* New York: Routledge.

Sarama, J., & Clements, D. H. (2009b, April). *Scaling up successful interventions: Multidisciplinary perspectives.* Paper presented at the American Educational Research Association, San Diego, CA.

Sarama, J., Clements, D. H., Starkey, P., Klein, A., & Wakeley, A. (2008). Scaling up the implementation of a pre-kindergarten mathematics curriculum: Teaching for understanding with trajectories and technologies. *Journal of Research on Educational Effectiveness, 1,* 89–119.

Sarama, J., Clements, D. H., & Vukelic, E. B. (1996). The role of a computer manipulative in fostering specific psychological/mathematical processes. In E. Jakubowski, D. Watkins, & H. Biske (Eds.), *Proceedings of the 18th annual meeting of the North America Chapter of the International Group for Psychology in Mathematics Education* (Vol. 2, pp. 567–572). Columbus, OH: ERIC Clearinghouse for Science, Mathematics, and Environmental Education.

Sarama, J., & DiBiase, A.-M. (2004). The professional development challenge in preschool mathematics. In D. H. Clements, J. Sarama, & A.-M. DiBiase (Eds.), *Engaging young children in mathematics: Standards for early childhood mathematics education* (pp. 415–446). Mahwah, NJ: Lawrence Erlbaum Associates.

Schoen, H. L., Cebulla, K. J., Finn, K. F., & Fi, C. (2003). Teacher variables that relate to student achievement when using a standards-based curriculum. *Journal for Research in Mathematics Education, 34*(3), 228–259.

Shepard, L. A. (2005). Assessment. In L. Darling-Hammond & J. Bransford (Eds.), *Preparing teachers for a changing world* (pp. 275–326). San Francisco: Jossey-Bass.

Shulman, L. S. (1986). Those who understand: Knowledge growth in teaching. *Educational Researcher, 15*(2), 4–14.

Sinclair, H. (1988). Forward. In L. P. Steffe & P. Cobb (Eds.), *Construction of arithmetical meanings and strategies* (pp. v–vi). New York: Springer-Verlag.

Skemp, R. (1976). Relational understanding and instrumental understanding. *Mathematics Teaching, 77,* 20–26.

Sophian, C. (2004). A prospective developmental perspective on early mathematics instruction. In D. H. Clements, J. Sarama, & A.-M. DiBiase (Eds.), *Engaging young children in mathematics: Standards for early childhood mathematics education* (pp. 253–266). Mahwah, NJ: Lawrence Erlbaum Associates.

Sowell, E. J. (1989). Effects of manipulative materials in mathematics instruction. *Journal for Research in Mathematics Education, 20,* 498–505.

Steffe, L. P. (2004). *PSSM* from a constructivist perspective. In D. H. Clements, J. Sarama, & A.-M. DiBiase (Eds.), *Engaging young children in mathematics: Standards for early childhood mathematics education* (pp. 221–251). Mahwah, NJ: Lawrence Erlbaum Associates.

Stone, T. T., III. (1996). The academic impact of classroom computer usage upon middle-class primary grade level elementary school children. *Dissertation Abstracts International, 57*(6), 2450.

Suydam, M. N. (1986). Manipulative materials and achievement. *Arithmetic Teacher, 33*(6), 10, 32.

Swanson, H. L., & Hoskyn, M. (1998). Experimental intervention research on students with learning disabilities: A meta-analysis of treatment outcomes. *Review of Educational Research, 68*(3), 277–321.

Thomas, G., & Tagg, A. (2004). *An evaluation of the Early Numeracy Project 2003.* Wellington, Australia: Ministry of Education.

Thomson, S., Rowe, K., Underwood, C., & Peck, R. (2005). *Numeracy in the early years: Project Good Start.* Camberwell, Victoria: Australian Council for Educational Research.

Tournaki, N. (2003). The differential effects of teaching addition through strategy instruction versus drill and practice to students with and without learning disabilities. *Journal of Learning Disabilities, 36*(5), 449–458.

Verschaffel, L., Greer, B., & De Corte, E. (2007). Whole number concepts and operations. In F. K. Lester, Jr. (Ed.), *Second handbook of research on mathematics teaching and learning* (Vol. 1, pp. 557–628). New York: Information Age Publishing.

Wadlington, E., & Burns, J. M. (1993). Instructional practices within preschool/kindergarten gifted programs. *Journal for the Education of the Gifted, 17*(1), 41–52.

Watson, J. A., Lange, G., & Brinkley, V. M. (1992). Logo mastery and spatial problem-solving by young children: Effects of Logo language training, route-strategy training, and learning styles on immediate learning and transfer. *Journal of Educational Computing Research, 8,* 521–540.

Weiner, B. (1986). *An attributional theory of motivation and emotion.* New York: Springer-Verlag.

Wilkinson, L. A., Martino, A., & Camilli, G. (1994). Groups that work: Social factors in elementary students mathematics problem solving. In J. E. H. Van Luit (Ed.), *Research on learning and instruction of mathematics in kindergarten and primary school* (pp. 75–105). Doetinchem, The Netherlands: Graviant.

Wright, R. J., Martland, J., Stafford, A. K., & Stanger, G. (2002). *Teaching number: Advancing children's skills and strategies.* London: Paul Chapman Publications/Sage.

Wright, R. J., Stanger, G., Stafford, A. K., & Martland, J. (2006). *Teaching number in the classroom with 4–8 year olds.* London: Paul Chapman Publications/Sage.

Young-Loveridge, J. M. (2004). *Patterns of performance and progress on the Numeracy Projects 2001–2003: Further analysis of the Numeracy Project data.* Wellington, Australia: Ministry of Education.

Zumeta, R. O. (2009). Remediating number combination and word problem deficits among students with mathematics difficulties: A randomized control trial. *Journal of Educational Psychology, 101,* 561–576. (PMC2768320 NIH136631; PMID 19865600)

CHAPTER 8

COMMENTS ON LEARNING AND TEACHING EARLY AND ELEMENTARY MATHEMATICS

Arthur J. Baroody, David J. Purpura, and Erin E. Reid
University of Illinois at Urbana-Champaign

Clements and Sarama's informative review centers on three key questions for improving mathematics education: How do students learn mathematics? What pedagogical strategies are supported by research? What approaches to professional development are supported by research? Their review of the first and third issues is brief. Similarly, our comments will focus on the second issue.

HOW DO STUDENTS LEARN MATHEMATICS?

This section fittingly focused on the importance of learning trajectories as a guide to understanding children's mathematical learning. Such guides are invaluable for formative assessment and instructional planning by helping to answer such questions as, What prior knowledge does a student need to know to achieve a particular goal? What should a child be taught next? A learning trajectory is particularly important when students run into difficulty and can

Instructional Strategies for Improving Students' Learning, pages 163–175

help teachers think backwards to remedy the source(s) of a learning problem. For example, if a child cannot identify the larger of two number neighbors (e.g., "Which is more 8 or 7?"), a key issue is whether the child is ready for instruction in this skill or needs to master more basic prerequisites. That is, does the child understand the counting-based rule for comparing numbers and accurately apply it to small numbers (e.g., "4" is more than "3" because "4" comes after "3" when we count)? Does the child know the counting sequence well enough to readily determine the number that comes after another (e.g., after 7 comes 8)? Does the child even understand the comparative term "more" or the meaning of number words such as "three" and "four?"

Ideally, standards and learning trajectories would explicitly highlight "big ideas" and how they can help students make sense of mathematics (Baroody, Cibulskis, Lai, & Li, 2004; Baroody, Feil, & Johnson, 2007). As big ideas are overarching concepts that interconnect various concepts and procedures within a domain and across domains, they can help educators and students alike recognize that mathematical knowledge is not merely a collection of unrelated facts, definitions, and procedures, but that it has structure and coherence. Comprehension of a big idea can enable students to learn new concepts and procedures meaningfully and more readily. For example, the really big idea of equally dividing up a whole ("equal partitioning") is a basis for such diverse concepts as division, fractions, measurement (the concept of unit), and the unit principle of natural numbers (all such numbers can be built up from the unit; e.g., $5 = 1 + 1 + 1 + 1 + 1$). Its informal analogy of fair sharing provides a model for comprehending or constructing a concept of division or fractions. For instance, $12 \div 3$ can be informally viewed as fairly sharing 12 items among three people. The fraction 2/3 can be viewed as the size of each person's share if two cookies are shared fairly among three people: two of three *equal* parts of a cookie.

The *Curriculum Focal Points, Common Core State Standards*, and learning trajectories cited by Sarama and Clements (2009) all mention understanding division through various representations, including equal-sized groups, fractions as representing parts of a whole, linear measurement in terms of "underlying concepts such as partitioning (the mental activity of slicing the length of an object into equal-sized units), and area measurement as "finding the total number of same-sized units" ... that cover the shape without gaps or overlaps" (NCTM, 2006, pp. 15, 15, 14, 16, respectively). Not underscored, though, is (a) that these concepts/domains have a common structure (equal partitioning) and (b) why and how this commonality applies to a concept. Division of $12 \div 3$ can be thought of as reverse of an "equal-groups" meaning of multiplication. For example, if $3 \times 4 = 12$ represents: three groups of four, such as three people have four items per person for a total of 12 items, then $12 \div 3$ represents undoing the equal grouping process. Specifically, if the total of 12 items is given back to the three people evenly, the result is each person's share is four again). In order to quantify a part of a whole in a manner that can be easily communicated and understood, fractions involve specifying the number of parts of interest in the special case where a whole is divided into equal-size parts (shared equally), not any partitioning of a whole. Measurement entails dividing a continuous (and otherwise uncountable) quantity into equal size pieces (units) that can then be counted. A child who comprehends this rationale would understand why you iteratively apply a chosen unit over an entire quantity and why you cannot have gaps or overlaps when determining length or area, instead of merely memorizing this procedure and constraint by rote.

Ideally, a review of how students learn mathematics would also include at least a brief mention of how children construct meaningful knowledge by making connections. Connections can be formed via assimilation (connecting new information to existing knowledge) or integration (connecting two previously unrelated ideas). In his 1892 *Talk to Teachers*, William James (1958) elegantly summarized the importance of the former—of building on previous knowledge:

> when we wish to fix a new thing in...a pupil's mind, our conscious effort should not be so much to *impress* and *retain* it as to *connect* it with something already there...if we attend clearly to the connection, the connected thing will certainly be likely to remain within recall. (emphasis added; pp. 101–102)

WHAT PEDAGOGICAL STRATEGIES ARE SUPPORTED BY RESEARCH?

We strongly agree with most of the conclusions in this section. Below we focus on differences or concerns.

False Dichotomies?

We agree that either/or debates, such as whether student-centered or teacher-directed instruction is better, are typically not productive. However, genuine philosophical differences about teaching and learning cannot be overlooked, and the meaningful teaching/memorization versus teaching/ memorizing by rote dichotomy does make sense (e.g., Hatano, 2003; Katona, 1967; Wertheimer, 1959).

Student-Centered or Teacher-Directed Instruction. Citing the results of the Fuson and Briars (1990) study, Clements and Sarama concluded that the key is attending explicitly to concepts, not the particular approach. Although this evidence is suggestive, it is far from clear and convincing.[1] Even so, their conclusion appears to be borne out by a recent meta-analysis (Alfieri, Brooks, Aldrich, & Tenenbaum, 2010) that indicated explicit instruction resulted in more favorable outcomes than unassisted discovery learning, but that assisted discovery learning was more effective than the two other forms of instruction (unassisted discovery and explicit instruction). In other words, "unassisted discovery does not benefit learners, whereas feedback, worked examples, scaffolding, and elicited explanations do" (p. 1).

However, we need to guard against overly general conclusions about teaching approaches. As Table 8.1 indicates, the amount of teacher or child involvement is better understood as a continuum; there is not a single middle-ground position; and there are significant differences in the middle-ground positions. These differences should not be camouflaged because they raise important questions that need to be researched. For example, proponents of conceptual and investigative approaches (the middle-ground views in Table 8.1) both recommend carefully connecting algorithms to manipulative models. However, they differ appreciably about how this should be done. In a conceptual approach, the teacher models the manipulative-based procedure and points out how the concrete model parallels each step of its analogous written algorithm. This is the approach used by Fuson and Briars (1990; cited by by Clements and Sarama on page 119) and used in many U.S. and Asian curricula. However, a potential problem is some, many, or even most students will not comprehend the direct instruction and modeling and therefore may learn the concrete procedure by rote, only in part, or not at all. In contrast, in the investigative approach, students are presented problems, encouraged to develop their own manipulative-based procedures, and then prompted to devise written procedures that parallel their concrete strategies.

Some evidence suggests that the effectiveness of an approach, *including* unassisted discovery learning (the problem-solving approach in Table 8.1) may vary depending on content and student developmental level. For example, explicit instruction and modeling appear to be effective in promoting the learning of relatively basic addition counting strategies that more or less directly model children's informal view of addition but are ineffective in doing so with abstract strategies that do not. For instance, such an approach can quickly lead 5- to 7-year-olds to appreciate and use concrete counting-all or concrete counting-on (e.g., Baroody, 1987; Fuson & Secada, 1986) but not abstract counting-on (Baroody, 1984; Baroody, Tiillikainen, & Tai, 2006). In contrast, third graders (albeit with mathematical learning difficulties) appeared to benefit from explicit instruction and modeling of abstract counting-on (Fuchs et al., 2009).

Another study found that, when compared to business as usual, both structured and unstructured discovery learning improved at-risk first graders' fluency and transfer with add-one combinations at a statistically significant level (Baroody, Eiland, Pauli, Bajwa, & Baroody, 2010; Baroody, Purpura, & Eiland,

TABLE 8.1 Different Views of the Skills and Concepts Debate and Four Different Approaches to Instruction

Skills only ↓	Skills first	Concepts with Skills	Concepts first	Concepts only ↑
Traditional authoritarian "skills approach"	Semi-direct "conceptual approach"	Semi-indirect "investigative approach"	Laissez-faire "problem-solving approach"	
Dualistic philosophy: One correct procedure/answer	Pluralistic philosophy: Alternatives tolerated but focus is on one best procedure/answer	Instrumentalism: Choice of perhaps several equally effective procedures/sensible answers	Extreme relativism: All procedures/answers equally valid	
Completely teacher directed: Teacher = authoritative source of all knowledge	Somewhat teacher directed: Teacher = strong guide	Somewhat child-centered: Teacher = gentle "guide on the side"	Completely child-centered: Teacher → little or no information/feedback	
Aim: Mastery of basic skills (facts, definitions, procedures, rules, and formulas) by rote (content oriented)	Aim: Mastery of basic skills with understanding and (some) mathematical thinking (content oriented; some process)	Aim: Mastery of basic skills with understanding and mathematical thinking (content and process oriented)	Aim: Foster mathematical thinking (problem solving, reasoning, conjecturing, etc.) and understanding (process oriented)	
Direct instruction (lecture & demonstrations) and drill (e.g., worksheets)	Teacher demonstration concrete models and explicitly connects to written algorithms; guided discovery	Variety of worthwhile (purposeful, meaningful, and inquiry-based) tasks (e.g., math games, projects; challenging problems, science experiments); children invent own concrete models and symbolic procedures; guided discovery	Unguided discovery learning; rich (complicated, multitopic) projects	

under review). The aim of the structured condition was to relate adding-up to number-after relations in the counting sequence so that children could construct the *number-after rule*: "the sum of $n + 1$ is the number after n in the counting sequence." This was accomplished by sequencing practice items so that adding-one items followed related number-after questions and juxtaposing adding-one equations with number-after results (e.g., a block with $7 + 1 \rightarrow 8$ was stacked on top of a block with number-after $7 \rightarrow 8$, where the $\rightarrow$ meant "is"). The unstructured discovery learning had no such scaffolding and involved haphazard practice of number-after relations and adding-one items. Both conditions had contrasting items such as adding zero or a number larger than 1, and neither involved explicitly pointing out the relation between adding-one and number-after. The two conditions did not differ statistically in effectiveness. Children in the unstructured condition apparently discovered the relatively straightforward number-after rule for adding one *if* they were developmentally ready for it (e.g., know number-after relations).

In brief, although it makes sense to reject the extreme positions that instruction should *always* be either completely student or teacher centered, what works best and when and how much to use each is not yet clear. That is, whether a conceptual, investigative, or problem-solving approach (or their blends) might "work" better—i.e., promote more efficient and effective meaningful learning and transfer—with what content and student (e.g., developmental level) needs to be empirically tested.

Meaningful Teaching or "Drill-and-Kill." Although "drill-and-kill" is a divisive label, skills-only instruction accompanied by "repeated experiencing" is embodied in real curricula such as the Kumon Math Program (see http://www.Kumon.com) and Saxon Math published by Houghton, Mifflin, Harcourt (see http://saxonpublishers.hmhco.com) and teaching practices. For example, the memorization of basic combinations by rote—what Brownell (1935) called the "drill" approach—is still all too common practice. Moreover, there is ample evidence—as Clements and Sarama note—to suggest that meaningful instruction is preferable to meaningless instruction and practice. For example, citing Henry and Brown's (2008) research, they concluded, "We can see that memorization without understanding...is a bad idea" (p. 116). On page 120, they observed, "Teaching for relational understanding gives 'teachers two for the price of one'" (conceptual understanding and skill fluency). In effect, Clements and Sarama repeatedly advocate (correctly so) the meaningful teaching/practice position over meaningless instruction/drill view.

Clear Guidelines for Using Practice?

According to Clements and Sarama, clear guidelines for using practice are that (a) "substantial practice is required for learning certain knowledge

and skills" (p. 115), (b) distributed practice is better than massed practiced, and (c) conceptual foundations and meaningful strategies should
be developed first. We agree wholeheartedly with the third guideline but
have three reservations about the first two. One is that the evidence for the
first two conclusions is based largely on research that involved memorizing
information by rote. Second, left unclear is what aspects of knowledge and
skill require repeated experiencing. A third reservation is that the nature
of the practice—as perceived by students (purposeful or engaging practice
versus pointless and tedious practice)—may be at least as important as practice frequency or regularity.

Regarding our first two reservations, the National Mathematics Advisory
Panel (NMAP, 2008) identified memorizing the basic number facts and solving algebraic equations as needing extensive practice.[2] Yet even these com-
monsense suggestions are debatable. As James (1958) implied, if educators
build on what students know, impressing knowledge on their memories via
repeated experiencing is much less necessary. For example, once children
construct the number-after rule for adding one, repeated practice is unnecessary for their mastery, because it permits them to efficiently deduce the
sum of any $n + 1$ combination for which they know the counting sequence,
including those with a multidigit addend not previously practiced, such as
$97 + 1$, $197 + 1$, or $1,097 + 1$ (Baroody et al., 2010; Eiland & Baroody, 2010).
James' advice applies to cases involving larger numbers and other operations. For instance, the first author learned $6 \times 8 = 48$ by realizing the U.S.
flag at the time had six rows of eight stars each and knowing there were 48
states. Similarly, the *meaningful* learning/memorization of algebraic procedures can be achieved without extensive practice by building on one's
understanding of equivalence and arithmetic (see Baroody & Coslick, 1998,
for specific details and examples). In short, meaningful memorization can
greatly reduce the amount of practice required for learning.

Regarding our third reservation, Piaget and Inhelder (1969) observed that
cognition and affect ("energetics") are "inseparable and complementary"
(p. 21). Psychologists have long known that a highly salient experience need
happen but once to be remembered. In both the short and long runs, salient and "eventful practice" may be more efficient and effective than merely
massed, distributed, or even meaningful practice. What needs to be studied
further (and emphasized more in teacher training) is how teachers can make
instruction and practice of various aspects of content salient or eventful for
children (i.e., purposeful, engaging, and highly motivating for them). For example, Carpenter, Fennema, Peterson, Chiang, and Loef (1989) found that
purposeful practice with word problems promoted significantly greater fluency with basic combinations than drill. In order to help his younger daugh-
ter, Arianne, achieve fluency with basic multiplication combinations, the first
author had the family create a baseball simulation in which the product of

two dice indicated the outcome for a batter. For example, the product 36 indicated a homerun. Arianne very quickly recognized that 6×6 is 36.

In brief, the recommendations for substantial and distributed practice seem clearly appropriate *if* the goal is memorizing content by rote, but less so if the goal is its meaningful memorization. However, there is relatively little in the preschool and elementary mathematics curricula that requires memorization by rote (e.g., the counting sequence to "12"). Nearly all facts, definitions, procedures, and formulas can be learned or discovered in a meaningful fashion (Baroody & Coslick, 1998). This is not to say that practice is unimportant to meaningful memorization. Meaningful and purposeful practice computing sums via counting, for instance, can provide opportunities for discovering patterns or relations that may serve as the basis for reasoning strategies, especially if children are encouraged to look for and share regularities. In turn, meaningful and purposeful practice of reasoning strategies such as the number-after rule for adding-one may promote their automatic application.

Beyond Dichotomies?

Clearly, "different teaching methods are effective for different learning goals" (p. 118). However, we have two concerns with this conclusion.

One is that it merely puts off, rather than settles, the debate about whether to focus on skills, concepts, or (probably better yet) some combination of both, because an implicit premise is that all learning goals are equally worthwhile. When would it be worthwhile to focus on skills only (or even mainly on skills) and use rapid-paced instruction, including modeling, and substantial amounts of error-free practice (Hiebert & Grouws, 2007)? As the previous section and various reviews (e.g., Kilpatrick, Swafford, & Findell, 2001; Clements & Sarama, this volume) suggest, mathematics instruction should focus on promoting both skills and understanding in an intertwined manner. From a research perspective, there needs to be a greater emphasis on work that identifies what teaching method works best for which concepts and for which children (e.g., for what developmental level).

A second concern is that the recommendation seems to suggest that an instructional strategy be based on a single external factor (the goals of instruction) instead of a variety of both external *and* internal factors. Dewey (1963) concluded that to promote educative experiences, educators must ensure that external factors mesh with *internal* (psychological) *factors*. A key factor that can affect the ease of learning and hence the instructional strategy used is the *salience* of a pattern, relation, strategy, or other learning goal. Salience, in turn, depends on the relative complexity of a goal (an external factor) and a child's existing knowledge and interest or motivation in the given instructional activity (internal factors). In addition to the cases of adding-one and counting-on already discussed, consider that young children can—without explicit instruction—readily discover the relatively apparent commutativity principle but not the relatively abstruse addition-subtraction complement principle (e.g., $5 - 3 = ?$ can be thought of as $? + 3 = 5$; Baroody, Ginsburg, & Waxman, 1983).

Students with Special Needs

We agree wholeheartedly with Clement and Sarama's conclusion that "until more is known, students should be labeled as 'MLD' only with great caution and after good instruction has been provided" (p. 121). All too many children identified as MLD simply lack the opportunity to learn. Note, though, that benefitting from good instruction does not exclude the possibility that a child has a genuine MLD, because such instruction can help all children reach their potential.

Of particular concern is the often-repeated hypothesis that difficulty retrieving basic combinations so characteristic of children with MLD is due to internal deficits such as "limited working memory" or "speed of cognitive processing." There seems to be a tendency to view such cognitive processes as having a fixed capacity for a child. An alternative possibility is that they have a fluid capacity and vary depending on the nature of the task (e.g., working memory may accommodate more meaningful knowledge than isolated and meaningless information). Another alternative possibility is that such cognitive deficits may be the by-product, rather than the cause, of a learning difficulty, and that many, or perhaps most, impairments of fluency with the basic combinations are due to inadequate number sense (Baroody, Bajwa, & Eiland, 2009). An inadequate number sense, in turn, can be due to a lack of prerequisite informal knowledge and a formal learning environment that focuses on memorization by rote rather than the search for and use of patterns and relations.

Clements and Sarama conclude that the evidence "indicates the benefit of teaching a strategy, not just providing more practice, especially for LD students" (p. 123). As with typically developing children, the teaching approach or method may depend on external factors such as the specific content and internal factors such as a child's developmental readiness. For example, consistent with Clement and Sarama's point, Baroody (1996) found that direct instruction and modeling was effective in helping children with mental retardation learn a concrete counting-all procedure. Inconsistent with their point, addition practice with no further strategy instruction resulted in such children inventing more advanced concrete strategies—and in a few cases even an abstract strategy.

WHAT APPROACHES TO PROFESSIONAL DEVELOPMENT ARE SUPPORTED BY RESEARCH?

Simply stated by Clements and Sarama, "teachers make a difference." Regardless of the efforts made to identify developmental trajectories and appropriate instructional strategies, without identifying how best to "teach the teachers" to use this information, these efforts are for naught. Of the three major questions posed by Clements and Sarama, this is the domain they indicate is least researched. Too often, professional development efforts are too brief and not focused on what teachers want or need to learn. This concern stems from both a lack of understanding how to implement an effective training session as well as the conceptual basis for holding professional development sessions.

Although there is much we do not know regarding professional development (or know does not work), Clements and Sarama indicate several principles of professional development that we do know. These principles also follow closely along with the general learning principles embodied throughout the chapter on teaching children mathematics. First, focusing on teachers' behaviors—or the *procedural* aspects of teaching—results in fewer positive effects on students than focusing on *conceptual* information such as how the students learn. Second, preservice teachers benefit the most from instruction in pedagogy. Third, the instruction must be meaningful to the teachers. It should be focused on information that is applied to their professional experiences, engaging, and the instruction should be ongoing (i.e., supported with additional coaching after the initial sessions). Overall, instruction during professional development must be meaningful to the teachers, connected to what they know and need to know, and engaging—much the same as they are being trained in how to instruct their students.

CONCLUSION

Although reviews such as Clement and Sarama's can provide useful instructional guidelines, much about mathematical teaching and learning early and elementary mathematics remains to be systematically and carefully examined. A systematic and empirically defined learning trajectory of mathematical concepts must be constructed through identifying *causal connections* in mathematics development. With such a learning trajectory, targeted assessment strategies can be developed to identify children's acquired level of number sense, and the resulting information can direct appropriate and individualized (but still empirically supported) instruction. Finally, there is still a great need for work to be done to identify how best to "teach the teachers" in applying these strategies to their everyday academic instruction.

ACKNOWLEDGMENT

Preparation of this work was supported by a grant #R305A080479 ("Fostering Fluency with Basic Addition and Subtraction Facts") from the Institute of Education Science, U.S. Department of Education and grant # R01-HD051538-01 ("Computer-guided Comprehensive Mathematics Assessment for Young Children") from the National Institutes of Health. The opinions expressed are solely those of the authors and do not necessarily reflect the position, policy, or endorsement of the Institute of Education Science (Department of Education) or the National Institutes of Health.

NOTES

1. The Fuson and Briars study did not have a control group, and thus, history, maturation, testing effects, and other confounds cannot be discounted. Fidelity was not measured, and so it is not entirely clear what participating teachers did. Adding to the uncertainty, teachers did not finish all of the lessons, could pick and choose which ones to introduce, and did so at different times of the year.
2. According to the NMAP (2008), "students should be provided opportunities for extensive practice in use of newly learned strategies and skills (p. xxiii); "sufficient and appropriate practice [is necessary] to develop automatic recall of addition and related subtraction facts, and of multiplication and related subtraction facts" (p. 33), and "many students will need extensive practice at solving algebraic equations" (p. 33). The evidence on the former largely involved older children or young adults, and the evidence for both domains did not necessarily involve meaningful learning.

REFERENCES

Alfieri, L., Brooks, P. J., Aldrich, N. J., & Tenenbaum, H. R. (2010, November 15). Does discovery-based instruction enhance learning? *Journal of Educational Psychology*. Advance online publication. doi: 10.1037/a0021017.

Baroody, A. J. (1984). The case of Felicia: A young child's strategies for reducing memory demands during mental addition. *Cognition and Instruction, 1,* 109–116.

Baroody, A. J. (1987). The development of counting strategies for single-digit addition. *Journal for Research in Mathematics Education, 18,* 141–157.

Baroody, A. J. (1996). Self-invented addition strategies by children classified as mentally handicapped. *American Journal on Mental Retardation, 101,* 72–89.

Baroody, A. J., Bajwa, N. P., & Eiland, M. (2009). Why can't Johnny remember the basic facts? *Developmental Disabilities Research Reviews, 15,* 69–79.

Baroody, A. J., Cibulskis, M., Lai, M.-L., & Li, X. (2004). Comments on the use of learning trajectories in curriculum development and research. *Mathematical Thinking and Learning, 6,* 227–260.

Baroody, A. J., & Coslick, R. T. (1998). *Fostering children's mathematical power: An investigative approach to K–8 mathematics instruction.* Mahwah, NJ: Lawrence Erlbaum Associates.

Baroody, A. J., Eiland, M. D, Pauli, V., Bajwa, N. P., & Baroody, S. C. (2010, March). Fostering at-risk primary-grade children's fluency with basic addition combinations. In C. Chin & R. Ochsendorf (Co-chairs), *Evaluations of interventions in early elementary math.* Symposium conducted at the annual meeting of the Society for Research on Educational Effectiveness, Washington, DC.

Baroody, A. J., Feil, Y., & Johnson, A. R. (2007). An alternative reconceptualization of procedural and conceptual knowledge. *Journal for Research in Mathematics Education, 38,* 115–131.

Baroody, A. J., Ginsburg, H. P., & Waxman, B. (1983). Children's use of mathematical structure. *Journal for Research in Mathematics Education, 14,* 156–168.

Baroody, A. J., Purpura, D. J., & Eiland, M. D. (under review). *Can computer-assisted discovery learning foster first graders' fluency with basic addition combinations?*

Baroody, A. J., Tiilikainen, S. H., & Tai, Y. (2006). The application and development of an addition goal sketch. *Cognition and Instruction, 24,* 123–170.

Brownell, W. A. (1935). Psychological considerations in the learning and the teaching of arithmetic. In W. D. Reeve (Ed.), *The teaching of arithmetic* (10th yearbook, National Council of Teachers of Mathematics, pp. 1–31). New York: Columbia University, Teachers College, Bureau of Publications.

Carpenter, T. P., Fennema, E., Peterson, P. L., Chiang, C. P., & Loef, M. (1989). Using knowledge of children's mathematics thinking in classroom teaching: An experimental study. *American Educational Research Journal, 26,* 499–532.

Dewey, J. (1963). *Experience and education.* New York: Collier.

Eiland, M. D., & Baroody, A. J. (2010, April). Fostering at-risk kindergartners' number sense. In D. P. Bryant (Chair), *Preventing early mathematics difficulties: Findings from kindergarten curriculum and intervention studies to foster number competence.* Symposium at the annual meeting of the American Educational Research Association, Denver, CO.

Fuchs, L., Powell, S. R., Seethaler, P. M., Cirino, P. T., Fletcher, J. M., Fuchs, D., & Hamlett, C. L. (2009). The effects of strategic counting instruction, with and without deliberate practice, on number combination skill among students with mathematics difficulties. *Learning and Individual Differences, 20,* 89–100

Fuson, K. C., & Briars, D. J. (1990). Using a base-ten blocks learning/teaching approach for first- and second-grade place-value and multidigit addition and subtraction. *Journal for Research in Mathematics Education, 21,* 180–206.

Fuson, K. C., & Secada, W. G. (1986). Teaching children to add by counting-on with one-handed finger patterns. *Cognition and Instruction, 3,* 229–260.

Hatano, G. (2003). Forward. In A. J. Baroody & A. Dowker (Eds.), *The development of arithmetic concepts and skills: Constructing adaptive expertise* (pp. xi–xiii). Mahwah, NJ: Erlbaum.

Henry, V., & Brown, R. (2008). First-grade basic facts. *Journal for Research in Mathematics Education, 39,* 153–183.

Hiebert, J. C., & Grouws, D. A. (2007). The effects of classroom mathematics teaching on students' learning. In F. K. Lester, Jr. (Ed.), *Second handbook of research on mathematics teaching and learning* (Vol. 1, pp. 371–404). Charlotte, NC: Information Age.

James, W. (1958). *Talks to teachers on psychology and to students on some of life's ideals.* New York: W. W. Norton & Company. (Original talk presented 1892)

Katona, G. (1967). Organizing and memorizing: Studies in the psychology of learning and teaching. New York: Hafner. (Original work published 1940)

Kilpatrick, J., Swafford, J., & Findell, B. (Eds.). (2001). *Adding it up: Helping children learn mathematics.* Washington, DC: National Academy Press.

National Council of Teachers of Mathematics. (2006). *Curriculum focal points for prekindergarten through grade 8 mathematics.* Reston, VA: Author.

National Mathematics Advisory Panel. (2008). *Foundations for success.* Washington, DC: U.S. Department of Education.

Piaget, J., & Inhelder, B. (1969). *The psychology of the child.* New York: Basic Books.

Sarama, J., & Clements, D. H. (2009). *Early childhood mathematics education research: Learning trajectories for young children.* New York: Routledge.

Wertheimer, M. (1959). *Productive thinking.* New York: Harper & Row. (Original work published 1945)

CHAPTER 9

THE COMMON CORE MATHEMATICS STANDARDS AS SUPPORTS FOR LEARNING AND TEACHING EARLY AND ELEMENTARY MATHEMATICS

Karen C. Fuson
Northwestern University

The Clements and Sarama chapter is an excellent research summary about effective mathematics learning and teaching in preschool and the early elementary grades. This brief commentary will build on that summary to identify some ways in which the new Common Core Mathematics Standards can improve teaching and learning. Because standards do not describe learning activities, they do not describe a learning trajectory in the Clements and Sarama sense, because their term includes learning activities. Therefore, this commentary uses the term learning path to mean the experiential progression of knowledge built by a coherent appropriate program of learning activities.

Instructional Strategies for Improving Students' Learning, pages 177–186
Copyright © 2012 by Information Age Publishing
All rights of reproduction in any form reserved.

As was emphasized in the research summary, and in all recent national reports, understanding and fluency are both crucial foci of teaching. Aspects of both understanding and fluency are mentioned specifically in the standards. Most importantly, the standards are focused and coherent across grades, and so there is time for teachers to concentrate on both understanding and fluency. At each grade level, the standards focus on fewer standards than in most previous state standards, and these standards build on each other across grades. Therefore, teachers can have enough time for grade-level mastery of core topics, and teachers of the next grade can concentrate on the goals for that grade level, as is common in other countries. Reducing the present pattern of the huge waste of time now spent in earlier grade-level reviewing (over 40% by some estimates) and the confusion about exactly which grade-level teacher is responsible for what topics will be a major positive result from the standards.

Reasoning is explicitly mentioned in the standards and such reasoning is supported by visual/conceptual aspects of the standards; therefore, age-appropriate learning paths exist. The research reviewed in the Clements and Sarama chapter indicates that it is crucial to base math teaching and learning (and math programs prepared by publishers) on learning paths (trajectories). These learning paths are particularly visible in the Common Core Standards for two of the most crucial domains for early learning: operations and algebraic thinking (OA) and number base-ten (NBT).

The OA operations and algebraic thinking standards lay out an ambitious learning path, with word problem types as the basis for understanding of operations $(+ - \times \div)$. These main types of word problems (see Tables 1 and 2 on pages 88 and 89 of the Standards document) are situations in the real world that give rise to addition, subtraction, multiplication, and division. There is a huge amount of worldwide research literature on learning paths within these word problem types and on methods that students use to represent and solve such problems. The standards reflect this research literature for grades K, 1, and 2. They identify grade-appropriate levels at which students work with the various problem types and with unknowns for all three of the quantities. The standards appropriately specify that students use drawn models and equations with a symbol for the unknown number to represent the problem (*situation equations* such as $5 + \square = 8$). Thus, students will have the crucial experience with algebraic problems from grade 1 on. Algebraic problems are those where the situation equation, such as $\square + 4 = 9$, is not the same as the *solution equation*, $4 + \square = 9$ or $9 - 4 = \square$. Importantly, students also work in kindergarten with forms of equations with one number on the left (e.g., $5 = 2 + 3$ and $5 = 4 + 1$) as they decompose a given number (here, 5) and record each decomposition by a drawing or equation. Experience with these various forms of equations can eliminate the usual difficulty that U.S. students have with equations in algebra, where their limited experience with one form of equation leads them to expect only equations with one number on the right.

The operations and algebraic thinking (OA) standards outline a learning path of three levels of addition/subtraction solution methods that students use at grades K, 1, and 2: (1) direct model, (2) count-on, and (3) make-a-ten and other derived-fact methods. These levels provide a bridge between algebraic problem solving and NBT because these strategies are used in multidigit adding and subtracting also. This learning path comes right from research. Prerequisites for more-advanced strategies are identified as standards in kindergarten so that students in grades 1 and 2 can learn these strategies. Furthermore, the standards specify that subtraction is to be understood as an unknown-addend problem, and division as an unknown-factor problem. These emphasize the inverse relationships between addition and subtraction and between multiplication and division. This perspective enables programs and teachers to emphasize solving subtraction by forward methods such as counting-on to find the unknown addend; for example, $14 - 8 = \square$ is thought of as $8 + \square = 14$ and can be found by keeping track of how many counted-on from 8 to reach 14: (take away) 8, then 9, 10, 11, 12, 13, 14, so six more; or make a 10: find $8 + \square = 14$ as $8 + 2 + 4 = 10 + 4$ and $2 + 4 = 6$, so the unknown addend is 6. Forward counting methods are much easier and less error prone for children than are methods involving counting down.

The number and operations in NBT standards outline a learning path for multidigit computation based on research. Core components of this learning path are that students are

- to use concrete models or drawings and strategies based on place value and properties of operations;
- to relate the strategy to a written method and explain the reasoning used (explanations may be supported by drawings or objects); and
- to develop, discuss, and use efficient, accurate, and generalizable methods including the standard algorithm.

Thus, students simultaneously build and use understanding of place value concepts of ones, tens, and hundreds in adding and subtracting numbers that are composed of these units.

This learning path adjusts the impression given by the research summarized in Clements and Sarama about student invention of strategies versus teaching the standard algorithm first. Many of these studies present Clements and Sarama's "false dichotomy" in two ways. First, in the invent situations, students were to invent, but also they were to make sense of and discuss and explain their methods. In the teach algorithms first conditions, sense making was not necessarily a priority or even supported. Also, there are a limited number of methods for solving any problem and so most students in a given classroom do not actually invent a new method. They see it used and explained by a classmate. In a classroom where invention is stressed, students rather than the teacher model and explain methods. So what is crucial is making sense of methods and providing supports for such sense making, such as manipulatives or drawings that show tens and ones, and requiring and supporting discussion of methods. The standards require such sense making.

Second, many studies or programs calling for students to invent methods have an extended period of invention without much explicit teacher or fellow-student intervention (teaching). Teaching here is viewed as necessarily interfering with sense making by students (for more about this issue, see Fuson, 2009). Such a view can result in extended periods in which some or even many students use only primitive methods, even counting all of the objects for a 2-digit problem as late as third grade. This is detrimental to less-advanced students and is unnecessary. There is a middle view called "learning-path teaching," which emphasizes sense-making that is not traditional rote teaching and is not extended invention without help to move students to more-advanced methods. Learning-path teaching stems from major NRC reports (Donovan & Bransford, 2005; Kilpatrick, Swafford, & Findell, 2001), from the NCTM process standards (NCTM, 2000), and from research on teaching in Japan and in this country (Fuson & Murata, 2007; Murata & Fuson, 2006).

A summary of such teaching referring to aspects of these reports is given in Table 9.1. The top of the table summarizes the classroom environment supported by research that creates understanding. Details of ways to build such a sense-making math talk environment are summarized in Fuson, Atler, Roedel, & Zaccariello (2009). The Common Core Standards specify mathematical practices that are similar to the NCTM process standards and that are consistent with the learning-path teaching summarized in Table 9.1. The learning trajectory approach described in the Clements and Sarama chapter and their instructional strategies based on their learning trajectories are also consistent with this learning-path teaching.

TABLE 9.1 NRC Principles and NCTM Standards Summarizing the Class Learning Path Model

OVERALL: Create the year-long nurturing meaning-making math-talk community.

The Teacher orchestrates collaborative instructional conversations focused on the mathematical thinking of classroom members (*How Students Learn Principle 1* and *NCTM Process Standards: Problem Solving, Reasoning & Proof, Communication*). Students and the Teacher use seven responsive means of assistance that facilitate learning and teaching by all (several may be used together): engaging and involving, managing, and coaching, which involves the five subcategories of modeling, cognitive restructuring and clarifying, instructing/explaining, questioning, and feedback.

TABLE 9.1 (continued)   NRC Principles and NCTM Standards Summarizing the Class Learning Path Model

FOR EACH MATH TOPIC: Use inquiry learning-path teaching and learning.

The Teacher supports the meaning-making of all classroom members by using and assisting students to use and relate (interform) coherent mathematical situations, pedagogical forms, and cultural mathematical forms (*NCTM Process Standards: Connections & Representation*) and uses *four class learning zone teaching phases* within a coherent in-depth sequence of problems and activities to help students move through their own learning paths within the class learning zone:

Phase 1. Guided Introducing: Supported by the coherent forms, the Teacher elicits and the class works with understandings that students bring to a topic (*How Students Learn Principle 1*).

   a. Teacher and students value and discuss student ideas and methods ["*individual internal forms (IIFs)* in action"].

   b. Teacher identifies different levels of solution methods used by students and typical errors and ensures that these are seen and discussed by the class.

Phase 2. Learning Unfolding (Major Meaning-Making Phase): The Teacher helps students form emergent networks of forms-in-action (*How Students Learn Principle 2*).

   a. Explanations of methods and of mathematical issues continue to use math drawings and other pedagogical supports to stimulate correct relating (interforming) of the forms.

   b. Teacher focuses on or introduces mathematically desirable and accessible method(s).

   c. Erroneous methods are analyzed and repaired with explanations.

   d. Advantages and disadvantages of various methods including the current common method are discussed so that central mathematical aspects of the topic become explicit.

Phase 3. Kneading Knowledge: The Teacher helps students gain fluency with desired method(s); students may choose a method; fluency includes being able to explain the method; some reflection and explaining still continue (kneading the individual internal forms); students stop making math drawings when they do not need them (*Adding It Up: Fluency & Understanding*).

Phase 4. Maintaining Fluency and Relating to Later Topics: The Teacher assists remembering by giving occasional problems and initiates and orchestrates instructional discussions to assist re-forming IIFs to support (form-under) and stimulate new IIF "nets for action" for related topics.

RESULT: Together, these achieve the overall high-level goal for all: Build resourceful self-regulating problem solvers (*How Students Learn Principle 3*) by continually intertwining the 5 strands of mathematical proficiency: conceptual understanding, procedural fluency, strategic competence, adaptive reasoning, productive disposition (*Adding It Up*).

Note: This is a later version of the table in Fuson and Murata (2007). This table appears in the work of Fuson, Murata, and Abrahamson (2011), in which we sought to bring together perspectives on understanding and fluency and provide language to do so. We characterized Piaget's and Vygotsky's conceptual activity as involving three types of external math forms: *situational, pedagogical,* and *cultural math forms.* We specified that each learner continually forms and reforms *individual internal forms (IIFs)* that are interpretations of the external forms. This parallel use of the word *forms* links the external and internal forms but emphasizes that each individual internal form may vary from the external form because the internal form is an interpretation. Doing math is using "IIFs in action" to form actions with *external forms.*

The middle part specifying the four phases of inquiry learning-path teaching is the balanced antidote to the nonproductive extremes of "invent for a long time" and traditional rote teaching. For any topic, one begins by eliciting student thinking. This might be brief for a short topic. For a major topic like single-digit or multidigit addition or subtraction, students would initially develop and use or choose their own methods in a classroom environment where they already have prerequisite knowledge and have visual supports for discussing their thinking. But soon (within a couple of days so as not to let less advanced students flounder for days) research-based mathematically desirable and accessible methods are introduced to the class if such methods have not arisen from students. These methods have been found by classroom research to be easily understood by students (more easily understood than the current common ways of writing a standard algorithm), to generalize to larger numbers readily, and to make salient important mathematical issues (e.g., moving from left to right vs. right to left or using expanded notation) that are fruitful for classroom discussion; for more details, see Fuson & Murata (2007), Kilpatrick et al. (2001), and NCTM (2011).

The Common Core Standards recognize that the methods invented by students often are generalized from counting methods and work for numbers within 100. Some methods, however, become more difficult for totals between 101 and 1000 (see details in NCTM, 2011). Therefore, the standards require students in grade 2 to add and subtract totals between 101 and 1000 (called "within 1000" in the Common Core Standards) in order to experience and generalize methods to larger numbers. Many other countries add and subtract such numbers at grade two for similar reasons.

Because the term "standard algorithm" has been such a flashpoint for the "math wars," I also wish to reiterate the crucial point made in the NRC report, "Adding It Up" (Kilpatrick et al., 2001) and in the Clements and Sarama research summary indicating that there is no single recognized "standard algorithm" for any operation. Many different forms have been used in this country and are currently being used around the world. The term "the standard algorithm" actually refers to the major mathematical features of the process and not to the details of how these are written. For example, multidigit addition and subtraction have two components: (a) adding or subtracting like units; and (b) when needed, group ten of a unit to make one of the next-left unit or ungroup one unit to make ten of the next-right unit. There are more and less accessible ways to write these steps, and students should see and be able to use more accessible versions. These are often minor variations that produce major decreases in errors and increases in understanding. Figure 7.3 in the Clements and Sarama chapter shows a subtraction standard algorithm that is much easier for students because they concentrate on any needed ungrouping first and then do all of the subtracting. Figure 9.1 here shows an easier addition standard algo-

456 +167 ─────	456 +167 ──1── 3	456 +167 ──1 1── 23	456 +167 ──1 1── 623
	Add 6 ones and 7 ones, write thirteen (one, ten, three ones), with the three in the ones place and the 1 ten *under* the tens column.	Add 5 tens and 6 tens to make 11 tens, and 1 more ten makes 12 tens. Write 12 tens, with the 2 tens in the tens column and the 10 tens (100) *under* the hundreds column.	Add 4 hundreds and 1 hundred to make 5 hundreds; add 1 more hundred to make 6 hundreds.

Figure 9.1 A mathematically desirable and accessible addition algorithm.

rithm. Writing the new tens or hundreds below in the next-left place makes it easier to add the numbers in those places (you can just add the two numbers you see and increase that total by one), shows the 2-digit totals clearly because their numbers are close to each other (13 ones and 12 tens), and allows students to write a teen number in their usual way (13 as write 1 then 3, not write the 3 and carry the 1). Both figures show how drawings of hundreds, tens, and ones can support the BAMT (break apart to make ten) methods by grouping numbers within 5-groups that show how much more to make a ten.

Because so much of the Common Core Standards reflect learning progressions and specify general kinds of visual supports for meaning making, these progressions and visual supports will need to be in standards-based math programs. Therefore, professional development (PD) can be more successful because more programs can be used as the basis of PD because more programs will contain many of the features described for successful PD at the end of the Clements and Sarama chapter.

The final two points concern the nature of the crucial bases for sense making in the classroom, visual teaching/learning supports. One important function of national reports and of the Common Core Standards has been to stimulate the use of such visual teaching/learning supports connected to mathematical notation and reasoning because so much research supports such use. However, sometimes crucial supports do not even exist. In such cases, reports and the standards can identify the need for them. Most of the illustrations given in the geometry learning trajectory in the Clements and Sarama chapter are not about the central 2-D shapes used in geometry (e.g., right-angled shapes such as squares, rectangles, and right triangles, which form the basis for conceptualizing area as the number of contiguous squares and for finding the formulas for the area of most shapes used widely in geometry). Only two illustrations used at ages 7 and 8 use squares, rectangles, and right triangles. Most earlier illustrations used shapes made from equilateral triangles. This is because physical sets of such shapes (often called "pattern blocks") have been available and widely used for a long time. It was the National Research Council's report on early childhood math, *Mathematics Learning in Early Childhood: Paths Toward Excellence and Equity* (2009), that identified the need for such materials for preschool and early elementary students. Students can engage in all of the levels in the geometry progression with a right-angled set of pattern blocks made from a few key squares, rectangles, and right triangles all based on a square of one inch. This enables them to build important informal knowledge leading to many of the Common Core geometry and measure standards.

Finally, teaching/learning supports and solution strategies interact with the language the child is speaking. The BAMT method shown in Clements and Sarama's Figure 7.1 is an excellent general method that can be viewed (and is viewed in East Asian countries) as the first step in multidigit adding and subtracting (you are already grouping or ungrouping). However, this method is more difficult in English than in East Asian languages, where teen words are said in a regular form such as *ten two* for 12. When 8 + 6 is recomposed to be 10 + 4, that is said as *ten four* in regular East Asian words, and so the conceptual step from *ten and four* to *ten four* is small (but not nonexistent; see Ho and Fuson, 1998). In English, children must take a larger step from *ten and four* to *fourteen* or, even more difficult, *ten and two* to *twelve*. So they must become fluent in all of the different numerical examples for teen numbers; the importance of this conceptual work is recognized in the kindergarten standards.

Likewise, the empty number line shown in Clement and Sarama's Figure 7.2 is used in The Netherlands with a language that says all 2-digit words with a reversal of the tens and ones. The example of 85 − 68 shown there would be said by the children as *five and eighty* minus *eight and sixty*. Therefore, a counting method and visual counting support that keep together the two-digit number is quite useful in dealing with the reversals between the written and spoken 2-digit numbers. Such methods are less necessary in English, where children can use counting-on methods by using math drawings of tens and ones to keep track of how many are counted on (NCTM, 2011; Fuson, Smith, & Lo Cicero, 1997). Of course, forward methods can also be supported by any visual supports: Many children find it easier to find 85 − 68 = □ by adding on ones and tens to 68 to make 85 (68 + □ = 85) using the concept of subtraction as finding the unknown addend, as described in the Common Core Standards.

Because the Clements and Sarama chapter focuses on preschool and early elementary mathematics, this commentary closes with a reminder about the crucial importance of the research summaries and recommendations of the NRC report on early childhood math of 2009 for creating a national environment of learning in the preschool years so that all kindergarten children can meet the Common Core Standards. Teaching approaches that implement these NRC recommendations are given in the books for teachers published by the National Council of Teachers of Mathematics (2010a, 2010b, 2009, 2011). Use of such research-based approaches in educational and care centers can help close the equity gap and can help all children achieve at a high level in early and elementary mathematics.

REFERENCES

Donovan, M. S., & Bransford, J. D. (Eds.). (2005). *How students learn: Mathematics in the classroom.* Washington, DC: National Academies Press.

Fuson, K. C. (2009). Avoiding misinterpretations of Piaget and Vygotsky: Mathematical teaching without learning, learning without teaching, or helpful learning-path teaching? *Cognitive Development, 24,* 343–361. doi:10.1016/j.cogdev.2009.09.009

Fuson, K. C., Atler, T., Roedel, S., & Zaccariello, J. (2009, May). Building a nurturing, visual, Math-Talk teaching-learning community to support learning by English language learners and students from backgrounds of poverty. *New England Mathematics Journal, XLI,* 6–16.

Fuson, K. C. & Murata, A. (2007). Integrating NRC principles and the NCTM Process Standards to form a Class Learning Path Model that individualizes within whole-class activities. *National Council of Supervisors of Mathematics Journal of Mathematics Education Leadership, 10*(1), 72–91.

Fuson, K. C., Murata, A., & Abrahamson, D. (2007). *Forming minds to do math: Ending the math wars through understanding and fluency for all.* Paper under revision.

Fuson, K. C., Smith, S. T., & Lo Cicero, A. (1997). Supporting Latino first graders' ten-structured thinking in urban classrooms. *Journal for Research in Mathematics Education, 28,* 738–766.

Ho, C. S., & Fuson, K. C. (1998). Effects of language characteristics on children's knowledge of teens quantities as tens and ones: Comparisons of Chinese, British, and American kindergartners. *Journal of Educational Psychology, 90,* 536–544.

Kilpatrick, J., Swafford, J., & Findell, B. (Eds.). (2001). *Adding it up: Helping children learn mathematics.* Mathematics Learning Study Committee. Center for Education, Division of Behavioral and Social Sciences and Education. Washington, DC: National Academies Press.

Murata, A., & Fuson, K. C. (2006). Teaching as assisting individual constructive paths within an interdependent class learning zone: Japanese first graders learning to add using ten. *Journal for Research in Mathematics Education, 37*(5), 421–456.

National Council of Teachers of Mathematics. (2000). *Principles and standards for school mathematics.* Reston, VA: Author.

National Council of Teachers of Mathematics. (2009). *Focus in grade 1.* Reston, VA: NCTM.

National Council of Teachers of Mathematics. (2010a). *Focus in prekindergarten.* Reston, VA: NCTM.

National Council of Teachers of Mathematics. (2010b). *Focus in kindergarten.* Reston, VA: NCTM.

National Council of Teachers of Mathematics. (2011). *Focus in grade 2.* Reston, VA: NCTM.

National Research Council. (2009). Mathematics learning in early childhood: Paths toward excellence and equity. C. T. Cross, T. A. Woods, & H. Schweingruber, (Eds.), *Center for Education, Division of Behavioral and Social Sciences and Education.* Washington, DC: National Academies Press.

CHAPTER 10

YOU CAN'T PLAY
20 QUESTIONS WITH
MATHEMATICS TEACHING
AND LEARNING, AND WIN

James W. Stigler and Belinda J. Thompson
University of California, Los Angeles

In their review of how mathematics is taught and learned, Clements and Sarama decry the "false dichotomies" that have impeded the progress of research and perhaps slowed down the emergence of smart policy and practice. Everyone has experienced the heat generated by debates over the right way to teach mathematics: "student centered" vs. "teacher directed," "direct" vs. "inquiry," "traditional" vs. "reform," "meaningful" vs. "drill-and-kill." The problem is that these debates detract attention from what really is important; namely, understanding how instruction actually works to promote learning. What kinds of learning opportunities can teachers create for students, how do students experience and interact with these learning opportunities, and what do they actually learn?

The late psychologist and computer scientist Alan Newell made a similar point in his classic 1973 paper, "You Can't Play 20 Questions with Nature

Instructional Strategies for Improving Students' Learning, pages 187–195
Copyright © 2012 by Information Age Publishing
All rights of reproduction in any form reserved.

and Win." He was referring, in his title, to the game *20 Questions*, in which players try to guess an object by asking a series of yes/no questions, starting with general ones and then getting more specific. In psychology, the dichotomies that guide research are not the same ones that define the mathematics education debate. They include things like "nature" vs. "nurture," and "serial" vs. "parallel" processing. But Newell's point applies equally well to mathematics teaching and learning. Psychology, writes Newell, tries to proceed by laying out a general dichotomy, then conducting an experiment that will help the field decide between the two alternatives. The only problem, according to Newell, is that the field doesn't usually make progress in this way, despite the common perception.

Newell's proposal, for psychology, was to shift the focus away from asking general dichotomous questions to trying to understand how people actually learn to perform complex tasks that matter. In the field of education, the pendulum swing of policies and initiatives generated by chasing the answers to these false dichotomies has not provided many widely accepted teaching practices. Rather, as these dichotomies are presented and debated, those who do the teaching are often presented with a mandate to implement or discard certain practices with no real direction. Further, these teachers grow weary of riding the swing, and few instructional changes occur, much less stick.

Mathematics, in general, consists of a number of important and complex tasks. We need to shift the research agenda beyond attempts to declare one side or the other of a false dichotomy as the winner. Instead, we need to figure out what the important learning goals are for school mathematics; what various students know at any particular time in the course of progressing toward the goals; what kinds of instruction are effective at helping students progress; and, ideally, what the mechanisms are that underlie the effects of instruction on learning. In short, we need to build the research and development enterprise not around big dichotomies but around something like *learning trajectories*.

Learning Trajectories: Great Potential

The concept of learning trajectories, as introduced here by Clements and Sarama and elsewhere (Confrey, Maloney, Nguyen, Mojica, & Myers, 2009; Simon and Tzur, 2004) has great potential for organizing and focusing research on mathematics teaching and learning. The main reason for our enthusiasm lies in the domain-specific nature of teaching and learning. In math-war discussions, we can argue skills vs. understanding. But in real classrooms, the term "understanding" must be replaced by something more specific: Students don't understand mathematics; they understand, for example, that divisions of integers can be expressed as fractions; that the denominator of a fraction conveys the number of equal sized pieces that a quantity is divided into; that 8 times 3 can be decomposed into 8 times 2 plus 8, and so on. Part of what has impeded a true focus on teaching for understanding has been the too-general nature of the recommendations given to teachers. Use of manipulatives or visual representations does not necessarily lead to understanding. But understanding of fractions and how they relate to division can be supported by use of a number line. It is the details that matter, and building research around learning trajectories forces us to keep the details in focus. This kind of thinking has been used effectively by Clements and Sarama as they sort through the various dichotomies that have shaped the research agenda in mathematics education. In general, what they find is this: the way teaching and learning actually work cannot be described well in such general terms. If forced to choose between "meaningful teaching" and "drill-and-kill," teachers and researchers would miss the subtle dynamics involved in learning the basic addition and subtraction facts. Research clearly shows that practice is critical for mastering the basic facts. But it also shows that *what* and *how* students practice are what determines success (Ericsson & Charness, 1994). If practice means simply repeated association of two digits with a sum, for example, there is evidence that this will not work (Henry & Brown, 2008). But if practice means repeated analysis of digit pairs in a thoughtful way, coming up with different addition strategies, linked with core concepts (such as place value), then practice is almost everything. The more we dig into the details, the more we find that multiple complementary instructional strategies must be integrated in order to achieve mathematical proficiency in a domain.

Learning trajectories, as defined by Clements and Sarama, afford a number of opportunities for teachers to improve their practice. Because learning trajectories are defined, first of all, by clear and explicit learning goals for students, they facilitate productive sharing of instructional ideas among teachers who are working toward similar goals. If one teacher is seeking to teach a procedure (e.g., invert and multiply for division of fractions) while another is seeking to teach a concept (e.g., understanding why 2/3 is the same as 2 divided by 3), their sharing of ideas will necessarily happen at a general level. But if both teachers are focused on the same concept, they can be highly specific in their conversation. In the example just mentioned, teachers might share their experiences teaching 2/3 as 2 divided by 3 compared with teaching it as 2 • (1 ÷ 3). This kind of conversation will not devolve into ideological math-wars type discourse, but will stay at a level that is both practical and important. Learning trajectories can help to move teachers from discussions of *teaching* to discussions of *how to teach x well.*

Of course, a learning trajectory is more than a goal. It also includes a sequence of subgoals—what Clements and Sarama refer to as "levels of thinking"—that chart a pathway students can follow to achieve a final goal. Parts of this longitudinal pathway may happen during the course of one school year and would naturally be addressed by teachers of students at the same grade level. These sequences may very likely cut across multiple grade levels, facilitating important "vertical" discussions across teachers of different grade levels within a school. Having these kinds of discussions adds a new sense of purpose as teachers interpret the curriculum, not only for the grade level they are assigned to teach, but also for prior and future grade levels. Take, for example, the teaching of basic geometric shapes. In the United States, we teach students to name shapes in the early grades— triangle, rectangle, square, and so on—but we do not give teachers compelling reasons for why this goal is important at a particular grade level. In Japan, where the curriculum has long been conceived as a learning trajectory, early elementary school students are taught to decompose and recompose geometric shapes, e.g., rectangles into triangles. The early-grade teachers, through their study of the curriculum and discussions with colleagues teaching the later grades, understand that composition and decomposition of shapes is not important just by itself, but because it will be used later as a foundation on which to build methods and formulas for finding the areas of geometric shapes. Explicit learning trajectories allow each teacher to see their own work in perspective as just one key part of a developmental progression that spans multiple grade levels.

An even more specific example of a carefully planned trajectory is the development leading up to equivalent fractions in the Japanese curriculum in grades 3, 4, and 5 (Takahashi, Watanabe, & Yoshida, 2008). At first glance, the presentation of equivalent fractions in this particular Japanese curriculum does not look much different from that in most U.S. curricula. Illustrations on the pages might show two rectangles divided into two different numbers of equal sized pieces with the same amount of area shaded. For instance, Figure 10.1 shows how the fractions 1/3 and 2/6 might be illustrated in grade 3 to show that each fraction covers the same amount of area.

However, where the Japanese curriculum differs is in the development of equivalence, in particular the deliberate connection of equivalent fractions with related concepts of multiplication and division. In grade 3, the development begins with the treatment of division, and the introduction of fractions as the result of division. Unit fractions are initially introduced as a number, one, divided into some number of equal parts. So, ¼ is the same

Figure 10.1 Illustration of equivalent fractions as shaded regions of the same unit.

We know that 21 ÷ 7 = 3. If we multiply 21 × 10 and 7 × 10, the
quotient is still 3. We can verify that by dividing 210 ÷ 70 = 3.

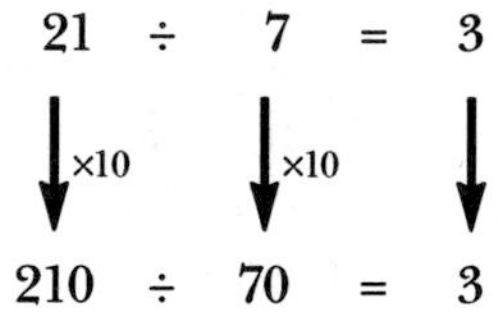

$$21 \quad \div \quad 7 \quad = \quad 3$$

$$\downarrow{\scriptstyle \times 10} \qquad \downarrow{\scriptstyle \times 10} \qquad \downarrow$$

$$210 \quad \div \quad 70 \quad = \quad 3$$

Figure 10.2 An important result in division: if the dividend and divisor are each
multiplied by the same number, the quotient is unchanged.

Multiplying the numerator and denominator of the fraction
by the same number does not change the size of the fraction.

$$\frac{1}{3} = \frac{1\times2}{3\times2} = \frac{2}{6}$$

Figure 10.3 Using multiplication to create an equivalent fraction.

as 1 divided 4, which can be represented by shading 1 of four equal parts
of an area or dividing a length of 1 meter into 4 equal part, naming each
part 1/4 meter.

In grade 4, students learn about an important result in division: that
if the dividend and divisor are each multiplied by the same number, the
quotient is unchanged (Figure 10.2). Then, in grade 5, when equivalent
fractions are introduced, this connection of division, fractions, and the important result come together to produce a mathematically compelling basis
on which to create or verify equivalent fractions (Figure 10.3). From there
it is straightforward to see that equivalent fractions can be understood as
divisions that have the same quotient and that two fractions are equivalent because the multiplicative relationship between the numerator and
denominator is unchanged.

The idea of learning trajectories also is evident in the South Korean curriculum. In the teachers' edition of the textbook, teachers are advised on
how to handle the most common error students make when learning to
add fractions with different denominators, which is to add, separately, the
numerators and the denominators. Most American teachers would simply
remind students that they need to first find a common denominator. Korean teachers are specifically warned against this practice, however, told instead to address fundamental misunderstandings that might lead students
to make the mistake in the first place. According to the South Korean materials, students who make this error do so because they are thinking of a
fraction as two numbers instead of one. They are advised to go back to the
fundamental concept of fraction, help students to see it as representing a

single number or quantity, and then reintroduce the problem of adding fractions, moving back through the learning trajectory that has been found effective.

Whether or not the Japanese or South Korean curriculum design matches the true learning trajectory of the concepts mentioned here is an empirical question. However, we argue that the coherent development and connected presentation of concepts, both within and across grade levels, provides a reasonable starting point for examining whether the sequence of tasks and conceptual explanations provided in a curriculum helps students to understand the concepts presented.

We see evidence of emerging learning trajectories in the Common Core Standards, as teachers are given specific guidance on introducing fractions using number lines in a specific way. Understanding first that a fraction is a number is a critical first step in learning to operate on and with fractions. If students cannot clear the hurdle of incorporating fractions into their idea of numbers, then operations with fractions are virtually meaningless. Teachers at subsequent grades will know how students have learned about fractions and can use this information to choose instructional strategies and assessments. Finally, well-mapped learning trajectories make it possible to provide teachers with specific strategies to address the specific level of each individual student. When teachers have only general goals of the sort provided by state or district content standards, it is hard to know which specific instructional approach is indicated. Sequences of specific learning goals, on the other hand, linked with students' levels of thinking, make it possible to develop targeted formative assessments that indicate each student's level. These formative assessments in turn become highly practical guides to inform instruction.

Learning Trajectories: A Deeper Look

As useful as learning trajectories are, there are some issues that must be directly addressed. The most important of these is this: Learning trajectories are not natural objects to be discovered. They are, instead, invented cultural artifacts. If only they were natural objects, we could discover them using the normal methods of psychological science. But learning trajectories are invented, either gradually over time within a culture or by an innovator who simply has a better idea on how to help students get from point A to point B. They are complex and dependent on students' prior experiences. A student who grows up in Japan may look similar to one who has grown up in the United States in terms of their level of thinking about fractions or addition, but because they arrived in the same place by different routes, there may well be different routes they have to follow next in order to achieve a common level of mathematical proficiency.

The work by Henry and Brown (2008) describes a fascinating case in point. U.S. curriculum proceeds from counting to find simple sums, to then memorizing the basic sums for rapid retrieval. In Japan, on the other hand, the curriculum lays out a learning trajectory with more levels, proceeding from counting to sums of less than 10, then to breaking apart larger sums to make 10 as a strategy for finding sums greater than 10, and finally to retrieval. Japanese students are taught that they can solve $7 + 5$ by decomposing the 5 into $3 + 2$, combining the 3 with the 7 to make 10, then adding back the remaining 2 to get 12. It's not that American students never do this, but Japanese educators have determined that this particular sequence leads to a better outcome. Not only do Japanese students master the single-digit addition facts more quickly, but they also get to practice relational thinking concepts that may prepare them for other topics such as algebra.

Clearly, this particular learning trajectory is not natural but cultural. It was invented and then developed over a long period of time in Japan (and other Asian countries too). The fact that learning trajectories are invented, not discovered, makes identifying and using them far more complex than it otherwise would be. We cannot simply watch students learn in order to identify learning progressions. We must also watch students learn in different cultures and different curricula to see what options are possible, and try out different instructional sequences that we invent. Trying out an instructional sequence is hard work; not only must we come up with a plausible sequence to test, but we must design and deploy an education program, sometimes over an extended period of time, just to see what its effects are. If the program requires a skilled teacher to implement it, we also need to give teachers the opportunity to learn how to implement the program—something that can take a long time and lots of effort to achieve.

It is also quite likely that there are multiple pathways students can take to reach a common learning goal. Just because we can map out and validate one pathway does not mean that all students need to go through the same levels in the same order. It may be that most students can benefit by learning to work with 10s after they learn to count and before they work with larger numbers. But there may be some students who don't need to go through the intermediate stage, or some who could be more successful if they took a completely different pathway, perhaps even one that has not yet been invented. And how should the domain of mathematics be carved up into learning trajectories in the first place? Should counting be a separate learning trajectory, or should it be just one part of a larger learning trajectory that leads to overall concepts of number and quantity? We know that making conceptual connections is important if we want to create flexible and usable knowledge. But how do we represent the specific connections students need to make, especially when these connections may often cut across multiple learning trajectories (e.g., connecting the concept of linear function with the concept of direct proportion)?

The invented and cultural nature of learning trajectories has significant implications for research. It means that we need to shift from a pure research focus to a research and development focus, using methods of design, engineering, innovation, and improvement. Whereas a psychologist or mathematics educator may be equipped to simply study existing learning trajectories, it will take a team with broad expertise to invent, test, refine, and improve new learning trajectories. This approach does not allow for the broad pendulum swings between skills and understanding, or teacher-centered and student-centered. Rather, it gives all involved permission to experiment with purpose, to ask questions, and to gain even more specificity in the trajectories being defined. However, along with this permission to experiment comes the responsibility to share knowledge. Therefore, it seems crucial to the development and refinement of learning trajectories to thoughtfully create and diligently implement a mechanism for sharing within and across all entities involved.

The increasing reliance on technology for building learning environments actually provides a fertile context for the design and development of learning trajectories, including shareability of knowledge. Educational programs that can be delivered on mobile devices can easily be reconfigured to test different orders of tasks and instruction. This makes it possible to compare the effects of different learning trajectories across individual students within the same class and to engage in rapid improvement cycles in which instructional products and their underlying theories are tested and refined.

Learning trajectories provide us with a tool to organize the work of improvement and to move beyond the game of 20 Questions. We need to stop spending our time debating whether instruction should focus on skills or on concepts and start building and testing instructional systems that produce mathematical proficiency in students. We need to focus, first, on clearly defining what we mean by mathematical proficiency, and stating clear learning goals for students. We next need to develop measures of proficiency that we can use to chart our progress, using these measures as a means of organizing large collaborative efforts in which all kinds of expertise are brought to bear on the problem of improving mathematical proficiency. Within this context, we must invent and/or discover learning trajectories that can be tried out and improved, or discarded if they prove ineffective. And we must then devise ways of implementing the learning trajectories in instruction of all kinds—face-to-face and technology-delivered.

REFERENCES

Confrey, J., Maloney, A., Nguyen, K., Mojica, G., & Myers, M. (2009). Equipartitioning/splitting as a foundation of rational number reasoning using learning trajectories. *33rd conference of the International Group for the Psychology of Mathematics Education,* Thessaloniki, Greece.

Ericsson, K. A., & Charness, N. (1994). Expert performance: Its structure and acquisition. *American Psychologist, 49*(8), 725–747.

Henry, V. J., & Brown, R. S. (2008). First-grade basic facts: An investigation into teaching and learning of an accelerated, high-demand memorization standard. *Journal for Research in Mathematics Education, 39,* 153–183.

Newell, A. (1973). You can't play twenty questions with nature and win: Projective comments on the papers of this symposium. In W. G. Chase (Ed.), *Visual information processing* (pp. 283–308). New York: Academic.

Simon, M., & Tzur, R. (2004). Explicating the role of mathematical tasks in conceptual learning: An elaboration of the hypothetical learning trajectory. *Mathematical Thinking and Learning, 6*(2), 91–104.

Takahashi, A., Watanabe, T., & Yoshida, M. (2008). *English translation of the Japanese mathematics curricula in the course of study.* Madison, NJ: Global Education Resources.

CHAPTER 11

LEARNING TRAJECTORIES THROUGH A SOCIOCULTURAL LENS[1]

Anita A. Wager and Thomas P. Carpenter
University of Wisconsin-Madison

In their chapter, "Learning and Teaching Early and Elementary Mathematics" (this volume), Clements and Sarama provide a comprehensive review of research on the teaching and learning of mathematics in preschool and the primary grades. In this chapter, we build on their review to address perhaps the most critical question facing the teaching and learning of early mathematics: providing equitable learning opportunities to an increasingly diverse student population. As Clements and Sarama (2007) have discussed in prior work, students of color and students of poverty do not always come to school with the same mathematical skills as their more advantaged peers. We are concerned that too often these differences are positioned as deficiencies. Rather, we suggest that it is the responsibility of schooling to address the differences in the children's skillsets by adapting a perspective of school readiness in which differences in children's skills are not perceived as lacking but as different. To that end, this review offers an extension of Clements and Sarama's chapter by incorporating a sociocultural perspective to explicitly address this challenge.[2]

Instructional Strategies for Improving Students' Learning, pages 197–204
Copyright © 2012 by Information Age Publishing
All rights of reproduction in any form reserved.

197

Clements and Sarama organize their chapter around three fundamental questions: (a) How do students learn mathematics? (b) What pedagogical strategies for teaching early mathematics are supported by research? and (c) What approaches to professional development are supported by research? We have organized our review along the same three themes. In each section, we address the ideas raised by the authors and then consider the constraints of a purely cognitive approach and the opportunities afforded by a sociocultural view to consider the contexts in which children live and learn.

How Do Students Learn Mathematics?

The section on how students learn mathematics in Clements and Sarama's chapter focuses on the learning trajectories that students follow to attain mathematical competence. Learning trajectories link developmental progression, example behavior, and associated instructional tasks with age levels and, as the authors point out, learning trajectories are being adopted in policy documents such as the Common Core State Standards (CCSSO/NGA, 2010) and the Curriculum Focal Points for Pre-Kindergarten through Grade 8 Mathematics (NCTM, 2006). Learning trajectories are a cognitive construct based on certain assumptions about the cognitive nature of knowledge. As a consequence, they do not fully account for the situated nature of children's learning. The three parts of learning trajectories—the goal, developmental progression, and instructional activities—are delineated into four components in Clements and Sarama's chapter (Table 7.1 on pp. 109–111). Drawing on these four components, we raise important considerations for how they should be used in a way that considers and connects to students' experiences. We find this consideration of particular importance, given the increasing focus on learning trajectories in shaping policy. The first component, age, suggests the approximate age at which children should reach each level in the developmental progression. Although ascribing age limits to a particular progression offers teachers a baseline against which to assess student knowledge, the downside can be significant when those children who are not meeting the projection are positioned as deficient. In attending to age levels at which students should attain particular tasks without a critical view, we are "legitimating the factors and circumstances that gave rise to those disparities" (Secada, 1991, p. 17). With these age limits as normative, they become the norm and they position those children outside as "deviant and marginal" (p. 21). The second and third components, developmental progression and example behavior, describe the levels through which children pass on the road to achieving understanding of a particular concept. This progression and the activities that students use to demonstrate the progression may vary depending on the experiences of the child and the context in which the progression is observed. Although mathematics is often viewed as "culture-free," and teachers find it difficult to relate mathematics to students' cultural backgrounds (Secada & Berman, 1999), researchers have repeatedly shown how cultural context matters in students' understanding of mathematics (Carraher, Carraher, & Schliemann, 1985; D'Ambrosio 1985; de Abreu, 1995; Guberman, 1996; Nunes, Schliemann, & Carraher, 1993; Saxe, 1988). By setting particular expectations for demonstrating "progression" and assuming that all children proceed in the same way, we ignore children's participation in cultural practices (Rogoff & Gutiérrez, 2003).

Finally, instructional tasks need to be culturally responsive and relevant. We elaborate further on this in the next section, in which we address pedagogical strategies. We do not pose the above as dichotomies to the practices presented in Clements and Sarama's chapter; rather we suggest that in using learning trajectories, teachers and researchers should be mindful of the potentially deficit views they may encourage and extend the ideas to consider the cultural and sociopolitical contexts children experience.

What Pedagogical Strategies are Supported by Research?

Clements and Sarama make a strong case for avoiding the false dichotomies often raised in discussions of mathematics pedagogical knowledge. We support the authors' notion of a balanced approach to instruction that weaves together the teachers' and students' roles in developing both understanding and skills, and also suggest incorporating pedagogical strategies that specifically address the needs of students from diverse linguistic, ethnic, and socioeconomic backgrounds.

In their pedagogical strategies section, Clements and Sarama link learning trajectories to Shulman's (1986) pedagogical content knowledge. We propose that the notion of pedagogical content knowledge, as described by Shulman, needs to be expanded to consider scholarship that examines teachers' understanding and use of children's cultural resources (Barta & Brenner, 2010; Ladson-Billings, 1995; Wager, 2010).

Many students have difficulty seeing the connection between mathematics in the classroom and the mathematics they experience out of school (Masingila, 2002). The failure of schools to recognize the mathematical strengths that students bring to school widens the gap between in- and out-of-school mathematical competencies. Scholars have shown that what we teach and the representations we use may not connect to the ways in which many students engage in mathematics outside school; and that representations, activities, and norms of interaction may privilege some students over others (de Abreu, 1995; Taylor, 2004). This may be especially true when the cultural backgrounds of students differ from that of their teachers. Masingila (p. 31) argued, "In order to help students connect mathematics in school and mathematics out-of-school, we need to know how students actually use—and how they perceive that they use—mathematics in everyday situations." The foundational work in this area is based on the concept of *funds of knowledge* (Civil, 2002; González, Andrade, Civil, & Moll, 2001; Moll, Amanti, Neff, & González, 1992). This concept refers to the "historically accumulated and culturally developed bodies of knowledge and skills essential for household or individual functioning and well-being" (Moll et al., 1992, p. 133). This suggests that for mathematics pedagogy to be effective, teachers must (a) learn what mathematical practices their students engage in outside school and (b) connect these practices to what is taught in school.

In responding to the question, What pedagogical strategies are supported by research? we cannot provide a blanket response generalizable to all children in all classrooms. We can, however, offer examples of scholarship on practices that have been successful in particular classrooms. Scholars such as Leonard (2008), Gutiérrez (2007), and Gutstein (2006) have observed either others or themselves in mathematics classrooms that are culturally responsive. Their findings share a common theme in that "context matters": the context of the children's lives, the classrooms they are in, and the tools they use to perform mathematical tasks. Thus, we suggest that we broaden pedagogical content knowledge to capture those contexts; as Gutiérrez (p. 2) proposes, we need to consider "the nature of effective teaching and learning contexts, not just their distilled characteristics." Examples of how this may be accomplished through culturally sensitive professional development are included in the following section.

In their discussion of pedagogical content knowledge, Clements and Sarama position trajectories at the core. We are proposing that we attend not just to knowledge of trajectories but also to the contexts in which students develop their understanding and the entailments and situated nature of it. We consider our perspective as expanding, rather than being in conflict with, pedagogical content knowledge.

What Approaches to Professional Development Are Supported by Research?

We agree with Clements and Sarama regarding the structures of professional development that do and do not work. In their chapter, they focus on professional development explicitly in terms of learning trajectories, which we have already argued come from a particularly cognitive view. Clements and Sarama offer examples of successful professional development to support teachers' understanding of children's trajectories. We add to these ideas by providing examples of professional development that also consider how to support teachers' understanding of equity in the teaching and learning of mathematics.

There is an increasing base of research on professional development programs that considers both the teaching and learning of mathematics and equity. These programs reflect the guidelines for successful professional development outlined by Clements and Sarama (pp. 149–150), but center attention on addressing equity and diversity concerns. Although these programs address a broad range of issues of equity and diversity, we highlight those that support teachers' use of funds of knowledge. (For details on additional professional development programs incorporating equity and mathematics, see Foote, 2010).

As we have suggested in the previous section, using students' funds of knowledge to teach mathematics provides a meaningful connection to what is learned in school and what is experienced in the home. Several professional development programs offer explicit examples of how to support teachers in developing the dispositions and strategies for using students' funds of knowledge as a resource. Some of these examples include using students' native language and culture (Celedón-Pattichis, Musanti, & Marshall, 2010) and connecting school mathematics to everyday practices (Wager, in press).

In a 4-year longitudinal study of professional development for K–2 bilingual teachers, Celedón-Pattichis et al. (2010) examined how instruction in students' native language and aligning curriculum with the cultural experiences of the children and families supported children's problem-solving strategies. The professional development was based on the cognitively guided instruction framework (CGI; Carpenter, Fennema, Franke, Levi, & Empson, 1999) but incorporated the role of native language and funds of knowledge. The researchers found that teachers came to recognize how the development of students' academic language in Spanish supported their mathematical thinking and reasoning. Drawing on research on the use of native language and their experiences in their classrooms, the teachers found that given the chance to learn the academic language of mathematics in Spanish, children were able to then transfer that understanding to English by assigning "new labels to their already formed understandings" (Celedón-Pattichis et al., 2010, p. 11). In examining the mismatch between the contexts provided in the curriculum and children's experiences in their homes, the teachers discovered that using a reform curriculum translated into Spanish was not enough, and that the context of the problems and assignments had to be changed. Further, the teachers recognized the importance of engaging the families through workshops and by providing resources to support families' understandings of the mathematics.

In another professional development program connecting the teaching and learning of mathematics to funds of knowledge, Wager (in press) provided a framework for incorporating children's out-of-school practices with those practices in school. In research facilitating professional development, she found that teachers draw on children's out-of-school practices in four distinct ways: (a) using context, (b) teacher-initiated situated settings, (c) out-of-school activities related to school mathematics, and (d) embedded mathematical practices. For this discussion, we focus on embedded mathematical practices. Embedded practices refer to situations in which the context drives the mathematics. In these situations, students develop informal strategies to accomplish their tasks that often differ substantially from the mathematical strategies typically taught in school (Carraher et al., 1985; Guberman, 1996; Saxe, 1988). For example, cooking is a common context for teaching fractions. This practice often involves using measuring cups, ingredients, and pots or pans. Yet, as others have also found, not all families use measuring cups and may cook "a ojo" (by eyeballing) (Celedón-Pattichis et al., 2010, p. 21) or measure with their hands. Thus, in using cooking as a context, teachers need to understand how children witness or experience cooking in their own homes, what mathematics is used (estimation, proportion, etc.), and what strategies the children use. In examining the strategies and mathematical practices that children use in everyday activities and then building on those practices in the classroom, teachers validate those practices and provide children with a way to connect their everyday lives to school mathematics.

Conclusions

In their chapter, Clements and Sarama address three questions regarding the teaching and learning of mathematics. Their perspective in responding to the questions of how mathematics is learned, how it is taught, and how teachers learn to teach it is grounded in the research on learning trajectories. Although we agree with views presented, we believe they need to be extended to incorporate a sociocultural lens, thereby minimizing the opportunity for deficit views of children and families, and offering more equitable learning opportunities for all.

NOTES

1. The preparation of this paper was supported in part by a grant from the National Science Foundation (144-PRJ38LF). The opinions expressed in this

paper do not necessarily reflect the position, policy, or endorsement of the National Science Foundation.

2. In another review, Clements and Sarama (2007) also incorporate a synthesis of theoretical frameworks that includes social constructivism, although we place somewhat greater emphasis on the sociocultural dimension than they do. They also have addressed providing equitable learning opportunities to an increasingly diverse student population.

REFERENCES

Barta, J., & Brenner, M. E. (2009). Seeing with many eyes: Connections between anthropology and education. In B. Greer, S. Mukhopadhyay, S. Nelson-Barber, & A. Powell (Eds.), *Culturally responsive mathematics education.* New York: Routledge/Taylor & Francis.

Carpenter, T. C., Fennema, E., Franke, M. L., Levi, L., & Empson, S. (1999). *Children's mathematics: Cognitively guided instruction.* Portsmouth, NH: Heinemann.

Carraher, T. N., Carraher, D. W., & Schliemann, A. D. (1985). Mathematics in the streets and in the schools. *British Journal of Developmental Psychology, 3,* 21–29.

CCSSO/NGA. (2010). *Common Core State Standards for mathematics.* Washington, DC: Council of Chief State School Officers and the National Governors Association Center for Best Practices.

Celedón-Pattichis, S., Musanti, S. I., & Marshall, M. E. (2010). Bilingual elementary teachers' reflections on using students' native language and culture to teach mathematics. In M. Q. Foote (Ed.) *Mathematics teaching & learning in K–12: Equity and professional development.* New York: Palgrave MacMillan.

Civil, M. (2002). Everyday mathematics, mathematician's mathematics, and school mathematics: Can we bring them together? In M. E. Brenner & J. N. Moschkovich (Eds.), *Journal for research in mathematics education: Everyday and academic mathematics in the classroom.* Reston, VA: National Council of Teachers of Mathematics.

Clements, D. H., & Sarama, J. (2007). Early childhood mathematics learning. In F. Lester (Ed.), *Second handbook of research on mathematics teaching and learning* (pp. 461–555). Charlotte, NC: Information Age.

D'Ambrosio, U. (1985). Ethnomathematics and its place in the history and pedagogy of mathematics. *For the Learning of Mathematics 5,* 44–48.

de Abreu, G. (1995). Understanding how children experience the relationship between home and school mathematics. *Mind, Culture, and Activity, 2,* 119–142.

Foote, M. Q. (2010). *Mathematics teaching & learning in K–12: Equity and professional development.* New York: Palgrave MacMillan.

González, N., Andrade, R., Civil, M., & Moll, L. (2001). Bridging funds of distributed knowledge: Creating zones of practices in mathematics. *Journal of Education for Students Placed At Risk, 6*(1 & 2), 115–132.

Guberman, S. (1996). The development of everyday mathematics in Brazilian children with limited formal education. *Child Development, 67,* 1609–1623.

Gutiérrez, R. (2007, October). Context matters: Equity, success, and the future of mathematics education. In T. Lamberg & L. R. Wiest (Eds.), *Proceedings of the*

29th annual meeting of the North American Chapter of the International Group for the Psychology of Mathematics Education, Stateline (Lake Tahoe), NV: University of Nevada, Reno.

Gutstein, E. (2006). *Reading and writing the world with mathematics.* New York: Routledge.

Ladson-Billings, G. (1995). Toward a theory of culturally relevant pedagogy. *American Educational Research Journal, 32,* 465–491.

Leonard, J. (2008). *Culturally specific pedagogy in the mathematics classroom: Strategies for teachers and students.* New York: Routledge/Taylor & Francis.

Masingila, J. O. (2002). Examining students' perceptions of their everyday mathematics practice. In M. E. Brenner & J. N. Moschkovich (Eds.), *Journal for research in mathematics education: Everyday and academic mathematics in the classroom.* Reston, VA: National Council of Teachers of Mathematics.

Moll, L., Amanti, C., Neff, D., & González, N. (1992). Funds of knowledge for teaching: Using a qualitative approach to connect homes and classrooms. *Theory into Practice, 31,* 132–141.

NCTM. (2006). *Curriculum focal points for prekindergarten through grade 8 mathematics: A quest for coherence.* Reston, VA: National Council of Teachers of Mathematics.

Nunes, T. Schliemann, A., & Carrahar, D. (1993) *Street mathematics and school mathematics.* New York: Cambridge University Press.

Rogoff, B. & Gutiérrez, K. (2003). Cultural ways of learning: Individual traits or repertoires of practice. *Educational Research, 23*(5), 19–25.

Saxe, G. B. (1988). Candy selling and mathematical learning. *Educational Researcher, 17*(6), 14–21.

Secada, W. (1991). Diversity, equity, and cognitivist research. In E. Fennema, T. P. Carpenter, & S. J. Lamon (Eds.). *Integrating research on teaching and learning mathematics* (pp. 17–54). Albany, NY: SUNY Press.

Secada, W. G., & Berman, P. W. (1999). Equity as a value-added dimension in teaching for understanding in school mathematics. In E. Fennema & T. A. Romberg (Eds.), *Mathematics classrooms that promote understanding* (pp. 19–32). Mahwah, NJ: Lawrence Erlbaum Associates.

Shulman, L. S. (1986). Those who understand: Knowledge growth in teaching. *Educational Researcher, 15*(2), 4–14.

Taylor, E. V. (2004, April). *Engagement in currency exchange as support for multi-unit understanding in African American children.* Paper presented at the annual meeting of the American Educational Research Association, San Diego, CA.

Wager, A. (in press). Incorporating out-of-school mathematics: From cultural context to embedded practice. *Journal of Mathematics Teacher Education.*

CHAPTER 12

WALKING THE SAME *BROAD* PATH (WITH SIDE TRIPS)

Response to Comments

Julie Sarama and Douglas H. Clements
University at Buffalo, SUNY

Researchers must become "thick-skinned" in reading criticisms of their writing. Reviewers can be harsh, even brutal, but most writers admit that they have learned more from such criticisms than from almost anything else they have read.

It is with particular pleasure, then, to read these illuminating—*and* kind—reviews by premier researchers in the field. We think this book speaks to the growing maturity of the field, in that there is sufficient empirical evidence that guides most of us to walk the same path, albeit with considerable room for differences in perspectives and foci (e.g., what bumps are most troubling) and allowances for important side trips.

Art Baroody, David Purpura, and Erin Reid emphasize the importance of the "big ideas" of mathematics—a notion with which we agree. Indeed, we

Instructional Strategies for Improving Students' Learning, pages 205–212
Copyright © 2012 by Information Age Publishing
All rights of reproduction in any form reserved.

have previously co-authored a structure for these big ideas in collaboration with Baroody in the past (see especially Part 1 in Clements, Sarama, & DiBiase, 2004) and have incorporated such structures directly and specifically into our notion of learning trajectories (Clements & Sarama, 2009; Sarama & Clements, in press). Baroody, Purpura, and Reid correctly go beyond describing these big ideas to the additional implication that standards, curricula, professional development, and teaching must not only be structured around such big ideas but should help *students* recognize and use these ideas to connect seemingly disparate domains of mathematics.

We believe that there are few practical differences between our position and that of Baroody, Purpura, and Reid on the educational implications. The main difference seems to rest with the nature of dichotomies. We agree that "genuine philosophical differences about teaching and learning" exist and are of fundamental importance. Still, we do not believe that the "meaningful teaching/memorization versus teaching/memorizing by rote" *dichotomy* is completely valid and useful. That is, as a continuum, this raises important issues. Research substantiates that too many U.S. mathematics classrooms are far closer to the "rote" end, with too little balance. Here we appear to agree. However, we regard a dichotomy as two disparate entities that are *opposed, entirely different,* and *mutually exclusive.* Only here do we disagree with Baroody, Purpura, and Reid. Although "rote" would rarely be in our description (except for certain limited cases of social-arbitrary knowledge such as number words to 10), we do not interpret meaningful learning as *opposed* to or mutually exclusive of learning through "repeated experiencing" or what Vygotsky (1934/1986) called spontaneous (everyday) knowledge.

Is this simply semantics? Somewhat. However, when we see how many teachers reject *any* repetition (practice, or what we prefer to call "repeated experiencing") *because* one has to "choose a side"—either "child centered" or "drill-and-kill,"—we believe there are significant practical ramifications to what we still call a false dichotomy. Of course, there are those who believe all early learning is by "rote," and only later becomes meaningful—an even more harmful application of the false dichotomy.

In this, we seem to be in agreement with Baroody, Purpura, and Reid, at least when they discuss other issues, such as "student-centered or teacher-directed instruction." However, these authors say we "recommend" a direct instruction approach. This is an overstatement. We cite research supporting that approach for children *with learning disabilities* or difficulties, and then we provide an extended discussion of reinterpretations (it is *explicit*, rather than "direct" instruction is supported by research), modifications, and alternate approaches. We believe that most of our recommendations are consistent with what the authors call the "investigative approach" (e.g., we state that "research supports the notion that inventing one's own procedures is often a good first phase in ensuring these advantages").

To repeat, we believe our practical implications are often consistent with those of Baroody, Purpura, and Reid. Further, we appreciate the additional details that their discussion offered, which we were not able to provide due to restrictions on the length of our chapter.

To resolve what may be seen as a difference between our position and that of Baroody, Purpura, and Reid in the notion of "practice," the reader should recognize that they have continued to define practice as drill-and-practice, whereas we redefined it as repeated experiencing, which *includes* all of what they call "meaningful learning/memorization." Repeated experiencing is not a euphemism for meaningless drill, but rather refers to experiencing the idea in multiple varied contexts, using it to solve problems (what Wirtz called "practice at the problem-solving level" [1974]), and incorporating it into the structure of mathematics. The research we cite on practice is not limited to meaningless drill, but the attainment of expertise. We do not accept our recommendations as a "straw man" of weak, unsubstantial, drill.

The authors appear to misunderstand Hiebert and Grouw's (2007) chapter and our brief review of it—nothing in either suggests that "teaching for skills only" is recommeded—it is simply a common practice that they describe. Indeed, if there were anything close to a true dichotomy, that of Hiebert and Grouws would be it.

We sincerely thank Anita Wager and Tom Carpenter for emphasizing a sociocultural perspective. Because we agree wholeheartedly with what they say, we feel we must point out that this perspective is honored in other publications (Clements & Sarama, 2009; Sarama & Clements, 2009), albeit not developed as thoroughly and as well as by others, including Wager and Carpenter.

Thus, we agree that cultural context matters to learning trajectories. We admit that Wager and Carpenter's statement that our learning trajectories are a cognitive construct and believe their caveats are well placed. However, we wish to add that our broader theory, *hierarchic interactionalism*, although also cognitivist, also considers sociocultural factors. We believe that thinking such factors have a profound effect and that "Different developmental courses are possible, depending on individual, environmental, and social confluences (Clements, Battista, & Sarama, 2001; Confrey & Kazak, 2006)" (Sarama & Clements, 2009, pp. 22–23). Further, one of the dozen tenets of the theory is precisely that "Environment and culture affect the pace and direction of the developmental courses" and "because environment, culture, and education affect developmental progressions, there is no single or 'ideal' developmental progression, and thus learning trajectory" (p. 23). To repeat, we agree that our chapter did not develop this perspective, and thus contend that Wager and Carpenter's comments are a necessary and useful complement to our review.

Wager and Carpenter correctly question the "age" column in our presentation structure for learning trajectories. In works focused on learning trajectories, we provide an elaboration, which is relevant to their concern. For example, we have previously stated that "the ages in the table are typical ages [at which] children develop these ideas. *But these are rough guides only*—children differ widely. Furthermore, the ages below are lower bounds on what children achieve without instruction. So, these *are "starting levels," not goals.* We have found that children who are provided high-quality mathematics experiences are capable of developing to levels one or more years beyond their peers" (Clements & Sarama, 2009, p. 6, emphasis in original).

More important, we would not agree with Wager and Carpenter's characterization of age as a "component"—it is simply a heuristic. That is, age is necessary in the initial formation of learning trajectories. Within and across topics, most studies involved children of a single age. Thus, we use age as a way of sequencing the levels in nascent learning trajectories. This is an explanation and also a caveat: Not all trajectories have been tested as comprehensive entities (ideally, with both cross-sectional and longitudinal designs). Thus, much work needs to be done. This work should be sensitive to Wager and Carpenter's concerns regarding the situated nature of children's learning and the need for a "critical view." However, we also believe that rejecting the view of children as "deviant" ("blaming the victim") does but should not imply that we, as an educational community, should accept that there are substantially different learning trajectories for some groups of children. First, this is too often translated into "my children learn more slowly and differently"—an insidious trap of low expectations disguised as sensitivity to cultural and individual differences. Second, we believe that the admittedly cognitive core of learning trajectories is valid with different cultural contexts.

Thus, we believe we are consistent with Wager and Carpenter in stating that learning trajectories can be the cognitive core that is instantiated in different ways in different sociocultural settings. The minor disagreements should not detract us from our appreciation of their perspective in expanding this core in necessary ways by emphasizing the importance of the sociocultural contexts of education and the growing research base that guides educators in using it to promote learning and equity. As such, their chapter is a critical complement to our own.

Karen Fuson's comments also go beyond our chapter to add valuable information about ways that the Common Core State Standards (CCSS) can improve teaching and learning in early and elementary schools. Fuson was a key figure in forming the algebraic thinking and number base-ten developmental progressions (what she calls "learning paths") on which those topics in the CCSS were based, and her discussion of them adds useful details to our review.

Because Fuson's chapter is an extension, there are few issues to which we need to respond. For example, we are pleased that her research is consistent with our theory of hierarchic interactionalism and its learning trajectories. One minor note: We believe the phrase "learning trajectories" is more accurate and useful than learning paths because the construct of learning trajectories (a) has an established theoretical and empirical history (Simon, 1995) with considerable research and development work (Clements & Sarama, 2004); (b) implies a direction and progression (whereas "paths" can simply meander); and (c) includes three well-defined components of goal, developmental progression, and instructional tasks.

Another issue needing clarification is that of geometric shapes. Although we agree with Fuson on the importance of many different categories of shapes, we disagree with her notion of what are "central 2-D shapes" and believe she has misinterpreted our chapter. First, the learning trajectory pictured in our chapter involves only shape composition. Second, the shapes for that learning trajectory are simply illustrations using the most commonly available shapes; the complete learning trajectory uses shapes with only multiples of 45° even in preschool (see Clements & Sarama, 2007, 2009). Third, our learning trajectories for geometric shapes (beyond simply composition) include all the shape categories she mentions as being illustrated in our chapter, all the shape categories she describes as "central," and many others. Children are miseducated when they are overexposed to any limited set of shapes, no matter how useful for some purposes (Clements, 2003).

Finally, we also appreciate the comments of James Stigler and Belinda Thompson, especially their extended discussion of false dichotomies, and the detrimental role they have played in research and practice in both education and psychology. They too see potential in the learning trajectory construct and add to the discussion by showing how learning trajectories focus on the details of both learning and teaching, undermining the "dumbbell theories" (Minsky, 1986) that false dichotomies propagate. They emphasize, for example, how the structure and focus on details learning trajectories can provide help teachers engage in more productive discussions. Like the other authors, they provide useful examples that illustrate their arguments, notably in their interesting international comparisons.

Several of the examples Stigler and Thompson provide emphasize the development of the subject-matter content (what we in the Common Core State Standards writing team call "mathematical progressions"). However, some of their other examples that simultaneously emphasize the children's understanding and learning, such as the notion that students who add the numerators and then add the denominators when adding fractions probably need more than reminders of the procedure. They may need to move back a level if they are not conceptualizing the fraction as a single number. Such simultaneous consideration of the development of mathematical content and the developmental course of cognitive growth is what we call the developmental progression component of a learning trajectory.

In their "deeper look" into learning trajectories, Stigler and Thompson address this characteristic directly, stating that they "are not natural objects to be discovered" but "are, instead, invented cultural artifacts." We believe there is much truth there, although our theory of hierarchic interactionalism does not dichotomize these two sources. Rather, we believe that natural progressions of thinking do exist. Even the trajectory Stigler and Thompson call "clearly not natural" follows developmental guidelines, as our research review shows. Indeed, this is why that trajectory developed the way it did in Japan—it *was* a natural developmental progression (even if it did not emerge on that basis explicitly), and was therefore particularly successful. However, we also agree that learning trajectories must be educationally engineered. In our theory, developmental progressions are born from cognitive psychology, and thus they

> play a special role in children's cognition and learning because they define sequences of levels of thinking for a specific content domain, each of which is built upon children's general intuitive knowledge and cognitive processes as they apply to the domain, as well as their previously developed patterns of thinking and learning within that domain. That is, although influenced by educational experiences and broader cultural factors, there are reliable sequences of levels of thinking, defined by identifiable patterns of mental processes and conceptual objects (actions-on-objects), through which most children progress as they learn about and gain competence. These patterns of thinking are natural to the extent that the extant biological and cognitive affordances (e.g., innate competencies) and constraints (e.g., information-processing limits and other "guidelines" described by cognitive and developmental psychology) privilege certain conceptual structures and solution strategies at certain developmental/cognitive levels and connections between contiguous levels privilege the developmental progression defined as the sequence of those levels. (Sarama & Clements, in press)

However, as Stigler and Thompson point out, learning trajectories also must be engineered. Several different curricular sequences may follow the guidelines set down by such "natural" patterns of thinking and some may be more mathematically coherent and productive than others. Thus, the demands of the subject are honored equally when constructing one or more complete developmental progression. Similarly, the third component of learning trajectories, the instructional tasks, must be invented. In our theory,

Based on the hypothesized, specific, mental constructions (mental actions-on-objects) and patterns of thinking that constitute children's thinking, curriculum developers design instructional tasks that include external objects and actions that mirror the hypothesized mathematical activity of children as closely as possible. These tasks are sequenced, with each corresponding to a level of the developmental progressions, to complete the hypothesized learning trajectory. Such tasks will theoretically constitute a particularly efficacious educational program; however, there is no implication that the task sequence is the only path for learning and teaching; only that it is hypothesized to be one fecund route. Indeed, moving from early childhood to adulthood, experience-expectant processes provide relatively fewer guides and the role of content concerns increases, but knowledge of human development and information processing contribute to the creation of effective learning trajectories at all ages. Tasks present a problem; people's actions and strategies to solve the problem are represented and discussed; reflection on whether the problem is solved, or partially solved, leads to new understandings (mental actions and objects, organized into strategies and structures) and actions. Specific learning trajectories are the main bridge that connects the "grand theory" of hierarchic interactionalism to particular theories and educational practice. (Sarama & Clements, in press)

Thus, learning trajectories have two parents, cognitive and educational psychology and educational engineering. Thus born, the initial learning trajectory is not a finished product. It must be refined based on an understanding of multiple phases of research and development (Clements, 2007) and incorporated into the local culture. The work must involve teams with varying expertise, as Stigler and Thompson state. Ideally, different learning trajectories should be developed and evaluated using such a research framework, and ultimately compared, integrated, and scaled up. We believe this consistent with Stigler and Thompson's position. Again, they extend this discussion with the point that technology allows more extensive and intense sharing, revision, and dissemination that previously possible.

In conclusion, we thank all the reactors for their thoughtful and valuable chapters. We are honored they would take the time to respond to our chapter. However, they all contribute much more than simple critiques: Each chapter extends our brief research review, with each chapter complementing the others.

REFERENCES

Clements, D. H. (2003). Teaching and learning geometry. In J. Kilpatrick, W. G. Martin, & D. Schifter (Eds.), *A research companion to Principles and Standards for School Mathematics* (pp. 151–178). Reston, VA: National Council of Teachers of Mathematics.

Clements, D. H. (2007). Curriculum research: Toward a framework for research-based curricula. *Journal for Research in Mathematics Education, 38,* 35–70.

Clements, D. H., Battista, M. T., & Sarama, J. (2001). Logo and geometry. *Journal for Research in Mathematics Education Monograph Series, 10.*

Clements, D. H., & Sarama, J. (Eds.). (2004). Hypothetical learning trajectories [Special issue]. *Mathematical Thinking and Learning, 6*(2), 81–260.

Clements, D. H., & Sarama, J. (2007). *Building blocks—SRA Real Math, grade pre-k.* Columbus, OH: SRA/McGraw-Hill.

Clements, D. H., & Sarama, J. (2009). *Learning and teaching early math: The learning trajectories approach.* New York: Routledge.

Clements, D. H., Sarama, J., & DiBiase, A.-M. (2004). *Engaging young children in mathematics: Standards for early childhood mathematics education.* Mahwah, NJ: Lawrence Erlbaum Associates.

Confrey, J., & Kazak, S. (2006). A thirty-year reflection on constructivism in mathematics education in PME. In A. Gutiérrez & P. Boero (Eds.), *Handbook of research on the psychology of mathematics education: Past, present, and future* (pp. 305–345). Rotterdam, The Netherlands: Sense Publishers.

Hiebert, J. C., & Grouws, D. A. (2007). The effects of classroom mathematics teaching on students' learning. In F. K. Lester, Jr. (Ed.), *Second handbook of research on mathematics teaching and learning* (Vol. 1, pp. 371–404). New York: Information Age Publishing.

Minsky, M. (1986). *The society of mind.* New York: Simon and Schuster.

Sarama, J., & Clements, D. H. (2009). *Early childhood mathematics education research: Learning trajectories for young children.* New York: Routledge.

Sarama, J., & Clements, D. H. (in press). Learning trajectories: Foundations for effective, research-based education. In J. Confrey, A. P. Maloney & K. Nguyen (Eds.), *Learning over time: Learning trajectories in mathematics education.* Charlotte, NC: Information Age.

Simon, M. A. (1995). Reconstructing mathematics pedagogy from a constructivist perspective. *Journal for Research in Mathematics Education, 26*(2), 114–145.

Vygotsky, L. S. (1934/1986). *Thought and language.* Cambridge, MA: MIT Press.

Wirtz, R. W. (1974). *Drill and practice at the problem solving level: Activity pages with comments for teachers* Washington, DC: Curriculum Development Associates.

ABOUT THE EDITORS

Jerry S. Carlson (PhD, University of California, Berkeley) is professor emeritus of educational psychology at the University of California-Riverside. His main research interests are in cognition and individual differences in mental abilities, their assessment, and applications to school learning. He has authored or coauthored over 160 articles and research reports and 11 authored or edited books. He was founding editor of the journal *Issues in Education: Contributions from Educational Psychology* and, with Joel Levin, co-edits the book series titled *Psychological Perspectives on Contemporary Educational Issues*. He has twice served as president of the International Association for Cognitive Education and Psychology and has been awarded a senior Fulbright lectureship as well as an Alexander von Humboldt Stiftung senior scholar fellowship. In addition to UC-Riverside, he has taught or served in administrative positions at the universities in Trier and Goettingen, Germany, the University of Washington, and the University of California-Santa Barbara. He is a Fellow of the Association for Psychological Science.

Joel R. Levin (PhD, University of California, Berkeley) is professor emeritus of educational psychology at the University of Arizona and the University of Wisconsin-Madison. One strand of his research has focused on the experimental investigation of instructional strategies and materials that are presumed to improve students' information processing and retention. Another research strand is in the field of quantitative methods in education and psychology, where he has developed a variety of inferential statistical procedures that are applicable in large-sample, small-sample, and single-case time-series designs. He is a Fellow of both the educational psychology

Instructional Strategies for Improving Students' Learning, pages 213–216

and evaluation, measurement, and statistics divisions of the American Psychological Association (APA) and a former editor of APA's *Journal of Educational Psychology*. With more than 385 scholarly publications to his credit, he has received both local and national recognition for his research, teaching, and professional service contributions.